THE BEST OF

San Francisco

Don W. Martin
Betty Woo Martin

Chronicle Books ■ San Francisco

To Kym and Dan
You must give wings to your dreams

Library of Congress Cataloging-in-Publication Data

Martin, Don W., 1934-
  The best of San Francisco / Don W. Martin, Betty Woo Martin.
    p.   cm.
"Completely revised and expanded" — Cover.
  ISBN 0-87701-660-7
  1. San Francisco (Calif.) — Description — Guide-books.   I. Martin, Betty Woo.
II Title.
F869.S33M37   1989
917.94'610453 — dc20   89-17315
                                                                      CIP

Editing: Carolyn Miller
Book and cover design: Nielsen/O'Brien
Cover illustration: Ed Taber
Cartography: Charles L. Beucher, Jr. and Eureka Cartographers

10 9 8 7 6 5 4 3 2 1

Chronicle Books
275 Fifth Street
San Francisco, CA 94103

CONTENTS

INTRODUCTION

I'd rather be a busted lamp post on Battery Street, San Francisco, than the Waldorf-Astoria in New York. — Willie Britt

best adj. (Superlative of good)   1: excellent in the highest degree   2: most useful, correct, worthy, etc.

Our weathered *Webster's Dictionary* effectively sums up our reasons for offering you *The Best of San Francisco,* which we first wrote in 1986, then revised in 1989.

For decades, we've wandered the streets of this wonderful city, seeking the best it has to offer. We've consulted assorted guidebooks, tried hundreds of restaurants, and asked scores of cabbies and concierges a simple question: "Where can we find the best of San Francisco?"

That's not an easy question to answer. At last measure, there were more than 4,000 restaurants and just over 2,000 bars in the city. The AAA's *California-Nevada TourBook* contains 26 pages of San Francisco lodgings and restaurants, and another 14 pages of activities and attractions. Dozens of other city guidebooks offer additional dozens of pounds of information. Who has time to sort through all this material?

So we decided to write a special kind of guidebook: one that arbitrarily sifts through lengthy lists of attractions, restaurants, pubs, and such, to offer readers only the very best the city has to offer. We wanted a book that would tell you — at the flip of a page — where to find the ten best hamburgers, the liveliest bars, the best fillet of sole, the most awesome ice cream ever to cool your palate on a warm September afternoon.

We've updated and expanded our second edition to make it more useful, both as an insider's guide and as a general reference source for visitors and Bay Area residents. Our lists of attractions have been expanded, we've added more restaurants, and a new chapter features the ten best bed and breakfast inns and small hotels.

In compiling material for *The Best of San Francisco,* we enlisted the aid of seven city-wise friends, asking them to prepare lists of their personal favorites. Guided by their suggestions, we spent months in the field, sampling sundry seafoods, sushi, and soufflés; admiring each view of this handsome city; pedaling assorted bike paths.

The San Francisco Seven was then reconvened. We placed before them unlabeled samples of the city's best sourdough French bread, salami, chocolate chip cookies, gourmet ice cream, and other local delights. Then we stepped back quickly and watched while they nibbled, chewed, and gravely nodded their heads.

After extended discussions, frequent loud arguments and an occasional coin flip, we came up with *The Best of San Francisco*, a fun book of lists from America's favorite city.

Within each group of the Ten Best (except where items aren't directly related) we've picked our favorite: our personal No. 1. The other nine follow alphabetically, with no attempt at further rating. In this way, we have no losers among the Ten Best, only winners and runners-up.

Our selections are a mix of many new discoveries and longtime favorites. Naturally, in a city that offers so much, we were somewhat arbitrary in our final decisions. Choices were influenced by our personal interests and tastes, and these may differ from yours. If you prefer fish cooked to the consistency of an artgum eraser, or if your idea of amusement is to stroll about in a contemplative daze with a stereo cassette player plugged into your ears, you may not find this guide useful.

Incidentally, we solicited no free meals or admissions to attractions, so our selections — while arbitrary — are impartial.

Come join us in rediscovering America's favorite city.

To learn more about the city: Stop in at the San Francisco Visitor Information Center in Hallidie Plaza at Powell and Market streets (near the cable car turntable and Powell BART/Muni station). Hours are 9 a.m. to 5:30 p.m. Monday through Friday, 9 a.m. to 3 p.m. on Saturday, and 10 a.m. to 2 p.m. on Sunday; phone 974-6900.

GET A PASS, FAST! The best way to get around the city — particularly if you plan an extended visit — is to purchase a $28 Fast Pass. Available at City Hall, assorted stores, and several banks, they're good for a month of unlimited rides on the city's bus, streetcar, cable car, and Metro-Muni rail system, and on BART trains within the city. With cable car fares up to $2 and basic bus fares edging toward a dollar, the Fast Pass will quickly earn its keep.

A BIT ABOUT THE AUTHORS

1 Don W. Martin has been in, out, and about the San Francisco Bay area since 1958. He and his wife, Betty, have authored three guidebooks on California, and they contribute travel articles and photos to an assortment of magazines and major newspapers. A few eons ago, he served as a U.S. Marine correspondent in the Orient, then he spent several years as a reporter and editor for various California newspapers. He served as associate editor of *Motorland,* the travel magazine of the San Francisco-based California State Automobile Association until 1988, when he left to become a full-time free-lance writer.

2 Betty Woo Martin offers the curious credentials of a doctorate in pharmacy and a California real estate broker's license. But never mind that. She's also an expert in Asian cuisine, a student of culinary arts and hospitality management courses at California's Columbia College, a free-lance writer-photographer, and a native Californian with an extensive knowledge of the Bay Area.

...AND THE SAN FRANCISCO SEVEN

1 Charles L. Beucher, Jr. A publication of this caliber must have a person-about-town on its advisory panel. Chuck has peered into every cafe, pub, and South of Market club in a never-ending search for the total San Francisco experience (and intriguing women with whom to share that experience). When not raving about the discovery of a new watering hole, he works as an imaginative art director and production-design genius. He also created the original maps for our hiking and biking tours in this book.

2-3 Phil and Sally Kipper The Kippers are longtime residents of San Francisco's Glen Park district, from where they venture forth frequently to seek the best of the city's good life. They possess an uncanny knack for finding that tiny eight-table bistro and sharing their discovery with intimates before excessive publicity ruins it. As members of the Seven, they now actively participate in the ruination of such charming places. Phil teaches broadcasting at San Francisco State University, and Sally is a budget analyst for San Francisco Mayor Art Agnos.

4-5 Frank and Velda Gillespie A retired public relations man with Trans World Airlines, Frank brings an extensive background in travel and a keen knowledge of Californiana. Velda, former chief flight attendant for TWA, is a fourth-generation Californian, and her cooking skills are legendary. Her palate was invaluable in helping us choose San Francisco's best specialty foods. Frank possesses an inexhaustible supply of barroom jokes. Fortunately, none found their way into this book.

6-7 Ferdinand "Von" and Ginna Von Schlafke A friendly bear of a man, Von brings his expertise in art, museums, and galleries to these pages. Until his retirement in 1989, he exhibited his skills in artistry and design as a preparator for the San Francisco Museum of Modern Art. Ginna is a gourmet and an excellent cook, and she also is knowledgeable about art. She and Von can be seen frequently at museum and gallery openings.

THANK YOU

1 Marge Booker and Cynthia Westbrook Hu of the San Francisco Convention and Visitors Bureau, who generously shared their extensive knowledge of the city in reviewing the manuscript.

2 Public Service Officer Diane Palacio of the Recreation and Park Department, for helping us discover the wealth of parks, museums, and other attractions administered by the city.

3 Nicolas Finck, community affairs director of the San Francisco Municipal Railway, for helping us search out scenic Muni routes and for teaching us the best reason for using public transit: you don't have to look for a parking place.

4 Public information officer Michael Feinstein and various rangers for helping us learn about that amazing urban park called the Golden Gate National Recreation Area.

5 Susan Swift of the Oakland Convention and Visitors Bureau for helping us prove that there is a there there.

6 Robert Byrne, author of *The Other 637 Best Things Anybody Ever Said* (New York: Atheneum, 1984). We consulted many sources for our chapter-heading quotes, but we found his book to be particularly helpful — and a delight to read.

7 Elizabeth Martin, former wine and gourmet foods specialist for Macy's California, for her guidance in our chapter on food.

8 — and especially the San Francisco Seven, without whose help this book would have been considerably thinner.

The Ten Best Attractions in San Francisco

...THAT YOUR OTHER INSIDER'S GUIDES MAY
HAVE OVERLOOKED.

A bay, a channel and ocean city — small in size, intense
upon its hills, haunted by fog and the bawling horns of it.
— William Saroyan

It's not a big city, actually.

With fewer than 800,000 souls, it ranks only 13th in population among America's cities; San Diego, San Jose, and Phoenix are larger. Yet San Francisco is a world-class city in every sense: a delightful cosmopolitan clutter of great museums, fine restaurants, urban parks, and intriguing ethnic enclaves.

It's amazingly complex and compact, second only to New York in population density. Tucked into this 46.48-square-mile metropolis are many world-renowned attractions — and a few neat little jewels that visitors often overlook. Some of our favorite things rate only a sentence in other guidebooks, or fail to make them at all.

After prowling the streets of San Francisco off and on since 1958, we've made these discoveries: our ten favorite things to see and do.

1   **WATCH THE SURF CRASH AT FORT POINT**   *Call 556-1693 to learn about* Fort Point *activities and exhibits. Fort open from 10 a.m. to 5 p.m. daily.* Like a storm-tossed ship, San Francisco is most beautiful and exciting with the wind in her face.

When a Pacific squall surges through the Golden Gate, great waves slam into the seawall at Fort Point, sending fans of water high into the air. Above the red-brick mass of the old fort, the slender span of the bridge may disappear into the gathering storm, like a pathway to infinity. Out on the bay, Alcatraz is a huddled dark shape, like a cat caught in a downpour. Beyond, the

1

city skyline broods under glowering clouds.

Fort Point is a nice sunny-day place, too. It draws rather light crowds even as visitors trip over one another at the Golden Gate Bridge viewpoint just above. Yet it offers some of the city's finest vistas — panoramas of sea, bridge, city, and headland — particularly from the old cannon batteries atop its eight-foot-thick walls.

The fort is a national historic site and park rangers dressed in period soldier suits demonstrate what army life was like a century ago: loading cannons and conducting rifle drills. You can prowl the great echoing corridors of the fort and capture stop-action glimpses of the city through its windows and gun ports.

Eight years and several million bricks were required to build this mighty bastion in the 1850s. One hundred twenty-six cannons, capable of hurling 128-pound balls two miles, were trained on the Golden Gate passage, waiting for menacing ships that never came. The armament was withdrawn around the turn of the century. Then the U.S. Army reoccupied the fort during World War II, and leveled its howitzers on the narrow passage, waiting for Japanese ships that never came.

2 **AMBLE ABOUT ALAMO SQUARE** *This historic district of Victorian homes is bounded by Webster, Fell, and Divisadero streets and Golden Gate Avenue, ten blocks west of the Civic Center.* They're called the Painted Ladies: those cheerfully colored Victorian row houses in the 700 block of Steiner Street. You may have seen them on postcards and magazine covers, with the city's modern skyline rising behind.

However, the Ladies are only six of several hundred Victorian-era houses still standing in this neighborhood. Indeed, these slender bay-windowed homes with their ornate wooden cornices, gables, and porticoes are scattered throughout San Francisco. The greatest concentration extends in a several-block radius around Alamo Square, a landscaped park at Steiner and Hayes streets.

Simply by zigging and zagging through this neighborhood, you'll see dozens of these San Francisco "Sticks." (See *San Francisco's Ten Most Handsome Victorians* in Chapter 20 and our *Victoriana-Haight Hike* in Chapter 21.) Most were constructed as tracts by contractors during a building boom lasting from the 1870s through the turn of the century. Nearly all were built of redwood, which is easily milled, sturdy, and fire-resistant. Redwood trees were plentiful then, which explains why they aren't now.

The ornate trim could be ordered through catalogues — anything from a fake sunburst gable to filigree, "doughnuts" and "drips." Many architectural writers of the day scoffed at the ornamental whimsy of the homes, which they sarcastically called the "Frisco-American" style.

"Why the curved piece with its radiating spindles over the porch?" fussed an early critic. "Why the meaningless little columns to the attic window which we know support nothing at all, and why so much cheap detail on the frieze and in the gable's peak?"

Although the great earthquake and fire of 1906 destroyed many of the city's Victorians, it stopped short of the Alamo Square area. In recent years, preservation-minded folks have been buying up and restoring the surviving filigreed homes. The houses often emerge with wonderfully gaudy paint jobs, adding a kaleidoscopic brilliance to the neighborhood.

3 **INHALE THE INCENSE AT A CHINESE TEMPLE** Norras Temple *is located at 109 Waverly Place,* **Tin How Temple** *is a few doors down at 125, and* **Jeng Sen Temple** *is across the alley at 146 Waverly.* Most Chinese don't practice their religion in the Western sense of attending regular services, listening to a sermon, then dropping coins into the collection plate. They visit their temples whenever the spiritual urge moves them. They may go to send prayers to their ancestors, or simply to sit quietly and reflect on their beliefs: generally a blend of Buddhism and Taoism, which venerates ancestors and the natural order of life.

The three temples listed above sit close together in Waverly Place, a busy alley between Washington, Grant, Clay, and Stockton streets in **Chinatown**. They are rather small places and difficult to find, located up narrow stairways and behind nondescript doorways. They do welcome visitors; ring a buzzer and you'll be admitted. You will enter a mystical, lavishly ornate world of red (the color of good fortune), black lacquer, and gold, where incense curls ceiling-ward from elaborate altars. After you have looked around a bit, a small contribution for the upkeep of the place will be appreciated.

4 **MAKE IT HAPPEN AT FORT MASON CENTER** *To learn what's happening at* Fort Mason Center, *call the 24-hour recording at 441-5705. For general information, contact Fort Mason Center Information Office, Building A, San Francisco, CA 94123; phone 441-5706.*

Make *what* happen?

Just about anything that culturally pleases you. Fort Mason Center is one of those "only in San Francisco" places: a gathering of galleries, museums, performing arts groups, and nonprofit organizations housed in a former waterfront army supply depot.

Members of the Fort Mason Foundation like to describe their unique enclave as a "year-around fair." Indeed, it hosts many special events in addition to housing art exhibits; music and drama workshops; a bookstore; a coffeehouse; and Greens, the noted Zen Buddhist vegetarian restaurant (see Chapter 8). For the casual stroller, it offers striking waterfront views, a chance to visit the restored liberty ship, S.S. *Jeremiah O'Brien* (see listing in this chapter), and a glimpse of interesting outdoor artworks including a curious mural of animals benignly taking over the San Francisco freeway system.

You can attend an aerobics class or a gallery opening, sit in on a music recital, fish for crab off the piers, or catch a play.

The center occupies several refurbished warehouses and piers at one corner of the former army post. The balance of the complex is a landscaped network of historic plantation-style army buildings housing the headquarters of the Golden Gate National Recreation Area (see Chapter 2), a still-functioning military officers' club, and a youth hostel.

The site of a Spanish garrison when San Francisco was a mission outpost in the 1770s, Fort Mason became an army embarkation depot in the 1930s. From its commodious piers, more than a million American servicemen and their supplies departed for the uncertain glories of combat in World War II and Korea. Then in a classic swords-to-plowshares move in 1972, many of the city's military facilities — including Fort Mason — became a part of the Golden Gate National Recreation Area. The Fort Mason Center Foundation was established to coordinate development of this former military base into a community haven for the arts and assorted nonprofit organizations. Nearly two million people visit each year to attend its events or stroll through its galleries and museums.

5   **ENJOY TGIF IN A FLOATING PUB**   *Golden Gate Ferry service runs daily from around 7 a.m. to 8:30 p.m. Sausalito ferry fare is $3.50 every day; Larkspur fare is $2.20 weekdays and $3 on weekends. For schedule information, call 332-6600.* Tired of hanging out with the same old crowd at the same old after-work bar? For a very few dollars, you can buy a ticket aboard a pub that goes somewhere: one of the Golden Gate Bridge District's passenger ferries operating between San Francisco and Marin County.

Golden Gate Ferry's fleet runs daily to Sausalito and Larkspur Landing from a dock behind the south wing of the San Francisco Ferry Building. When the ferries were put into operation several years ago, officials decided to install sea-going bars to attract the commuter crowd. They're still going strong. Drink prices are reasonable, and you get all that San Francisco waterfront scenery, a close-up of Alcatraz, and a peek at the pretty Marin shoreline. What saloon can offer as much?

The San Francisco-Sausalito run is our favorite; we like to explore that charming community's shops and attractive waterfront after going ashore; then we catch a later ferry back. The Larkspur Ferry has its appeal, too. The Larkspur Landing shopping center and a new Marriott Hotel are near the terminal, and daytime riders can walk to nearby Muzzie Marsh, a major waterfowl habitat.

4

We prefer boarding the ferries with the afternoon commuters instead of combating the heavy visitor crowds attracted to the boats on weekends. For thirsty Marin-bound yuppies, it's about a two-martini crossing.

6 **SHAKE WITH A QUAKE AND SMILE AT A CROCODILE** *California Academy of Sciences hours are 10 a.m. to 5 p.m. daily. Admission is $4 for adults, $2 for kids and seniors, and free for everyone on the first Wednesday of each month. Additional fees for planetarium and Laserium shows. Call 750-7145 (a recording) or 221-5100 for information on special exhibits.* We're recommending a science museum as a major tourist attraction? Certainly!

The California Academy of Sciences in Golden Gate Park is one of the most innovative and versatile institutions of its kind in the country. It's many good things under one big roof: a natural-science center with stuffed creatures in realistic settings, a planetarium, a hall of man that traces us from our banana-munching predecessors, and a major aquarium.

Exhibits change frequently, so there's never an excuse to stay away for more than a few months. One of the newest creations here is "Wild California," an entire hall devoted to the variety and drama of the state's landscape, which opened in late 1988. It offers thirteen dioramas of the Golden State's flora and fauna, including a remarkably realistic Farallon Islands display with a sea bird rookery, a 14,000-gallon aquarium, and life-sized elephant seals.

The Hall of Earth and Space Sciences, completed a few years ago, teaches visitors about plate tectonics and continental drift while Plexiglas planets circle overhead, following neon orbits. You can experience a "safequake" by stepping aboard a platform that jiggles you with nearly the same intensity as the city's destructive 1906 earthquake. In Morrison Planetarium, you can lean back in special tilted seats while a 5,000-pound star machine projects the heavens above, or watch a light-fantastic Laserium show.

In the Hall of Mammals, recorded grunts, groans, snorts, and chirps greet visitors at a realistic African watering hole. You can stare down at a swampful of grinning 'gators in the Steinhart Aquarium, then stand inside an unusual doughnut-shaped fish roundabout, where great schools of finned critters swim about you. The academy also offers a science- and nature-oriented gift and book shop.

7 **HAVE A LOOK AT A LIBERTY SHIP** *The S.S. Jeremiah O'Brien is open from 9 a.m. to 3 p.m. daily except major holidays; other elements of the National Maritime Museum are generally open from 10 a.m. to 5 p.m., with seasonal variations. For specifics on the O'Brien and other Maritime Museum exhibits, call 929-0202 or 556-8177.* They called them liberty ships:

those hastily assembled cargo carriers that kept our fighting troops supplied with ammo and Spam during World War II. Nearly 3,000 were built by legions of riveting Rosies; each ship was hammered and welded together in a few weeks from prefabricated parts.

Only one completely intact liberty ship survives, and she sits beside Pier 3 at Fort Mason. The S.S. *Jeremiah O'Brien* was built in 1943 and saw action as a troop and supply carrier during the Normandy Invasion. A few years ago, she was liberated from a floating ship storage area by a group called the National Liberty Ship Memorial, restored, and put on display. The outfit has succeeded in having good old *Jeremiah* listed on the National Register of Historic Places.

You can explore her welded metal decks from bow to stern, stand in the wheelhouse, peek into seamen's cabins, and prowl along the many catwalks in the cavernous engine room. A still-operational triple-expansion steam engine once pushed the heavy cargo ship through the waves at a leisurely 11 knots. Slow and vulnerable, she was armed with ten defense guns; two are still in place.

This is more than a static exhibit. On Open Ship Weekends, held about eight times a year, the crew cranks up the steam engines and demonstrates other workings of the historic freighter. The association also schedules annual cruises on San Francisco Bay.

The *O'Brien* is one of several yesterday ships exhibited along the city's waterfront: all part of the National Maritime Museum, which we cover in greater detail in Chapter 2.

8 **TAKE A WORLDLY TROLLEY CAR TOUR** *The San Francisco Trolley Festival operates from mid-May to mid-October, and the cars accept the same fares and transfers as the rest of the San Francisco Municipal Railway system. For details on all city transit services, call 673-MUNI.* **Note:** *Trolley service was temporarily suspended for the renovation of Market Street, but should be reinstated in 1990.*

You may do a double-take if you're standing at a streetcar stop on Market and an Australian trolley comes clanging along. But hop aboard, mate. It's part of the collection of international streetcars operated each summer by Muni.

The Trolley Car Festival began in 1983, sponsored by Muni and the San Francisco Chamber of Commerce. People liked riding the funny old cars so much that the festival was expanded the following year. Barring possible budget cuts, it is to be a regular feature of the San Francisco summer experience.

Fifteen vehicles are in the antique streetcar fleet, most of them city-owned; a few are leased. At least eight different trolleys are in operation on any given day. You can board that 1930 Australian streetcar, a breezy 1934 English open-air tram, or a 1912 antique trolley from Portugal. The star of the fleet is Old Car Number One, a tram that went into service in 1912 as Muni's first vehicle.

9 EXPLORE MARIN HEADLANDS' OUTER LIMITS *Marin Headlands is part of the Golden Gate National Recreation Area; for specifics on ranger hikes and other activities, call 331-1540.* A couple of decades ago, only a handful of people were aware of the road that climbs the Marin Headlands opposite the Golden Gate Bridge. Their reward was uncrowded and awesome vistas of the city, framed dramatically by the span. However, since the creation of GGNRA, droves of people drive up there. On a sunny weekend, it's a chore to find a parking place.

But there's much more to explore in this area. If you take a right onto McCullough Road from the main headlands road (Conzelman), you'll pass through a gap in the headlands and wind up in Rodeo Valley, a much less crowded area. Fort Cronkhite here, once an army post guarding the Golden Gate, is now headquarters for the Marin Headlands portion of the GGNRA. At a small visitor center, rangers will point you to a variety of trails to follow, some old artillery batteries to explore, and several viewpoints and picture spots. Ask them about a small picnic site on a ridge where you can munch your lunch while enjoying a splendid cityscape.

Rodeo Beach, a sandbar between the Pacific and Rodeo Lagoon, is surprisingly uncrowded, even on those rare warm August and September days when you might be tempted to dip a reluctant toe into the nippy Pacific.

Another neat headlands attraction is Point Bonita Light, which has been helping steer ships through the Golden Gate since 1855. It's now automated, but it still uses the same hand-ground Fresnel lens that was installed 130 years ago. The lighthouse occupies a dramatic niche at the tip of a razorback ridge; visitors reach it by walking through a tunnel and across a 120-foot-high bridge.

From this vantage point, the Golden Gate looms as the sea captains see it: a narrow waterway flanked by steep headlands, spanned by that magnificent bridge, and the very devil to find in a fog.

10 SHOP THE PRODUCE STANDS *The Heart of the City Farmers' Market is held in San Francisco's United Nations Plaza near the Civic Center on Sunday, Wednesday, and Friday from 8 a.m. to 5 p.m. The Alemany Farmers' Market off Alemany Boulevard south of the city functions from 6 a.m. to 6 p.m. Saturday and from 7:30 a.m. to 5 p.m. Tuesday through Friday; it's closed Sunday and Monday. Call toll free, (800) 952-5272, for details.*

7

It's nice to know that in the most sophisticated city west of Chicago, you can still buy a turnip directly from the turnip-grower. The Heart of the City Farmers' Market is held three days a week on United Nations Plaza, a wide promenade running from Market and Leavenworth streets to the Civic Center. Strolling past cheerful blue awnings, you can buy assorted fresh and dried fruits, vegetables, an entire tuna, honey still in the comb, and other products of soil, sea, and bee.

This market is a relative newcomer, however. The original Alemany Farmers' Market has been operating out of two long sheds south of the city since 1943; it's one of the oldest such markets in the state. Because of increased competition from other farmer-to-consumer marts (including downtown San Francisco's), only about a dozen stalls are busy here during weekdays. But on weekends, nearly every stall is filled. "The place really jumps," says manager Mary Vienot.

To find the Alemany market, head south from the city on U.S. 101, take Interstate 280 toward Daly City, then catch the first Alemany Boulevard exit. You'll hit a stop light on Alemany, and the market's just across the street.

Both marts are certified by the County Agricultural Commissioner, which means they can offer only commodities produced by the seller or immediate family members. California now has more than 90 farmers' markets; the program is coordinated by the Direct Marketing Program of the Department of Food and Agriculture.

If You Must Play Tourist

WHEN TO VISIT THE CITY'S MOST POPULAR ATTRACTIONS

It's an odd thing that anyone who disappeared was said to be seen in San Francisco. It must be a delightful city and possess all the attractions of the next world. — Oscar Wilde

Obviously, you'll want to see San Francisco's most famous attractions. Or if you've seen them all before, perhaps Cousin Ferdie is coming from Kansas, and he simply *must* experience Coit Tower.

It isn't necessary to compile a list of the city's Ten Best tourist lures. Anyone not familiar with the Golden Gate Bridge or Chinatown must be living in a Fresno fallout shelter. But they aren't much fun to visit if you have to shoulder through thick crowds and breathe tour bus fumes. And when was the last time you were able to find a parking place during a summer weekend visit to Fisherman's Wharf? (The famed wharf is not on our list. Two decades ago, it was ruined by developers with carnival midway mentalities; it has been slipping downhill since.)

What follows is a list of the best *times* to see the city's Ten Best attractions. July obviously isn't, because both the fog and visitors can become quite thick then. If you can't visit during the off-season, consider hitting the tourist high spots early in the morning or late in the day. There are no crowds, and there's a special quality to the light when the sun is low.

1 **GOLDEN GATE NATIONAL RECREATION AREA FROM DAWN TO DUSK, PREFERABLY IN THE FALL** *Details of GGNRA activities are available at the park's Fort Mason visitor center, open weekdays from 8:30 a.m. to 5 p.m. Write: GGNRA Headquarters, Fort Mason, San Francisco, CA 94123. Phone number for general information: 556-0560. Public transit serves many of GGNRA's attractions; call Muni at 673-MUNI and 332-6600 for Golden Gate Transit schedules in Marin County.* Who would have thought that the U.S. Army would function as a major force for conservation? It did so in San Francisco — mostly by accident.

A good part of the city's most beautiful terrain—beaches, headlands and the craggy shores of the Golden Gate—were taken over by the military as sites for forts and garrisons. Military occupation, in fact, dates back to the Spanish era. In all history, no ship ever approached the Gate in anger, so the forts ringing it never fired a retaliatory shot. On the other hand, none of the this land was available for private use, so it was spared "development."

In 1972, largely through the efforts of the late Congressman Phillip Burton, much of this prime military land—along with city, state, and privately owned property—was set aside as the Golden Gate National Recreation Area. The original park was expanded in succeeding years to its present size of 114 square miles: *triple* the area of the city itself! It's the world's largest urban park and the most-visited element of the U.S. National Park system. (This is no great trick, of course; so many units of the park rim the city and Marin County to the north that it's difficult *not* to tread on park soil.)

The GGNRA is not a solid unit but a wonderful patchwork of shorelines, viewpoints, eucalyptus groves, and history-ridden forts and buildings. Parcels include the north and south anchorages of the Golden Gate Bridge, Fort Point, most of the city's northern beaches, a collection of antique ships at Fisherman's Wharf, most of the Marin Headlands, and Muir Woods. The historic 1,500-acre Presidio of San Francisco is to become part of GGNRA when its deactivation as an army post is completed in the early 1990s. Park boundaries even stretch north to Tomales Bay, that dramatic inland waterway created by California's notorious San Andreas Fault. The GGNRA is headquartered at Fort Mason (see Fort Mason Center in Chapter 1).

The best time to enjoy the park's facilities is in the fall, simply because that's when San Francisco enjoys the clearest, most wind-free weather. So much of the park is visual: the panorama from the headlands, glimpses of the Golden Gate Bridge through Lincoln Boulevard's wind-sculpted cypress, city skyline views from the Coastal Trail.

GGNRA references are scattered throughout this book, since nine of its elements are worthy of National Historic Site status, and most of the city's best beaches are part and parcel of the park. As we said, it's difficult not to tread on GGNRA soil when visiting San Francisco.

And that's just great.

2 **ALCATRAZ ON A SUNNY WEEKDAY AFTERNOON** *Alcatraz-bound boats are operated by the Red and White Fleet, departing Pier 41 several times daily. Tickets are available at the pier or by reservation through Ticketron; call 556-0560 for Alcatraz information and 546-9400 for tickets. Advance reservations are recommended during weekends and the peak summer tourist season.*

You're no doubt familiar with the Birdman of Alcatraz: hulking Burt

Lancaster tenderly chucking sick canaries under the beak. But the real-life Robert Stroud didn't do his research on bird ailments at Alcatraz; most of that took place before he got there, during his stay at Fort Leavenworth Federal penitentiary in Kansas. But he certainly was an Alcatraz resident, along with Al Capone, killer Alvin "Creepy" Karpis, and a group of angry, disillusioned native Americans who took over the place in 1969 after it had been closed as a prison.

Alcatraz means "pelican" in Spanish; the name originally was intended for Yerba Buena Island, which links the two ends of the San Francisco–Oakland Bay Bridge. A nearsighted map-maker accidentally stuck the name on the large rock in the middle of the bay, which indeed pelicans had given their own personal patina. Alcatraz was an army prison from 1859 until 1933, then it became the infamous federal lock-up until it was closed in 1963.

Now it's part of the GGNRA; rangers will lead you through the grim cell blocks, regaling you with stories of inmates and Indians. Perhaps because of its intrigue — so close yet once so unapproachable — Alcatraz is one of the most popular units within the national park system. More than half a million people shuffle through there in a good year.

Naturally, visiting during the off-season is advantageous, since you can wait for one of those sunny afternoons that we recommend. It can get chilly on cloudy, windy days — in other words, during normal midsummer weather. But just wait until you get out there and catch the view back at the city!

3   **THE CABLE CARS AT SUNRISE**   *Cable car schedules are available by calling 673-MUNI.* All right, Andrew Smith Hallidie might have been a nice guy. However, it wasn't sympathy for horses pulling streetcars up the city's steep hills that inspired his development of the cable car. He owned a firm that manufactured wire rope (cable), which had been invented by his father in 1835. The development of a trolley with a device to grip an underground cable created a market for the product.

It is true that he saw a horse — part of a team pulling a freight wagon, not a streetcar — go fanny over teakettle down Jackson Street in 1869, but he was already at work on his invention when he witnessed that historic mishap.

He successfully tested his first cable car on Clay Street between Kearny and Jones on August 1, 1873. His assistant was supposed to take the grip, but he looked down the steep hill and said something like: "Forget it, Andy." The cars have been running ever since, but only three lines remain from about 30 routes once operated by private companies. They're now part of the city's Muni system.

If cable cars are legendary, so are the waiting lines during peak season. The famed turntable at Powell and Market has the longest queues of all. That's why we're getting up at such a ridiculous hour.

Early morning is the gentle and uncrowded time for catching cable cars. They begin running at 6 a.m. We like to board the California Street line at Van Ness Avenue. The air is cool and fresh at sun-up, not yet scented with grease and diesel, and the cacophony of traffic hasn't begun. Waiting to start their first run of the day, the cable car's gripman and conductor chat with the few passengers; most are regulars.

As the Hallidie Grip grabs the cable and the car lurches forward, you hear the sharp, distinctive sounds of this curious device at work: the metallic clink of wheel on rail, the whir of the cable beneath the street, the crisp clang of the bell. The car trundles along traffic-free California Street and climbs toward the sunrise as it tops Nob Hill. Soft shafts of first light burnish brick walls of the venerable Mark Hopkins and splash off Financial District towers below. It's a nice moment to be in San Francisco.

Even if you aren't moved to move out of bed so early, you can still escape lengthy prime-time queues. The California-Van Ness terminal is never as busy as the popular Powell-Market turntable. Once aboard, with transfer in hand, you can switch to a Powell Street car at California and Powell, beside the Fairmont Hotel. During peak periods, this transfer point gets pretty busy, too. But even if you have to wait a bit, it's better than standing wearily in a long line at Market Street, watching resident derelicts taking nips from their paper bags.

The funny little cars are in their second century, despite periodic efforts in the past to scuttle them. A $60 million restoration of the system was completed in 1984, then more money was needed to fix the overhaul.

San Franciscans fussed about the added cost, even as they fuss today about tourists crowding them off their cable cars. But they issued a collective sigh of relief with the assurance that the rattling old museum pieces will be around for another century or more.

4   **CHINATOWN BEFORE 8 A.M.**   At this point, you may have decided that this book wasn't intended for late-sleepers. Actually, I don't like rising with roosters either, but in San Francisco, the reward is generally worth the effort.

Chinatown awakens from its fitful sleep early. Merchants sweep the night's litter from sidewalks and delivery people hurry by, pushing hand-carts laden with cartons of tangerines, hairy melons, and mustard greens. At Chinatown's "produce corner" — Stockton and Broadway — diminutive housewives in quilted smocks pick apart fruit and vegetable displays that moments before had been neat pyramids of oranges and orderly rows of bok choy. At the seafood markets, merchants smooth mounds of shaved ice that soon will glitter with freshly caught fish.

There's no other place quite like San Francisco's Chinatown, not even in

China. Mainland Chinese cities tend to be low-lying and somewhat color-less. They definitely aren't choked with traffic, nor are they decorated with dragon-entwined lamp posts.

Despite claims of other cities, San Francisco's Chinatown is the largest Asian community outside the Orient, with population estimates ranging as high as 200,000. That's more than one in five San Franciscans. Chinese make up the city's oldest, largest, and most affluent ethnic group, and their self-contained city functions rather independently of San Francisco. It has its own chamber of commerce, banks, newspapers, and somewhat mystical service groups called benevolent associations.

Chinatown became a tourist attraction by accident. The first wave of Chinese immigrants came to California during the 1849 Gold Rush. Some found work near the hotels that ringed Portsmouth Square, cooking and doing laundry for macho white miners, who considered such chores to be women's work. Those early laundries and cafes laid the foundation for today's Chinatown.

Chinese were subjected to brutal discrimination, climaxed by the Oriental Exclusion Act of 1882, prohibiting further immigration. Unable to bring in brides, men turned to harlots and opium dens; bloody tong wars were fought over territorial rights, and a white slave trade thrived. Chinatown became a dark and sinister ghetto.

The 1906 earthquake and fire brought instant urban renewal, destroying the old slum. As the community rebuilt, it began attracting tourists. The Chinese opened curio shops and fancied up their restaurants to meet this new trade. With the addition of fake temple roofs and dragon lanterns in the 1950s and 1960s, modern Chinatown began to take shape.

It still has its scruffy side: dark but not really sinister alleys with sweat shops and mah-jongg parlors. But we hope the urban renewalists will stop trying to rehabilitate this place. Already the Golden Arches and themed shopping centers have invaded Grant Avenue, and more are threatened. Thankfully, a wax museum that opened in the 1970s melted into oblivion.

Incidentally, you should go to Chinatown the way the Chinese do: aboard the "Orient Express." That's the No. 30 Muni bus that travels along Stockton Street. Never mind what you heard in *Flower Drum Song;* Stockton, not Grant Avenue, is the real heart of this community. A good downtown place to catch the bus is on Stockton near Sutter, just before it enters the Stockton Tunnel.

5 **THE CIVIC CENTER DURING BUSINESS HOURS** *Civic Center guided tours are conducted on Mondays, and Davies Hall tours are held on Wednesdays; call 552-8338 for information.* San Franciscans like to boast that their city hall is taller than the nation's capitol—important only if you like statistics. It certainly is worth a look, with its French Renaissance columns and spired green copper dome. Step inside to admire the great rotunda and the sweeping grand stairway. Across Polk Street, in Civic Center Plaza, you can tune in on the latest protest rally or feed seagulls in the reflecting pool, while sidestepping pigeons and homeless people.

Opposite Civic Center Plaza is the outgrown but handsome San Francisco Public Library; stride up the central stairway beneath an ornate barrel-vaulted ceiling and check out special exhibits that usually line the wide mezzanine balcony. Across Van Ness Avenue from City Hall are the semi-similar War Memorial Opera House and Veterans Memorial Building. All are of French Renaissance design, selected by architects at the turn of the century to give the Civic Center a classic yet timeless appearance. The "Vet" houses the San Francisco Museum of Modern Art, a fine-art bookstore and a neat little cafe worthy of a lunch stop. The Opera House — obviously — is home field for the San Francisco Opera, the oldest and probably the finest west of the Rockies.

Considerably less timeless and hardly classic are the new structures of the Civic Center: Davies Symphony Hall, the San Francisco Ballet headquarters, and a state office building. They all have rounded, puffy Pillsbury-doughboy looks, better suited to avant-garde hotels than to civic structures. Davies Hall, showplace of the excellent San Francisco Symphony, is indeed handsome *inside,* with its multi-tiered foyer and elegant performance hall. Its steeply raked floor, wraparound balconies, and magnificent Ruffatti organ have earned it critical praise. But the exterior — with slender columns and odd vertical fins — looks like the grille of a 1956 Buick.

Worth stepping into, even if you aren't an auto club member, is the eight-story green-glass main office of the California State Automobile Association at Van Ness and Hayes. Its glass skin covers the original Spanish-California facade of the structure, built in 1925. The Latin look survives on the main floor, with its lace filigree, decorated arches, and ornate atrium ceiling. If you're really observant, you'll see a bas-relief of winged Mercury — holding a steering wheel.

We recommend visiting the Civic Center during business hours because that's when everything is open. Since tour buses rarely stop here, City Hall and the other buildings are never crowded, except possibly with attorneys.

6 **COIT TOWER AT MIDNIGHT** *The tower is open from 10 a.m. to 5:30 p.m., and an elevator takes visitors to the top for $3; call 362-8037 for details.* Lillie Hitchcock Coit was a tough lady who ran around in men's clothes, smoked cigars, and chased fire engines. Fire laddies admired her spit and spirit and made her a volunteer — uh — fireperson. When she died in 1929, she left funds to build a monument to volunteer firemen, but it wasn't the famous Coit Tower. It was a sculpture of three firefighters rescuing a woman, which still stands in Washington Square.

Her will also provided funds for "the purpose of adding to the beauty of San Francisco." From that bequest emerged Coit Tower atop Telegraph Hill, completed in 1933. Some say the fluted column resembles a fire nozzle, but historians insist this was not the designers' intent.

An elevator whisks visitors to the top for a dazzling city panorama; also, one can admire 1930s murals of California at work and browse through a souvenir shop on the lower floor.

But we prefer visiting at night, even though the tower is closed. There's no bumper-to-bumper traffic jamming the curving street leading to its parking lot and it can be very peaceful up there. For the proper nighttime approach (take a friend if you're the nervous type), start at Lombard and Hyde, drive down the squiggly "Crookedest Street in the World," and continue on Lombard until it blends into Telegraph Hill Boulevard.

The old fire nozzle glows warmly in the evening haze, bathed by floodlights. It's a place for lovers at night, locked in embrace on the leeward sides of trees; a place for dreamers standing in silence to admire the carpet of lights spread below. During quiet moments, sounds of the city drift upward like whispers in the night.

Incidentally, it isn't always that peaceful after dark. Young people often hang out in the parking lot at night, trying to blast out the windows of their low-riders with their car stereo systems. At least they scare away the muggers.

7 THE GOLDEN GATE BRIDGE AN HOUR BEFORE SUNSET Few visions in the world are more enchanting than the Golden Gate Bridge. Its architect, a little man named Joseph B. Strauss, was both an engineer and a poet: the sort of person who could create something bold and masculine, yet graceful and feminine.

The name Golden Gate was given to San Francisco Bay's narrow entrance by explorer John C. Fremont in 1846, nearly a century before the bridge was built. He apparently was moved by the golden sunsets in the open sea beyond the gate: the kind you may witness by spending a few quiet moments there late in the day. And no, the bridge isn't golden. The official name of the paint job is International Orange — picked because of its luminosity in a thick fog.

Avoid the bridge at midday when the ninth tour bus has spilled its cargo of camera-clutchers onto the viewing area near the toll plaza. The metered parking stalls will be filled, and herds of cars will be sitting at idle, waiting for someone to depart. If you want to take pictures, you'll have to wait until Martha from Madera — blocking your view of the Strauss statue — has finished grinning into her husband's Instamatic.

15

Go instead in the late afternoon after the others have left, when slanting rays cast shadow patterns across those lofty towers and down to the sea below. The bridge's pedestrian walkway is open from 6 a.m. to 9 p.m. Plan to arrive an hour or so before sunset, giving yourself time to take the three-mile round-trip stroll over to the Marin County side. Stare down at the water 200 feet below, where toy-sized sailboats weave cottony wakes as they head for safe harbor before dark. Watch the distant skyline become more sharply defined as late shadows accent the buildings.

Then retrieve your car and drive across the bridge to Vista Point. After absorbing the view from there, cross back under the freeway, but head up to the Marin Headlands instead of returning to Highway 101. Every bend of the winding road offers a stunning new view of bridge, bay, and city. Pull off at one of the many turnouts and sit quietly with someone special. Watch as the sun slips into its own glittery path, and lights of the city wink on like awakening fireflies.

You'll understand why people are moved to write poems and books about this city and its bridge.

8 **GOLDEN GATE PARK IN SPRINGTIME** *For information about park activities and free summer guided tours, call 221-1311.* Some flowers bloom the year around in Golden Gate Park, particularly in its wonderful century-old Conservatory of Flowers. But in springtime, the entire park is alive with multi-hued azaleas and rhododendrons. In the Japanese Tea Garden, delicate pink and white cherry blossoms timidly emerge for their brief two-week tenure from middle to late March.

This dramatic swatch of green, converted from windblown sand dunes, is one of the world's largest manmade parks, covering 1,017 acres (larger than New York's Central Park). And it's amazingly versatile. It shelters an outstanding Academy of Sciences (about which we've already raved), the world-noted de Young and Asian Art museums (see Chapter 17), a polo field, a nine-hole golf course, a buffalo paddock, an outdoor band shell, 11 lakes, ten gardens, biking and hiking paths, and statues of people we've never heard of. John McLaren, park superintendent for more than 40 years, hated those statues. Whenever city fathers erected one, he'd plant a climbing vine or bush in front of it.

San Franciscans live in their park, particularly on Sundays when the main thoroughfare, John F. Kennedy Drive, is closed to vehicles. It becomes a happy highway of cyclists, skateboarders, breakdancers, Frisbee flippers, runners, and power walkers.

Some park attractions not covered elsewhere in this book:

Conservatory of Flowers, *on Kennedy Drive, open daily from 9 a.m. to 5 p.m.; $1 for adults, 50 cents for seniors and kids.* Housing thousands of tropical plants and orchids, plus seasonal displays, it was built in 1879 and is the oldest structure in the park.

Japanese Tea Garden, *Martin Luther King, Jr. Drive, open daily from 9 a.m. to 6:30 p.m. March–September, 8:30 a.m. to 5:30 p.m. October–February; $2 for adults and $1 for kids and seniors.* Famed for its spring cherry blossom display, it's a prettily landscaped complex of pools, pagodas, and quiet walkways, plus a teahouse and a gift shop.

Strybing Arboretum, *Ninth Avenue at Lincoln Way; free; guided tours at 10:30 a.m. and 1:30 p.m.; horticultural library open weekdays from 8 a.m. to 4:30 p.m. and weekends and holidays from 10 a.m. to 5 p.m.* It features 6,000 plants from around the world, and has a Garden of Fragrance for the blind.

The Dutch Windmill *near the Great Highway and Lincoln* is one of two built early in this century to pump the park's water supply. It was restored in 1981 after sitting bladeless for decades; officials hope to raise funds to restore the nearby Murphy Windmill.

Children's Playground and carousel *near Kezar Drive. Carousel and gift shop hours 10 a.m. to 5 p.m. daily in summer and 10 a.m. to 4 p.m. Wednesday–Sunday the rest of the year; rides are $1 for adults, 25 cents for kids and free for tots; 558-4249.* The playground features the exquisitely restored 1912 Hershel-Spillman carousel, a gift shop, and innovative play equipment.

9 | MISSION SAN FRANCISCO DE ASIS DURING CELEBRATION OF THE EUCHARIST

Museum visitor hours are 9 a.m. to 4:30 p.m. May through October and 10 a.m. to 4 p.m. the rest of the year. Call 621-8203 for times of religious services and special events. The simple adobe mission at Dolores and Sixteenth Street isn't just an isolated curiosity and popular tour bus stop. It's part of a busy Catholic parish, although most activities are centered in the large basilica next door.

You'll enjoy sitting beneath the painted wooden beams of the old chapel during a service; you'll get the feel of life as it was before the Gold Rush, when this was the church of the little pueblo of Yerba Buena — the good herb. Currently, the only service regularly conducted in the chapel is Eucharist, celebrated every morning at 7:30. Later, you can tour the grounds and see relics of the city's Spanish mission era in the museum. Admission is free, but the nice folks here would appreciate a donation for the Maintenance and Education Fund.

After exploring the museum and its brilliantly flowered cemetery garden, step into the lofty sanctuary of the basilica. Soaring Moorish-Corinthian spires overshadow the little adobe chapel; some visitors think the basilica *is* the mission. Gaze upward into the vaulted arches and unusual domed ceiling and admire stained-glass windows depicting the 21 missions that led to the state's settlement.

San Francisco's history began in 1776, when Father Francisco Palou established California's sixth Spanish mission in a simple brushwood shelter on the banks of Arroyo de los Dolores (The Stream of Sorrows). He offered up the first Mass on June 29 just five days before American independence was declared in faraway Philadelphia. The fledgling mission was named for St. Francis of Assisi, founder of the Franciscan Order. It's more popularly known as Mission Dolores. The present chapel, completed in 1791, is two blocks from the original site, at the intersection of Guerrero and a scruffy residential alley called Camp Street; no monument marks the spot.

10 **SAN FRANCISCO ZOO DURING MEALTIME** *Sloat Boulevard near 45th Avenue; open daily from 10 a.m. to 5 p.m. Admission $2.50; kids with adults are free; seniors $1; Children's Zoo admission $1. Phone 661-2023 for special activities.* We mean the animals' mealtime, not yours. The lions are liveliest when they're being fed (daily at 2 p.m.); call for schedules of other animal mealtimes.

San Francisco's zoo, once a rather ordinary animal park, has developed in recent years into an excellent zoological complex. Particularly noteworthy is the Primate Discovery Center, with a nocturnal gallery that reverses the clock so visitors can watch night prowlers in action, and special exhibits telling you all you ever wanted to know about simians. Other realistic habitats have been constructed to give critters and visitors a feeling of place. Among these themed areas are Koala Crossing, with Australian flora and fauna; Musk Ox Meadows, for dwellers of the Alaskan tundra; Gorilla World, the world's largest gorilla habitat; and Wolf Woods, for North American mammals. Naturally, the penguin habitat is called Tuxedo Junction.

More than a thousand furred and feathered creatures call the zoo's 70 acres home, including rare snow leopards. A quick way to see it all is aboard the Zebra Zephyr train.

Ever felt the urge to pet a grasshopper? The Children's Zoo has an animal petting yard, nature trails, and an insect zoo where youngsters can get curious about creatures with six or more legs.

SAN FRANCISCO'S NEXT TEN BEST ATTRACTIONS

These are listed alphabetically, with no attempt at rating, since one visitor's curiosity is another tourist's turn-off. (Other specialty museums are featured in Chapter 17.)

1 **AMERICAN CAROUSEL MUSEUM** *Near Fisherman's Wharf at 633 Beach Street; open daily from 10 a.m. to 6 p.m.; $2 for adults and $1 for kids. Call 928-0550.* Visitors see a collection of hand-carved carousel critters, while listening to tunes from an antique Wurlitzer organ.

2 **BATTERY LOWELL A. CHAMBERLAIN** *At Baker Beach, part of the GGNRA; open weekends only; phone 556-0560 for hours.* Tracing two centuries of fortification of the bay entrance, this intriguing mini-museum is built into a coastal battery's thick concrete bunkers. It exhibits photos, sketches, a rare "disappearing rifle" artillery piece, shells, and other military regalia.

3 **CABLE CAR MUSEUM** *1201 Mason Street near Washington. Open daily from 10 a.m. to 6 p.m.; free admission; call 474-1887.* You'll learn how the archaic cable car system works in an underground viewing room. Study historic photos and admire a display of venerable cars, including Old Number One, built in 1873. The museum was completely redesigned during the 1983–84 rehabilitation of the cable car system.

4 **THE CLIFF HOUSE AND MUSÉE MECHANIQUE** *Great Highway and Point Lobos Avenue. Museum open weekdays 11 a.m. to 6 p.m., weekends 10 a.m. to 7 p.m.; free.* A Cliff House has clung to the rough coastal promontory above Seal Rocks since the 1860s; versions have been alternately destroyed and rebuilt. The current structure houses an information center of the GGNRA, a viewing platform for the seals of Seal Rocks, several restaurants, and a bar. **Musée Mechanique** features one of the world's largest collections of old-time nickelodeons, music boxes, and historic mechanical art. Take along some change and watch these Rube Goldberg devices do their thing.

5 **THE EXPLORATORIUM** *Behind the Palace of Fine Arts (enter at Bay and Lyon). Hours vary; call 561-0360. A six-month pass is $5 for adults, $1 for kids 6–17; a senior lifetime pass is $2.50. Additional fee for Tactile Dome, which requires reservations (561-0362).* This is a wonderful hands-on museum with more than 500 scientific exhibits happening right in front of you. Make your own personal lightning bolt or crawl through the blacked-out Tactile Dome and try to figure out what you're feeling.

6 **GRACE CATHEDRAL** *1051 Taylor Street at California, atop Nob Hill; visitors welcome and guided tours given; call 776-6611.* It's a virtual gallery of religious art as well as one of the oldest cathedrals in America, established in 1863. Seat of the Episcopal Bishop of California, the present neo-classic edifice was completed in 1964.

7 **JOSEPHINE D. RANDALL JUNIOR MUSEUM** *199 Museum Way (Roosevelt Way); 863-1399. Monday–Friday from 10 a.m. to 5 p.m. in summer, Tuesday–Saturday from 10 a.m. to 5 p.m. the rest of the year; free.* Displays in this student-oriented museum include scientific exhibits, and arts and crafts geared to the younger mind. Live critters provide amusement for city kids; the museum is run by the San Francisco Recreation and Parks Department.

8 **PALACE OF FINE ARTS** *Baker Street at Marina Boulevard; open during daylight; free.* Built in 1915 for $400,000 and restored in 1965 for ten times that amount, it's the last survivor of the 1915 Panama-Pacific International Exposition celebrating the opening the Panama Canal. The dramatic Beaux-Arts rotunda is as tall as a ten-story building. A reflecting pool and small park attract dozens of ducks and duck feeders; watch where you step.

9 **THE PRESIDIO OF SAN FRANCISCO** It dates to 1776 when the Spanish set up a military garrison to protect the nearby mission. The 1,500 landscaped acres, once headquarters for the U.S. Sixth Army, becomes part of the Golden Gate National Recreation Area following its 1990 deactivation. Its winding, tree-shaded streets are popular with strollers and cyclists, providing impressive views of the city and the Pacific. The Presidio Officers' Club, originally the Spanish commandant's headquarters, is the city's oldest building.

10 **SAN FRANCISCO MARITIME NATIONAL HISTORIC PARK** *It has several elements, all near Fisherman's Wharf: Hyde Street Pier at the foot of Hyde, admission $2 (kids under 17 and seniors free), daily from 10 a.m. to 5:30 p.m.; National Maritime Museum at the foot of Polk Street, free admission, daily from 10 a.m. to 5 p.m.; and the World War II submarine U.S.S. Pampanito at Pier 45, admission $3 for adults, $2 for juniors, and $1 for kids and seniors, daily from 10 a.m. to 5 p.m. Phone 929-0202 for details.* The assorted elements of the maritime historic park remind us of those days when lusty men — and women — went down to the sea in ships, or off to war.

Hyde Street Pier features America's largest collection of vintage ships, including a century-old lumber schooner, a San Francisco Bay ferry boat, and the square-rigged *Balclutha,* which once sailed around Cape Horn. The Maritime Museum, in a building shaped like the superstructure of an art deco ship, exhibits dozens of model vessels, paintings, photos, and other aquatic artifacts. The *Pampanito* at Pier 45 offers visitors the opportunity to crawl around the compact innards of a battle- scarred World War II submarine that sank six Japanese ships and damaged four others. Exhibits and a self-guided audio tour help explain the sub's complexities.

CHAPTER THREE

Where to Stare on a Clear Day

THE TEN BEST CITY VIEWS

Oh God, I was afraid it would be this beautiful!
— New York author Gail Sheehy, standing on Telegraph Hill

Built on seven hills perched on a peninsula, flanked by sea cliffs, San Francisco is a city of vistas. When columnist Walter Winchell visited here 45 years ago, he claimed the best view was from the men's room on the 22nd floor of the 111 Sutter Building. My research did indeed uncover a male rest stop there, but it's windowless. So much for legends.

However, we have discovered hundreds of other great places from which to admire this special city. Here are our ten favorites.

1 **The Best Overall View of San Francisco: TANK HILL**   Say what? That's right, not Twin Peaks, but Tank Hill, a lower promontory just beneath the famous pair of peaks. We prefer it for two reasons: It's practically deserted and provides a serene setting for eyeing the city, and it's a bit lower in elevation, offering a closer but equally impressive vista. You can see the entire cityscape from here with one slow-motion sweep of your eyes, from Point Reyes to Hunters Point.

To find this little-known lump, drive up Market to Castro, and veer slightly to the right onto 17th; follow this to Stanyan, turn left, and go up a steep grade to Belgrave. Go left again and — still climbing — drive a few blocks to the end of the street. Before you, on the left side of the street, is a trail sloping upward to Tank Hill. The best viewpoint is from a rocky promontory to your left. Just to your right, you'll discover the concrete base of an old water tank that gave this place its inelegant name.

When you reach the top of Tank Hill, the great sweep of the city is unveiled suddenly. It reminds us of the sensation experienced in a helicopter flight that tops a ridge to reveal a hidden panorama.

Reach for your camera and your adjectives. This is the place.

2 **The Best View of the City Skyline: JUST OUTSIDE THE TREASURE ISLAND NAVAL STATION ENTRANCE** From a vantage point near Treasure Island's main gate, you look flat across San Francisco Bay, and the skyline seems to rise from its choppy waters. In fact, many of the high-rises technically do that, for they're built on bay fill.

This viewpoint is easy to find. Just take the Treasure Island exit from the Bay Bridge, and drive to a parking area just outside the naval station. Many people, assuming that access to Treasure Island is restricted, bypass this spot. You do have to be a member of the military or have official reasons to enter the station itself, but the public has access to the parking area. The Treasure Island turnoff is marked from either direction on the bridge.

3 **The Best View of the Restless Sea: GGNRA'S COASTAL TRAIL OFF LINCOLN PARK** Many people are familiar with the Golden Gate Promenade, a pedestrian trail that extends from Aquatic Park near Fisherman's Wharf to Fort Point. Less known and probably more dramatic is GGNRA's Coastal Trail. (Both are suggested hikes in Chapter 21.)

A section of this trail just off Lincoln Park Golf Course offers wonderful vistas of the Pacific and its rocky shoreline; often, such views are filtered through veils of Monterey cypress. It's difficult to believe that you're in a major city — until you glance to your right and see the Golden Gate Bridge and skyline beyond.

The Lincoln Park section of the Coastal Trail begins to the right of El Camino del Mar, just after it emerges from the exclusive Sea Cliff residential area. Look for a sign reading "Welcome to the Golden Gate National Recreation Area." A path skirts the edge of the golf course and takes you to the Coastal Trail. Stroll in either direction on this wilderness-trail-in-a- city and enjoy the scenery.

4 **The Best View of the Waterfront: COIT TOWER** *Tower elevator hours are 10 a.m. to 5:30 p.m. daily; elevator fee is $3.* Certainly this is an insider's guide, full of hidden discoveries, but we can't always avoid the obvious. There's no quarrel that the best vantage point for the city's waterfront, with its wharfingers reaching out into the bay, is from Coit Tower atop Telegraph Hill.

The view is quite nice from the circular parking area below the tower, and the higher you go, the better it gets. So ignore our advice in Chapter 2 about coming here at night; plan a visit when the tower elevator is still operating.

During summer or any sunny weekend, avoid the bumper-thumper traffic by walking up; it's only a ten-minute stroll along a shady pedestrian path. The trail starts where Lombard Street blends into Telegraph Hill Boulevard.

Catch Muni's 39-Coit bus and get off here before it, too, gets stuck in the jam.

5 **The Best View of the Bay Bridge: THE EMBARCADERO PROMENADE** The San Francisco Port Commission has constructed a concrete promenade to the right of the Ferry Building along the Embarcadero. It's a great place from which to admire the bay. From this vantage point, the San Francisco–Oakland Bay Bridge stands boldly in front of you, with little in the foreground to clutter your vision.

6 **The Best View of the Golden Gate: MARIN HEADLANDS** We keep coming back to this ridge, but it *does* offer the most spectacular images of the Golden Gate Bridge and the city skyline.

Vistas of all varieties present themselves as you wind up the narrow road. Pause at the first turnout at Battery Spencer, where the bridge's north tower filters a cityscape through its suspension cables. Climb farther and you see its entire length below you, cradling the skyline in its curved main cables. Gazing at the center span, you may find it hard to believe that this slender reach of steel is a mile long.

If you think this is a beautiful vantage point on a sunny day, hurry up here when cottony tufts of fog roll over the hills and caress those towers, or at night when the city glimmers beyond the gate.

7 **The Best View of Sailboats at Play on the Bay: FORT POINT PIER** What *are* those little sailboats doing out there on the bay all day? Having fun, mostly. If you watch closely, you'll note that many of them are racing. Several sailing clubs stage weekly regattas, using buoy markers and landfalls to chart their liquid courses around the bay.

The best place to watch these races — and also get an eyeful of city, shoreline, and bridge — is from the end of Fort Point Pier. It's not actually at Fort Point, but about half a mile east, along the Presidio shoreline. You can stroll along the Golden Gate Promenade from the fort, or follow signs to the Crissy Field parking area and walk toward the old L-shaped pier, near a Coast Guard station.

This vantage point is just a few hundred feet from a buoy marking one of the race courses. Boats sailing toward the Golden Gate (usually against the wind) must tack sharply toward the buoy, leaning precariously as they work against the stiff breeze. You can hear their sails pop as they change tack, heel around the marker, and head downwind. Some unfurl their spinnakers like giant colored balloons and run with the spirited breeze toward the finish line.

24

8 **The Best View from on High: A LEFT WINDOW SEAT ON UNITED AIRLINES' FLIGHT 553 TO SEATTLE**   This flight leaves San Francisco International Airport at 4:10 p.m. and normally flies inland just over the bay. Left-seaters get a great glimpse of the city crowded onto its small peninsula; details are accentuated by late-afternoon shadows.

Travelers often miss the best aerial angles because the airport is south of the city and most routes go south, west or east. Isn't flying to Seattle a rather costly way to get a good view? Well, there's always United's Flight 1452 to Medford, Oregon.

9 **The Best Overall View of the Bay: GRIZZLY PEAK BOULEVARD ABOVE BERKELEY**   Grizzly Peak follows the Berkeley Hills ridge line, offering pretty pictures of the entire northern end of San Francisco Bay, from San Mateo to the Golden Gate to Belvedere. Several turnouts along this winding, forest-cloaked route invite you to stop and admire the entire San Francisco Peninsula and much of the Bay Area; it's like studying a giant topographic map. The best viewpoints are in Tilden Park, just above the University of California campus. Any good Oakland–Berkeley map will get you up there.

10 **The Best View of the Sunset: THE CAPTAIN PHINEAS T. BARNACLE**   The P.T. Barnacle is a made-to-look-funky pub in the Cliff House, providing a picture-window vision of Seal Rocks and the Pacific. It faces westward so you get the full grandeur of the sun sizzling into the sea. The trick here is to get a window table, because a lot of other folks agree with us and most spots are taken as sundown approaches.

There are many other vantage points around the Cliff House, including an assortment of terraced walks and a trail down to the site of the old Sutro Baths. (Be wary of the surf here; the stones can be slippery and dangerous if you try to work your way out toward Seal Rocks.)

If the Barnacle is full and you really must have a glass in hand to appreciate the sunset, walk up to Louis' Restaurant at 902 Point Lobos; maybe the people there can find room for you.

Where to Point Your Pentax

THE TEN BEST PHOTO SPOTS

'What is the use of a book,' thought Alice, 'without pictures?'
— Lewis Carroll, *Alice's Adventures in Wonderland*

Remember those "Kodak Picture Spot" signs scattered around Disneyland? They're supposed to make it easier for novice photographers to take better snapshots. In the same spirit, we offer you San Francisco's Ten Best picture spots.

Bear in mind that popular vista points don't necessarily produce the best photos. Skyline views usually are too shallow to photograph well, and high vantage points tend to flatten out the scenery. A good scenic photograph should have an interesting foreground, middle ground, and background. Sometimes it's nice to frame your subject with a twig or bright flower.

If you want Aunt Irma in the photo, dress her in something bright; yellows, reds, and oranges are good. And don't force her to squint into the sun. Photograph her with the sun behind you but far to your right or left; the angle will add shadow detail to her face and she won't look like she just ate a bad pizza.

Time of day also is important for photography. During early morning and late afternoon, shadows are sharper, bringing out more detail — particularly in buildings. Often, the atmosphere has a subtle golden quality late in the day, giving warm tones to subjects. At midday when the sun's rays shine straight down, objects look flat and uninteresting.

Dozens of professional photographers have taken hundreds of San Francisco photos that are more dramatic than anything we might produce. But by following our simple hints and finding some interesting vantage points, you'll be able to take home some images that are substantially better than the average snapshot.

What follows are the Ten Best vantage points from which to shoot some of the city's most popular settings. You can use an ordinary adjustable 35mm camera; a 35mm-80mm zoom lens couldn't hurt.

1 **Best Shot of Bridge and City: FROM KIRBY COVE**   The Golden Gate Bridge is the most photographed manmade object in the world. We can understand why. Like a beautiful woman, the bridge looks good from any angle. It's difficult to take a bad picture of it (although thousands of visitors succeed every year).

For our favorite photo, we're returning you to the Marin Headlands. But instead of heading for the heights, go down a dirt road from Battery Spencer (the first fortification you encounter on the headlands road) to Kirby Cove. A short hike through a campground takes you to Kirby Beach, and that beautiful cityscape reappears. This time, it's *under* the bridge span.

The composition is elegant: the beach in the foreground with some tree limbs for framing, the surf and bridge in the middle ground, and the city beyond. It's a late-afternoon horizontal shot; use a 28mm to 35mm lens to get the full expanse of the bridge. Shoot around sunset, when lights begin to twinkle in the city and the last rays of Old Sol highlight the bridge and paint the ocean a gunmetal gray.

The results can be stunning.

2 **Best Shot of Alcatraz: FROM THE AFT GUN DECK OF THE JEREMIAH O'BRIEN**   If the Golden Gate Bridge is the most photographed subject in the city, Alcatraz must be a close second.

We found an unusual angle aboard the old liberty ship S.S. *Jeremiah O'Brien* anchored at Fort Mason's Pier 3 (see Chapter 1). By framing the scowling old prison island under the barrel of a deck gun on the ship's stern, you can create a rather sinister-looking combination.

This can be either a vertical or horizontal; the gun is movable and its position might have changed since we were there. Your lens can vary from 35mm to 80mm. Photograph the ship as close to opening (9 a.m.) or closing (3 p.m.) hours as possible, to get those distinct shadows we've been talking about.

3 **Best Shot of the Bay Bridge: FROM YERBA BUENA IS-LAND**   You've probably seen this handsome view, with the bridge in the foreground and the familiar cityscape beyond. But from where was it taken?

That's the problem. This classic San Francisco scene can be captured only from an overpass just above the Bay Bridge tunnel through Yerba Buena Island, which is Navy property. Strolling around isn't encouraged, says the Treasure Island Public Affairs Office. This is a narrow road with no sidewalks and no place to park. Professional shutter-clickers can contact Public Affairs and be escorted up there, but the office understandably can't handle requests from the general public.

The solution? Have someone with a light foot drive you by slowly while you get a nice shot or two out the car window. To get there, take the Treasure Island turnoff from the Bay Bridge, drive down to the parking area outside the main gate, then turn around and go back up the road, following the signs to Oakland. That takes you across the overpass and you—as the passenger—will be on the proper side of the car to get the shot. The best angle is just beyond the overpass, placing the span between you and the city skyline. Please don't stop or block traffic, or we'll hear about it from the Navy.

The format is horizontal and it's a morning picture, using a 55mm to 80mm lens. Take it on a weekend, when the traffic is light.

4 **Best Shot of the City's Painted Ladies: FROM ALAMO SQUARE**   Once little known, this photo angle of six matching Victorian homes with a modern city skyline beyond has become very popular. Good grief, the area is now on the tour bus route.

The Ladies are on Steiner Street between Fulton and Hayes, opposite a hillside park called Alamo Square. To get your picture, walk up the sloping lawn of the park until you line up the Ladies with the city skyline. We like to shoot under a small evergreen to frame our shot in foliage.

This is a mid-afternoon photo, best as a horizontal; use an 80mm lens. Don't wait until too late in the day, or tree shadows will start obscuring the Ladies' bright makeup.

5 **Best Shot of Mission Dolores: FROM THE MISSION CEMETERY-GARDEN**   It's a challenge to get an effective photo of Mission Dolores from the street because of parked cars—and, frequently, tour buses—that distract from the historic aura of the old adobe. We found a nice angle from a back corner of the cemetery, which is planted in brilliant mums and other flowers.

This view picks up the ancient grave markers, a side of the mission with its old tile roof, and the twin spires of the basilica beyond. We shot it vertically with a 28mm lens in mid-afternoon.

6 **Best Long Shot of the City: FROM THE TIBURON MARINA**   A small marina paralleling Main Street in Tiburon offers an unusual perspective of the city's skyline, looking between Angel Island and Belvedere. You can shoot from several vantage points, including the Tiburon-Angel Island Ferry dock or from the patio of Sam's Anchor Cafe or Guaymas, two restaurants that open onto the marina.

The city is several miles away here, so wait for a clear day and reach for your long lens. You'll get a dramatic effect by shooting through the foreground masts of the marina. It's a vertical and requires at least a 150mm lens. Wait until late afternoon, since you'll need all the shadow accents you can get on that distant, hazy skyline.

7 Best Shot of Yesterday and Today: THE TRANSAMERICA PYRAMID AND ZOETROPE BUILDING FROM THE WINCHELL'S DONUT SIGN ON COLUMBUS AVENUE   A wonderfully ugly little old structure called the Sentinal Building stands on the corner of Columbus and Kearny, and the Transamerica Pyramid towers behind it.

The skinny, wedge-shaped office building, built in 1907 and painted old copper green, houses Francis Ford Coppola's Zoetrope Studios. A Captain Video store on the ground floor adds to the incongruity of blending this ancient building with the modern Pyramid.

If you step into the street just opposite the Winchell's Donut sign at 145 Columbus, you can capture a nice wide angle — about 35mm — of old and new architectural extremes. Late afternoon is best; make sure a passing car doesn't run over your foot.

8 Best Shot of Coit Tower: FROM 807 FRANCISCO STREET   We should have at least one simple little photo in our collection, and we found it with a nice, clean angle of Coit Tower, taken from Francisco Street.

After crossing Hyde Street, Francisco bumps into a cement wall above Leavenworth. Just short of the wall, at 807 Francisco, a bonsai-shaped pine tree leans into the street and forms a nice frame around Coit Tower, several blocks away. As we said, it's a simple shot: just the tower and the tree border. Take it in late afternoon, or in the morning if you want the tower silhouetted. This is a vertical, best photographed with an 80mm lens.

9 Best Shot of the Ferry Building and That Ugly Fountain: NEAR LOS CHILES CAFE   You either love the Vaillancourt Fountain in Justin Herman Plaza or you hate it, right? If you want to capture it on film, you might include the Ferry Building, because I can't think of anyone who doesn't like that.

A nice vantage point is just in front of Los Chiles, an outdoor restaurant in the No. 4 Embarcadero Center complex that borders Justin Herman Plaza. If you aim your camera toward the Ferry Building, the square-jointed fountain does a nice job of shielding the Embarcadero Freeway, which is even uglier than the fountain. A tree offers a pleasant foreground frame for the Ferry Building's clocktower. And watch out for that garbage can near the fountain on your left. This is an afternoon vertical; shoot it with a 55mm lens.

Incidentally, most folks know that Armand Vaillancourt is an artist with a curious sense of form, but who was Justin Herman? He was head of the San Francisco Redevelopment Agency and was largely responsible for waterfront area improvements. Originally called Embarcadero Plaza, this spot was renamed in his honor in 1974, three years after he died.

10 **Best Night Shot of the City: FROM THE VIEWPOINT NEAR TREASURE ISLAND NAVAL STATION ENTRANCE**   This is the same spot we recommended in Chapter 3 for the best view of the city skyline.

At night, cityscape colors glitter and ripple in the waters of the bay, offering creative photo opportunities. Also, those striking garlands of lights added to the cables of the Bay Bridge in 1987 provide a new dimension. The area is paved, so you've got level terrain for your tripod. Arrive about sundown with someone or something warm (both is best), because nightfall often brings up a chilly breeze. Set up and shoot a couple of rolls as the light changes. This can be horizontal or vertical — whatever amuses you.

Dining: The Inside Guide

LISTS OF THE TEN BEST SAN FRANCISCO RESTAURANTS

One cannot think well, love well, or sleep well if one hasn't dined well.
— Virginia Woolf

As a restaurant town, San Francisco has no equal in America. There are more than 4,000 eating establishments here — something like one for every 187.5 residents. The city has more restaurants per capita than any other city in the world.

Statistics say that San Franciscans dine out two-thirds more often than other Americans and that they spend twice as much on restaurant food as New Yorkers. Of course the city's dining spots draw people from throughout the Bay Area as well as tourists from all over the world, so statistics are distorted somewhat. Still, by every measure, the city is *the* nation's dining-out mecca.

Several factors contribute to this bounty. San Francisco is one of the world's most ethnically rich cities, and the nearby Pacific Ocean and the great San Joaquin Valley farm belt provide chefs with a variety of fresh ingredients. From this bounty has developed a contemporary American cuisine, called by most "California" cuisine. It's based on innovative combinations of simply prepared, interestingly spiced dishes using fresh, local ingredients. The movement got its start across the bay in Berkeley, with Alice Waters's now-legendary Chez Panisse, and quickly spread to San Francisco's Stars, Square One, Zuni Cafe, Rings, and others. Chef-owners of Stars and Square One, in fact, are Chez Panisse graduates.

For the next several chapters, we offer you the results of the most pleasant part of our research, dining out in San Francisco. We didn't get around to all 4,000 of the city's restaurants, but Betty and I or the San Francisco Seven have dined at every one mentioned in the pages that follow — except some of those that were recommended by hotel people and cabbies. We dined out nearly 200 times to research the first edition of this book, then tried scores more places in researching this update. We thus gained quite an insight into

31

the San Francisco dining scene.

Also about 15 pounds each.

Naturally, we have to be brazenly arbitrary to nominate a few restaurants out of 4,000. Some of our choices are old hangouts where we've eaten for years; others are new discoveries. Our criteria are simple: consistently good food, prepared as requested, served at the proper temperature, in interesting surroundings.

Our price range runs the gamut from some of the city's most expensive places to some of the least. Our judgment is not based on the bottom line on the check, but on value received.

As mentioned in the introduction, we've selected a No. 1 restaurant as our favorite; the rest are listed alphabetically, with no further ranking. (Credit card abbreviations are the obvious: MC for MasterCard, VISA for Visa, AMEX for American Express, CB for Carte Blanche, DC for Diners Club, and DIS for the new Discover card. "Major credit cards" indicates the two bank cards plus two or more of the others.)

Our price estimates work this way: **Expensive:** $30 or more per person for soup or salad and dinner entree (not including dessert, beverage or gratuity); **moderately expensive:** from $20 to $29; **moderate:** from $10 to $19; and **inexpensive:** under $10.

And now the good news: Thanks primarily to the efforts of former supervisor Carol Ruth Silver, an ordinance was passed in 1987 requiring all eating places to set aside separate sections for non-smokers. But the bad news: as we dined out, we noted that too many places ignore this law or at least fail—as the statute requires—to mark non-smoking areas and advise patrons that they have a choice. If a smoke-free atmosphere is important when you dine out, *insist* that the place obey the law. Or take your appetite somewhere else.

We begin our cafe chapters at the top, with the Ten Best restaurants in San Francisco.

SAN FRANCISCO'S TEN BEST RESTAURANTS

1 **DONATELLO RISTORANTE**   *501 Post Street (at Mason), 441-7182. Northern Italian; expensive; full bar. Open 11:30 a.m. to 2 p.m. and 6 to 10:15 p.m. daily. Reservations essential; major credit cards. Jacket and tie for lunch and dinner.* When we wrote the first edition of this book, we selected Donatello as San Francisco's finest all-around restaurant. Then when we compiled *San Francisco's Ultimate Dining Guide,* based primarily on surveys of people who work with the restaurant and travel trades, it was given the highest rating of any establishment in its price range.

The city's best must pass several tests. The food must be both interesting and superlative, the setting pleasant, and the service attentive. Since we Westerners have little patience with stuffiness, it must meet all these criteria without pretension.

Donatello continues to succeed in every measure. And now it has gone a delightful step further, permitting smoking only in its cocktail lounge. Part of the Donatello hotel (the former Pacific Plaza), this exquisite restaurant is divided into two intimate dining rooms, each simply decorated, but with elegant touches such as Fortuny silk wall coverings and delicate Venetian glass lamps. The setting enhances the food instead of competing with it. Service is efficient, alert, and congenial.

The Northern Italian cuisine is imaginative, delicious, and artfully presented; its flavors are complex yet subtle, not overwhelmed with thick sauces or heavy spicing. Chef Renato Rizzardi changes his menu frequently, featuring specialties from his native country. But he's not strictly a classicist; hints of California cuisine appear in his dishes with the accent on lightly cooked, fresh ingredients.

Donatello has a feature we'd like to see other establishments adopt: a table d'hôte with a different wine to complement each of four courses.

Buon appetito!

2 **ALEJANDRO'S SOCIEDAD GASTRONOMICA** *1840 Clement Street (at 19th Avenue), 668-1184. Latin; moderate; full bar. Open 5 to 11 p.m. Monday–Thursday, 5 p.m. to midnight Friday and Saturday, 4 to 11 p.m. Sunday. Reservations suggested; VISA, MC, AMEX, DC.* Alejandro's is one of those rare restaurants capable of turning an evening into an absolute delight. Patrons are greeted by a pleasing south-of-the-border eclectic decor: hand-painted Mexican tile, carved high-backed Peruvian chairs, Spanish mirrors, and walls busy with all sorts of bright and cheery objects. A mellow-voiced troubadour strolls among the diners, creating the perfect mood for sampling the intriguing menu.

Chef-proprietor Alejandro Espinosa describes his fare as Peruvian-Spanish-Mexican, but he stirs in a lot of Espinosan creativity. Try deep-fried "Alejandro" pastries with cheese, mild chilies, and egg; a cold-cooked cactus and shredded lettuce salad, tapas (spicy Spanish hors d'oeuvres); and entrees such as *paella valenciana* (rice with mussels and cracked crab) or trout wrapped in dried ham. Alejandro serves the best flan in town.

In case you're curious, Sociedad Gastronomica is an association of Latin epicures that convenes at the restaurant from time to time to pass judgment on the fare; menu items with the initials "S.G." have earned its highest ratings.

3 **THE CARNELIAN ROOM**   *Atop Bank of America, 555 California Street (at Montgomery), 443-7500. Continental; expensive; full bar. Open 6 to 10:30 p.m. daily; Sunday brunch from 10:30 a.m. Reservations suggested; all major credit cards; jacket and tie required.* The Carnelian Room has come of age. Initially considered a "view" restaurant only, it has matured into a genuine showplace that also serves consistently excellent food. And it has one of the largest wine cellars in the city. The menu is eclectic Continental, with curious but tasty things like McCorckle duckling with nectarines and raspberries and more predictable items such as veal sautéed with artichoke hearts.

The view from its 52nd-story perch is nothing short of spectacular; it looks *down* on most other sky rooms. When not gazing out the windows, you can admire the French antiques, exquisite tapestries and crystal chandeliers. It's truly a handsome place, inside and out.

We like to arrive early to enjoy a drink — and a different view — in the cocktail lounge before adjourning to dinner.

4 **FLEUR DE LYS**   *777 Sutter Street (at Jones), 673-7779. French; expensive; full bar. Open 6 to 9:30 p.m. Monday–Saturday. Reservations essential, well in advance; major credit cards. Jacket and tie required.* For decades, the city has been noted for its wonderfully posh French restaurants. But many remain in a culinary time capsule, still serving cholesterol- and calorie-rich haute cuisine despite the trend to lighter fare. Fleur de Lys broke out of this capsule a few years ago with the arrival of a new partner, French-born chef Hubert Keller, who has quickly restored it to a premiere position among the city's finer dining establishments. Chef Keller describes his cuisine as "haute nouvelle": frankly French, yet with light, innovative touches and a curious use of seasonings such as cilantro and ginger — curious at least for *cuisine de France.*

His three-star creations are served under a canopy of old world elegance; the cascading fabric ceiling and lavish Continental decor provide a lush setting for a pleasing evening out.

Fleur de Lys was voted the city's best restaurant in our poll of restaurant executives and celebrity chefs in our earlier book, *San Francisco's Ultimate Dining Guide,* and Chef Keller was voted one of the top three chefs in the Bay Area by *San Francisco Focus Magazine* in 1988.

5 **HARRIS'**   *2100 Van Ness Avenue (at Pacific), 673-1888. American (primarily steaks); moderately expensive; full bar. Lunch from 11:30 a.m. to 2 p.m. weekdays, dinner 5 to 11 p.m. Monday–Saturday and 4 to 10 p.m. Sunday. Reservations essential; major credit cards. Jackets required for dinner; tie optional.* Several years ago, owners of that giant feed lot called

Harris Ranch in the San Joaquin Valley hollowed out old Grisson's Steak House to create a handsome, plush, and spacious restaurant. It quickly became — and remains — the best place in the Bay Area to get excellent beef.

The American-style menu features fresh fish and other meats as well, but we go for the wonderful pepper steak and rare prime rib. Cooked vegetables arrive properly crisp, and the decadent desserts are to die for.

With its oak paneling, brass chandeliers, and large, deeply upholstered booths, the place has a masculine and rather clubby feel, but the friendly staff creates a congenial atmosphere.

6 **KULETO'S** *221 Powell Street (at Geary), 397-7720. California-Italian; moderate; full bar. Open from 7 a.m. to 11 p.m. daily. Reservations accepted; all major credit cards.* Normally, a restaurant has to survive the taste of time in order to make our Ten Best list. But Kuleto's, opened in 1987, has quickly become one of the most consistent, versatile *and* durable places in the city.

Functioning as the dining arm of the new Villa Florence Hotel, it serves innovative omelets to early-rising stockbrokers, California cuisine lunches and a mix of classic Italian and other Continental dinners.

It's a stylish yet cheerfully bright place, a pleasing blend of marble, copper, brass, and mahogany glowing under a striking vaulted plaster ceiling. The interior work was done by Pat Kuleto, set designer for Fog City Diner and the Corona Bar and Grill. He fashioned his namesake place working in partnership with hotelier Bill Kimpton, who created the adjacent Villa Florence.

7 **SQUARE ONE** *190 Pacific Avenue Mall (at Front), 788-1110. California-Mediterranean; moderately expensive; full bar. Lunch 11:30 a.m. to 2:30 p.m. weekdays; dinner 5:30 to 10 p.m. Monday–Thursday, 5:30 to 10:30 p.m. Friday–Saturday, and 5 to 9:30 p.m. Sunday. Reservations essential; MC, VISA, AMEX.* Joyce Goldstein, formerly with Alice Waters's Chez Panisse, says she goes back to "square one" every day to create things tasty in the nouvelle style.

The "Mediterranean" reference suggests lively spices and a tendency toward feta, but her dishes are, in fact, quite international. She bases her often-changing menu on whatever fresh, interesting ingredients are available. Pork brochettes in Indonesian peanut sauce; Brazilian mixed grill with black beans and rice; and grilled squab in honey, bourbon, and soy are examples. Steaks emerge with Korean ginger marinade, and grilled fish arrives Cajun style.

All this creativity occurs in an expansive, modern brick structure near the Golden Gateway just off the Embarcadero. Sitting opposite Waldon Park, the airy restaurant is a study in architectural nouvelle with brass, glass, natural woods, and warm fall colors. An open kitchen, the essential ingredient for trendy restaurants, issues its pleasant aromas to waiting diners; a high waffled ceiling softens the clang and clatter.

8 **STARS** *150 Redwood Alley (off Van Ness Avenue between McAllister and Golden Gate), 861-7827. California cuisine; moderately expensive; full bar. Lunch 11:30 a.m. to 2:30 p.m. weekdays only; dinner 5:30 to 10:30 p.m. Monday–Saturday and 5 to 10 p.m. Sunday (limited menu between lunch and dinner). Reservations essential; VISA, MC, AMEX.* The home of the power lunch continues to thrive. Opened in 1984 by Jeremiah Tower, another Chez Panisse graduate, Stars has become an institution. It remains the favorite haunt of power brokers, local celebrities, and faithful followers of Tower's creative California cuisine.

Green awnings and a neat little neon star logo are the only clues that a busy restaurant lurks in Redwood Alley (the more obvious entry on Golden Gate is the back door). Decor in the barnlike interior is upscale rudimentary: an occasional potted palm; a wall immodestly filled with framed awards, accolades, and clippings; and Tiffany-style fixtures dangling from the high ceiling. It is in the huge, open kitchen that creativity *really* thrives. The daily-changing menu features an innovative mix of new California creations with strong international accents.

The entrees are complex and handsomely presented; ingredients are impeccably fresh. Examples are sautéed chicken breasts over fried polenta with rosemary hollandaise; grilled scallops on shredded chilies, cilantro, and ginger with black bean sauce; and, for dessert, rich and creamy hazelnut parfait.

9 **TOMMY TOY'S HAUTE CUISINE CHINOISE** *655 Montgomery Street (at Clay), 397-4888. Chinese-French; expensive; full bar. Lunch 11:30 a.m. to 3 p.m. weekdays; dinner 6 to 10 p.m. Monday–Saturday. Reservations essential; major credit cards; jacket and tie required.* Critical comments on Tommy Toy's lavish dining palace range from "exquisite" to "Chinese excess." The food has been flawless during our several visits, and we *like* dining amidst elegance, even when it's almost overdone. Toy, who earned his marks as a restaurateur with his Imperial Palace in Chinatown, opened this "elegant 19th-century palace" in the heart of the Financial District in 1985.

The restaurant brims with Chinese art and affluence, a museum-quality collection of rare paintings in sandalwood frames, lacquered carvings, and blue porcelains. Booths and chairs are brocaded silk, and tables are set with delicate little porcelain Chinese bridal lamps.

Toy's menu is upscale Cantonese and Mandarin with strong French accents, and it's served European style in individual and beautifully presented entrees. Examples include Szechuan lamb, Maine lobster in ginger sauce and a wonderfully crispy Peking duck. For more of a Chinese-style "sampler" feast, try an eight-course prix fixe dinner.

10 **WASHINGTON SQUARE BAR AND GRILL**   *1707 Powell Street (at Union), 982-8123. American, tilted toward Italian; moderate; full bar. Lunch 10 a.m. to 3 p.m. Monday–Saturday; dinner 5:30 to 11:30 p.m. Sunday–Thursday, to midnight Friday and Saturday; Sunday brunch from 10 a.m. to 3 p.m. Reservations essential; VISA, MC, AMEX, DC.* Our personal prejudice reigns, and this durable place which regulars call "The Square" remains on our Ten Best list. Long a journalists' sanctuary and the city's unofficial press club, it's our favorite hangout. (The real San Francisco Press Club is frequented mostly by attorneys, politicians, and PR hustlers.)

Proprietors Ed and Mary Etta Moose have created the ultimate San Francisco bistro: a crowded and noisy place with friendly bartenders and black-jacketed waiters, white napery and a menu that ranges from amazing hamburgers to properly prepared fresh fish and traditional Italian fare.

The place is alive with activity, from penny-pitching contests to nightly jazz to Sunday brunch. It earns frequent ink in the local press with its globe-trotting *Les Lapins Sauvages* softball team, a group of middle-aged not-so-savage rabbits that recently introduced the game to Russia.

All of this happy commotion occurs just where it should: in a classy high-ceilinged Victorian opposite Washington Square, in the heart of old San Francisco.

THE TEN FAVORITE RESTAURANTS OF THOSE WHO REALLY KNOW

Who keeps closer tabs on the restaurant scene than hotel people and cab drivers? Every day, they're asked by visitors and residents to recommend a good place to eat. We polled concierges, managers, and others from the city's major hotels and drivers from five large cab companies, and asked them to select their favorite dining spots.

Incidentally, since this was a popularity contest among many voters, we rate them according to the order of finish.

The Hotel Folks' Ten Favorite Restaurants

Hotel people weren't permitted to nominate restaurants within their establishments. Interestingly, many selected cafes from other hotels, and two — Donatello and Campton Place — appear among the top ten vote-getters.

1 **THE CARNELIAN ROOM** *Atop Bank of America, 555 California Street (at Montgomery), 443-7500. Continental; expensive; full bar. Dinner 6 to 10:30 p.m. daily; Sunday brunch from 10:30 a.m. Reservations suggested; all major credit cards; jacket and tie required.* See details above.

2 **DONATELLO RISTORANTE** *501 Post Street (at Mason), 441-7182. Northern Italian; expensive; full bar. Open 11:30 a.m. to 2 p.m. and 6 to 10:15 p.m. daily. Reservations essential; major credit cards. Jacket and tie for lunch and dinner.* See details above.

3 **MAX'S OPERA CAFE** *601 Van Ness Avenue (at Golden Gate in Opera Plaza), 771-7300. Upscale deli; moderate; full bar. Open 11:30 a.m. to midnight Sunday–Thursday, 11:30 a.m. to 1:30 a.m. Friday–Saturday. All major credit cards.* A cross between a New York and California deli, Max's is popular for its lunches and light dinners. The waiters and waitresses pause periodically at night to entertain diners with a show tune, or even an aria.

4 **SQUARE ONE** *190 Pacific Avenue Mall (at Front), 788-1110. California-Mediterranean; moderately expensive; full bar. Lunch 11:30 a.m. to 2:30 p.m. weekdays; dinner 5:30 to 10 p.m. Monday–Thursday, 5:30 to 10:30 p.m. Friday–Saturday, and 5 to 9:30 p.m. Sunday. Reservations essential; MC, VISA, AMEX.* See details above.

5 **RISTORANTE MILANO** *1448 Pacific Avenue (at Hyde), 673-2961. Northern Italian; moderate; wine and beer. Dinner from 5:30 to 10:30 p.m. nightly; MC, VISA.* This *tres chic* restaurant with black and white decor dishes up subtle Milanese-style chicken, veal, and pastas; it's noted for excellent in-house desserts.

6 **CAMPTON PLACE** *340 Stockton Street (in the Campton Place Hotel, near Sutter), 781-5155. American nouvelle; expensive; full bar. Breakfast Monday–Friday 7 to 11 a.m.; Saturday 8 to 11:30 a.m.; lunch Monday–Friday 11:30 a.m. to 2:30 p.m., Saturday noon to 2:30 p.m., dinner Sunday–Thursday 5:30 to 10 p.m., Friday–Saturday from 5:30 to 10:30 p.m. All major credit cards; jackets suggested for lunch and dinner.* This opulent restaurant, a decorator's vision of gold leaf, brass, potted palms, and Chinese porcelain, serves excellent and inventive American regional cuisine.

7 **ZUNI CAFE**   *1658 Market Street (at Franklin), 552-2522. California-Mediterranean; moderate to moderately expensive; full bar. Open Tuesday–Friday 7:30 a.m. to midnight, Saturday 9 a.m. to midnight, Sunday 9 a.m. to 11 p.m. Reservations essential; MC, VISA, AMEX.* Begun as a Southwestern nouvelle restaurant, Zuni has widened its culinary horizon to include interesting international and contemporary American fare. It still retains its Southwestern motif, with warm colors and an occasional Navajo blanket.

8 **STARS**   *150 Redwood Alley (off Van Ness Avenue between McAllister and Golden Gate), 861-7827. California cuisine; moderately expensive; full bar. Lunch 11:30 a.m. to 2:30 p.m. weekdays only; dinner 5:30 to 10:30 p.m. Monday–Saturday and 5 to 10 p.m. Sunday (limited menu between lunch and dinner). Reservations essential; VISA, MC, AMEX.* See details above.

9 **TRADER VIC'S**   *20 Cosmo Place (between Post and Taylor), 776-2232. Oriental-Continental; moderately expensive; full bar. Lunch weekdays 11:30 a.m. to 2:30 p.m.; dinner Monday–Saturday from 5 p.m. to 12:30 a.m. Reservations essential; major credit cards.* Flagship of the late Victor Bergeron's restaurant fleet, it has been serving its mai tais and upscale Chinese-Polynesian cuisine to generations of the faithful. It's the favored haunt of old, moneyed San Francisco.

10 **DORO'S**   *714 Montgomery Street (at Washington), 397-6822. Continental; expensive; full bar. Lunch daily 11:30 a.m. to 2:30 p.m.; dinner daily 6 to 10:30 p.m. Reservations essential; all major credit cards; jackets recommended.* Don A. Dianda's handsome restaurant is another San Francisco institution, where residents and visitors settle into red leather banquettes to dine on haute cuisine from the Continent.

The Cab Drivers' Ten Favorite Restaurants

The city's cabbies picked Original Joe's as their favorite in the original edition of *The Best of San Francisco,* and they've done so again, obviously proving the durability and popularity of the place.

1 **ORIGINAL JOE'S**   *144 Taylor Street (at Turk), 775-4877. Italian-American; inexpensive; full bar. Open 10:30 a.m. to 1:30 a.m. daily. Reservations for five or more only; no credit cards.* It's the oldest surviving Italian-American "Joe" style restaurant in the city, opened in 1937 by Joe Morelio, three years after he established the first such place—New Joe's—

on Broadway. "We have some of the oldest waiters this side of Medicare," says present owner Marie Rodin Duggan, pointing out that some have been serving up Original Joe's pasta for 40 years.

2 ALFRED'S *886 Broadway (at Mason), 781-7058. Italian-steakhouse; moderately expensive; full bar. Dinner 5:30 to 10 p.m. nightly. Reservations recommended; jackets suggested for men; major credit cards.* Combine Harris' with an upscale Original Joe's and you get Alfred's: a restaurant dating back to 1928 that serves outstanding beef and reliable Italian-American fare.

3 GAYLORD *Ghirardelli Square, 900 North Point, 771-8822. Northern Indian; moderate to moderately expensive; full bar. Lunch noon to 2 p.m. daily; dinner 5 to 11 p.m. daily. Reservations essential; all major credit cards.* See Chapter 7 for details.

4 TADICH GRILL *240 California Street (at Front), 391-2373. American, primarily seafood; moderate to moderately expensive; full bar. Open Monday–Friday 11 a.m. to 9 p.m. No credit cards.* Established in 1849, Tadich is one of the city's oldest restaurants, yet its charcoal-broiled, lightly cooked fish is contemporary and delicious. San Francisco Giants' general manager Al Rosen calls it the best seafood house in San Francisco.

5 ZUNI CAFE *1658 Market Street (at Franklin), 552-2522. California-Mediterranean; moderate to moderately expensive; full bar. Open Tuesday–Friday 7:30 a.m. to midnight, Saturday 9 a.m. to midnight, Sunday 9 a.m. to 11 p.m. Reservations essential; MC, VISA, AMEX.* Also selected by hotel folks; see details above.

6 ALEJANDRO'S *1840 Clement Street (at 19th Avenue), 668- 1184. Latin; moderate; full bar. Open 5 to 11 p.m. Monday–Thursday, 5 p.m. to midnight Friday and Saturday, 4 to 11 p.m. Sunday. Reservations suggested; VISA, MC, AMEX, DC.* Details above.

7 SCOMA'S *Pier 47 (Fisherman's Wharf), 771-4383. Seafood; inexpensive to moderate; full bar. Open from 11:30 a.m. to 11 p.m. daily. Reservations accepted; major credit cards.* Many San Franciscans insist that venerable Scoma's is the best restaurant at Fisherman's Wharf; our cab drivers obviously agree.

8 **BEETHOVEN RESTAURANT**   *1707 Powell Street (at Union), 391-4488. Moderate; wine and beer. Open 5:30 to 10:30 p.m. Tuesday–Saturday. Reservations accepted; MC, VISA, AMEX.* See details in Chapter 7.

9 **NEPTUNE'S PALACE**   *Pier 39, 434-2260. Seafood; moderate to moderately expensive; full bar. Open 11 a.m. to 11 p.m. daily. Reservations advised during summer; major credit cards.* See details in Chapter 6.

10 **FIOR D'ITALIA**   *601 Union Street (at Columbus Avenue), 986-1886. Italian; moderate; full bar. Open 11 a.m. to 10:30 p.m. daily. Reservations accepted; major credit cards.* Occupying the same site since 1886, it's the city's oldest Italian restaurant: a North Beach landmark with high-backed booths, etched glass trim, and black-jacketed waiters.

CHAPTER SIX

Delights from the Deep

THE TEN BEST SEAFOOD CAFES

I like my oysters fried; That way I know my oysters died.
— Roy G. Blount, Jr.

A city surrounded on three sides by water had *better* offer good seafood restaurants, and San Francisco certainly does. It's not just the waterbound topography that has created this abundance of chowder houses. Fish was a dietary staple for two of our earliest immigrant groups, the Italians and Chinese, and they opened many of the city's first seafood restaurants.

Fisherman's Wharf, for instance, has been a focal point for Italian seafood restaurants for decades. However, we feel that many of them have become complacent; only one—Tarantino's—makes our list of the Ten Best fish spots. We've discovered more interesting restaurants with more innovative menus elsewhere.

Incidentally, many of San Francisco's larger seafood houses with extensive menus may serve frozen as well as fresh fish, so always ask what's just been reeled in. We usually get a frank answer, although some waitpeople use that wonderful self-canceling response: "Well, it's freshly frozen."

Our favorite seafood haven is a long way from the Wharf; the only water you can see from there is in your glass.

1 **HAYES STREET GRILL** *324 Hayes Street (at Franklin), 863-5545. Moderate to moderately expensive; full bar. Lunch 11:30 a.m. to 3 p.m. weekdays; dinner 5 to 10 p.m. Monday–Thursday, 5 to 11 p.m. Friday and 6 to 11 p.m. Saturday. Reservations essential; VISA, MC.* We've been going to Hayes Street Grill since it opened in 1979, and we've yet to be served poorly done fish. Although the city offers dozens of fine seafood parlors, several factors place this one a cut above the others.

Only fresh fish is served, and you have a choice of preparation: mesquite broiled, pan-fried, or whatever. It's *always* lightly done, and it's offered with an interesting selection of sauces, served on the side so you can nip at them carefully before committing your entire fish.

A California-oriented wine list features several full-flavored yet dry wines by the glass, selected with fish in mind.

The daily-changing menu is written on a blackboard, saving you the need to memorize a waiter's long incantation. A few meats and even an excellent burger and fries are included on the large menu; but essentially, this is *the* place for wonderfully fresh, simply prepared seafood.

2 **BENTLEY'S SEAFOOD GRILL & OYSTER BAR** *185 Sutter Street (at Kearny), 989-6895. Moderate; full bar. Lunch Monday–Saturday 11:30 a.m. to 3 p.m.; dinner Monday–Thursday 5 to 9:30 p.m. and Friday–Saturday 5 to 10:30 p.m. Reservations advised; major credit cards.* The dining arm of the art deco Galleria Park Hotel, Bentley's is the city's newest upscale seafood salon, combining a handsome 1920s look with a trendy seafood menu. If you've grown weary of basic fillet of sole, try intriguing dishes such as monkfish roasted with endive, chanterelles, and fried Jerusalem artichokes; linguine with cracked pepper, roasted tomatoes, and Dungeness crab, simmered in vodka; or blackened prawns with green onions and papaya bits. Entrees come with tasty house-baked corn muffins. The menu changes weekly to feature curious new kitchen creations; although the fare is primarily seafood, a few meat dishes are offered.

The place pleases the eye as well as the palate. The entrance is particularly striking: a 25-foot-high glass portal etched with seafood designs. The interior is done in salmon pink with shell wall sconces and black and white photos of Roaring Twenties scenes. A raw bar, a lively booze bar, and dining tables occupy the main floor; a more intimate dining area is tucked into a second-floor balcony.

3 **MAYE'S STEAK AND OYSTER HOUSE** *1233 Polk Street (at Sutter), 474-7674. Inexpensive to moderate; full bar. Open Monday–Saturday 11:30 a.m. to 9:30 p.m., Sunday 2 to 9:30 p.m. Reservations accepted; MC, VISA, AMEX.* Venerable Maye's, in business since 1867, is looking a bit brighter these days. New owners Bibi and Phyllis Fiorucci have redone the interior to lighten the old wainscoting and dark woods. But the old-fashioned deep, comfortable booths and crisp white linens remain, along with remarkably modest prices; Maye's is one of the city's least expensive seafood places.

The new owners have updated the kitchen as well, offering mesquite-grilled seafood and steaks, along with the traditional crab casseroles and steamed clams. We compliment their wisdom in buying a dining landmark, then — to quote the popular country song — knowing what to throw away and knowing what to keep.

43

4 **NEPTUNE'S PALACE** *Pier 39, 434-2260. Moderate to moderately expensive; full bar. Open 11 a.m. to 11 p.m. daily. Reservations advised during summer; major credit cards.* When we wrote the original *Best of San Francisco*, we selected Neptune's as the best seafood restaurant at the city's ultimate tourist trap, ticky-tacky Pier 39, and one of the Ten Best in the city. Subsequent meals haven't changed our vote.

Neptune's is one of the original Pier 39 restaurants, surviving where many others have failed. We like the fetching Victorian decor of this large, airy place and its fine end-of-the-pier vantage point offering great bay views. The kitchen still keeps pace with cooking trends, offering lightly done, subtly sauced seafood dishes.

We wouldn't send you to a chowder house just for the view (you have a choice of three dining rooms), but if you can combine wonderful vistas with good food, why not?

5 **PACIFIC CAFE** *Ghirardelli Square, 775-1173; also at 7000 Geary Boulevard, 387-7091. Inexpensive to moderate, full bar. Open 11:30 a.m. to 10:30 p.m. weekdays (to 11 p.m. Friday), 5 to 11 p.m. Saturday, 5 to 10 p.m. Sunday (shorter hours on Geary). Reservations accepted; all major credit cards.* Several cafes Pacific are scattered about the Bay Area; we've eaten at four different outlets and have received consistently good, inexpensive seafood and affable service.

Our favorite is the Ghirardelli branch, which looks right at home in this old brick complex with its semi-rustic natural wood decor and hanging plants. It's popular both with residents and tourists, and if it becomes too popular and you have to wait for your table, the barkeep will offer you a complimentary glass of wine. Nice touch.

The seafood is fresh and simply prepared, ranging from hard-to-find sand dabs (a favorite of ours) and Cajun-style snapper to lobster Newburg. Menu prices are curiously odd, such as $9.27 or $8.58. It's a harmless conversation piece, although tip calculations are a bit more difficult if you're the precise type.

6 **PACIFIC HEIGHTS BAR & GRILL** *2001 Fillmore (at Pine), 567-3337. Moderate; full bar. Lunch from 11:30 a.m. to 2:30 p.m. Monday–Friday; dinner 5 to 10 p.m. Sunday–Thursday and 5 to 11 p.m. Friday–Saturday; Sunday brunch 10:30 a.m. to 2:30 p.m. Reservations accepted; MC, VISA, AMEX.* Owners Susan and Craig Bashel claim their restaurant has the largest raw bar on the West Coast, offering 12 to 16 varieties of oysters daily. We didn't know those awful-looking things *came* in a dozen different types. But there they were, flashing crooked grins from their bed of shaved ice: blue points, Golden Mantels, Quilcenes, Appalachicolas,

Yaquina Bays and even New Zealand green-lipped mussels. The courageous can try them with an assortment of sauces, from sour cream dill to tomato herb salsa.

Those who don't care for such slippery fare can pick from a large selection of fish such as Hawaiian ono, a wonderfully rich and tasty spearfish; a mesquite-grilled catch of the day; peppered Louisiana redfish; Chilean sea bass; or even a hamburger. If you can handle black noodles, try the seafood pasta with squid ink — *much* tastier than it sounds.

Opened in 1984, the place is "contemporary California" in style, with cool pastel colors, brick accent walls, oak trim, and lots of mirrors; it's housed in a venerable Victorian along Fillmore Street's growing restaurant row. The raw bar set in the front window and the long liquor bar are popular yuppie hangouts, and the place can get noisy on Friday and Saturday nights. But the volume wasn't excessive when we visited, and the service was excellent.

7   **PISCES**   *2127 Polk Street (at Broadway), 771-0850. Moderate; wine and beer. Lunch 11:30 a.m. to 3 p.m. Monday–Saturday; dinner 5 to 10 p.m. Monday–Thursday, 5 to 10:45 p.m. Friday–Saturday and 4 to 10 p.m. Sunday. Reservations accepted; all major credit cards.* We recall when Pisces was the new dining discovery in Polk Gulch, but now it's on the verge of becoming an institution, having served consistently good seafood since 1977.

The owner and chef are Thai, but the seafood menu is more Continental than Asian. The moderately priced dinners are an excellent value, since they include chowder or salad, fresh vegetables and rice, or thick French fries. The menu offers a tasty range of fresh fish, calamari, lobster, and an excellent cioppino over rice.

The charming little place is casual and inexpensive yet intimate, with flickering candles and fresh-cut flowers on starched white napery; it's one of our San Francisco favorites.

8   **SCOTT'S LOMBARD**   *2400 Lombard Street (at Scott), 563-8988; also at No. 3 Embarcadero Center near the waterfront, 981-0622. Moderate to moderately expensive; full bar. Open 11:30 a.m. to 10:30 p.m. daily. Reservations accepted; MC, VISA, AMEX.* Scott's was one of the first major seafood restaurants to move away from downtown and the waterfront, locating along the city's "motel row" in 1976. It has since returned to the bay front to open a branch in Embarcadero Center. Each is a fashionable seafood restaurant with a strong local following.

We prefer the original Scott's, in a stylish Cape Cod–Victorian atmosphere with lots of brass, warm woods, and glass.

Both restaurants specialize in locally caught fish, plus a good fisherman's stew and various shellfish dishes. The versatile menu changes twice daily, with as many as a dozen fresh fish entrees, steaks and chops, several appetizers, a couple of pastas, and tasty in-house desserts.

9 **TARANTINO'S**   *206 Jefferson Street (above the boat basin at Fisherman's Wharf), 775-5600. Moderate; full bar. Open 11 a.m. to 11 p.m. daily. Reservations accepted; VISA, MC, AMEX.* We've been ordering fresh fish from Tarantino's since the 1950s, watching it change subtly with the times by lightening up on its sauces while maintaining its role as both a tourist lure and a comfortable haven for regulars.

It has kept its dignity amid the growing tackiness of the Wharf while offering good, honest seafood. Perhaps we favor the place because it was founded by a couple of Irish lads. When Gene McAteer and Dan Sweeney opened their place in 1946, they gave it an Italian name, since the area was dominated by the sons of Italy. The tip-off to Tarantino's genealogy is the green bow ties worn by the wait staff and green trim on the busboys' jackets.

Tarantino's second-floor location over a corner of the boat basin provides one of the best views on the Wharf; seating is tiered so all diners can share the vista. The seascape is equally appealing from a handsome little cocktail lounge.

10 **THE WATERFRONT**   *Pier 7 (Embarcadero at Broadway), 391-2696. Moderate to moderately expensive; full bar. Open 11:30 a.m. to 10:30 p.m. daily. Reservations accepted; major credit cards.* Combining fresh seafood, an elegant Old San Francisco decor, and a great bay view, Al Falchi's classy place has become *the* waterfront establishment for power lunches and first-rate dinners.

The menu is versatile, ranging from assorted grilled fish, scampi, and a mixed grill to pastas and an occasional steak. It's served in a pleasing environment of brass, natural woods, potted foliage, and crisp white linens. All this ambiance is housed in a sturdy old masonry building on the waterfront, with a glass-walled view of the Bay Bridge and Treasure Island; the dining room is steeply terraced so that everyone can see. And finally, Falchi offers a great wine selection, with more than a hundred California vintners represented.

Fare with an International Flair

THE TEN BEST ETHNIC RESTAURANTS

Nachman's rule: when it comes to foreign food, the less authentic the better.
— Gerald Nachman

Few people can agree on the authenticity of ethnic foods. What Americans consider Mexican cuisine has been altered by generations of Mexican-American cooks. On the other hand, many Chinese dishes retain their traditional style and are even superior to the original fare in China. Why? Because fresher ingredients are available in our more affluent society, and because Chinese farmers in the San Joaquin Valley grow the same hairy melons and long beans that are staple veggies of the old country.

However, the issue here is not authenticity, but variety. San Francisco probably has a greater range of international restaurants than any other city in the world.

How is it possible to choose the best from among the scores of ethnic places? Which of the several hundred Chinese restaurants — Cantonese, Hunan, Szechwan, Mandarin, Hakka — deserve top honors? Can one pot of properly prepared pasta really be more perfect than another? How does one decide among the many elegant little French restaurants where candles glimmer on white-clothed tables and mysterious sauces simmer in back kitchens?

An impossible task, you say?

Obviously.

We therefore rely on the divination that has served us so well in the past: personal preference. In arriving at our ethnic Ten Best, we applied criteria similar to those used in our earlier selections: good food, service, and value.

But we also made some arbitrary decisions, both in price range and style. Since the French produce the world's most elegant fare, we focused on upscale restaurants featuring haute cuisine. From Italy, we sought hearty trattorias, which are typical of San Francisco's Italian community (although we hastily add that some of the city's most elegant restaurants are Italian as well). Our Chinese selections reflect old-country cooking, not San Franciscanized chop suey. Since Chinese places represent the largest group in the city and their cuisine is quite divergent, we've divided them into two broad groups. Cantonese reflects the cooking style of Canton with its fresh, lightly seasoned fish and vegetables; Mandarin is our catch-all category covering the spicier cooking of the rest of China, including Szechwan and Hunan.

In limiting ourselves to ten varieties, we are unable to mention many of the foreign cuisines that can be savored in this city. We apologize to the Korean, Nicaraguan, Philippine, Thai, Polish, Salvadoran, Yugoslav, and many other ethnic restaurants that failed to make the list.

Those that *have* made it are tallied alphabetically.

1 **The Best Cantonese Restaurant: OCEAN**   *726 Clement Street (at Sixth Avenue), 221-3351. Inexpensive to moderate; wine and beer. Lunch 11:30 a.m. to 3 p.m. and dinner 4:30 to 9:30 p.m. daily. MC, VISA, AMEX.* Our favorite Cantonese restaurant isn't in Chinatown; it's among the growing ranks of Asian places in the Richmond District, along Clement Street. For the past decade, Chinese, Japanese, Korean, and Vietnamese restaurants have been shifting away from high-rent districts into more affordable neighborhoods. We've found them to be as good as (sometimes better than) their higher-priced downtown cousins.

The best of these is Ocean, which not only serves excellent Cantonese food, but serves it in a bright, cheerful environment. Many small family-run Asian restaurants are a bit scruffy, with Formica furnishings, but Ocean has been spruced up with pink tablecloths, blonde wood chairs, and clean white walls with large pastel floral prints.

As the name suggests, the Cantonese menu leans heavily toward seafood, and some of it is still alive in tanks in the kitchen, so there's no concern about freshness. Among offerings on the varied menu are rock cod over cooked lettuce, oysters with black bean sauce, and shrimp with sweet walnuts, plus the usual array of Cantonese vegetable, beef, and pork dishes. A few spicier dishes are available as well; try the excellent hot and sour seafood soup or Hunan crab hot pot. Portions are generous, with plenty of meat or fish, not stretched out with a lot of vegetables.

2 **The Best French Restaurant: MASA'S**   *648 Bush Street (at Powell), 989-7154. Expensive; full bar. Open Tuesday–Saturday 6 to 9:30 p.m. Reservations absolutely essential, well in advance; MC, VISA, AMEX, DIS; jackets required, ties optional.* It is the most opulent and expensive French restaurant in San Francisco and one of the finest west of the

Mississippi, and perhaps the Seine.

"Contemporary subdued elegance" is manager John Cunin's description of this posh restaurant founded in 1983 by the late Masataka Kobayashi. Present chef Julian Serrano and owner Bill Kimpton have successfully carried Masa's banner of excellence. Cost is no object, for it is passed on to eager diners, who cheerfully pay to be fed and pampered by a wait staff that outnumbers the guests.

The fare is classic Gallic, which is curious, since the founder was Japanese and the present chef is Italian. Yet the food is faultlessly French, with its rich sauces, served in a hushed environment of burgundy and gray, with textured wallpaper, gold-rimmed mirrors, a paneled ceiling, and subdued lighting. Smoking is not permitted, so you smell only those savory sauces.

With only a dozen or so tables to attend, alert waiters are at your side at the slightest arch of an eyebrow, but they never hover. Masa's remains the ultimate venue for special occasions and quiet celebrations.

3. The Best German Restaurant: BEETHOVEN RESTAURANT

1707 Powell Street (at Union), 391-4488. Moderate; wine and beer. Open 5:30 to 10:30 p.m. Tuesday–Saturday. Reservations accepted; MC, VISA, AMEX. We love the Black Forest ambiance of this place, with its old-fashioned wainscoting, fine-print wallpaper, ticking cuckoo clock, and violin music sighing softly in the background — presumably something by Beethoven. It's difficult to believe that busy Powell Street is just outside.

Host Alfred Baumann treats visitors like guests in his home, guiding them through the menu and suggesting a proper German wine with his rich fare. Among the more traditional entrees are a few Baumann innovations such as *paprikaschnitzel,* his spicier version of *wienerschnitzel.* Sauces are hearty and Germanic, touched with brandy, sherry, or wine to give them authority.

Despite its warm-wood elegance, Beethoven is remarkably inexpensive; complete meals with tasty soups and large salads are under $15. Two musts, no matter what else you order: potato pancakes with your entree, and, for dessert, apple strudel, with a filling so generous it's like eating deep-dish apple pie.

4. The Best Indian Restaurant: GAYLORD

Ghirardelli Square, 900 North Point, 771-8822; also at One Embarcadero Center, 397-7775. Moderate to moderately expensive; full bar. Lunch noon to 2 p.m.; dinner 5 to 11 p.m. daily. Reservations essential; major credit cards. This handsome restaurant's roots reach back to British colonial India, when the Gaylord family started its first dining palace in Bombay. Branches have since opened in a few other major cities, but the chefs are still India-trained.

Gaylord typifies the quiet elegance of finer Indian restaurants with a mix of old European and Eastern decor. A bonus at the Ghirardelli location is a striking view of the bay.

The two restaurants specialize in the tandoori cooking of northern India instead of the hot curries typical of southern regions. Meats are rubbed with light seasonings, then cooked at a high temperature in round clay tandoor ovens to preserve their juices. Your meal should be accompanied with a bread made of wheat, yogurt, and onion called *kulcha*, which is whomped against the side of the tandoor, where it is quick-baked and brought to your table still radiating that tantalizing aroma.

5 **The Best Italian Restaurant: BASTA PASTA** *1268 Grant Avenue (at Vallejo), 434-2248. Inexpensive to moderate; full bar. Open 11:45 a.m. to 2 a.m. daily. Reservations accepted; MC, VISA, AMEX.*

Picking the city's best Italian restaurant is as frustrating as selecting the top Chinese place; there are so many choices. But we'll vote for Basta Pasta, founded in 1977 and reopened in late 1988 with a sleek new look: off-white walls accented by green and burgundy ceramic tile strips, set off by dark wood trim. A ceramic tile wood-fed pizza and calzone oven is a focal point of the open kitchen downstairs. Upstairs, folks can dine beneath a skylight.

Only a bathtub painted with comic caricatures survives from the old, funkier Basta Pasta. But the versatile menu and long hours remain; we like to wander into this cheerful place at midnight and order a plate of predictable pasta. Although the menu lists hearty southern Italian fare such as fresh-made pastas, veal dishes, pizza, and calzone, its choicest entrees are fish, literally fresh off the boat. Owners Bruno Orsi and Lorenzo Petroni are part owners of a fishing boat. So if you seek really fresh seafood, ask what the *North Beach Star* brought in that morning.

6 **The Best Japanese Restaurant: YOSHIDA-YA** *2909 Webster Street (at Union), 346-3431. Moderate; full bar. Open 5 to 10 p.m. Sunday; 5:30 to 11 p.m. Monday–Thursday and 5:30 to midnight Friday–Saturday. Reservations advised; major credit cards.*

Japanese are masters at understated decor, and Yoshida-Ya captures this in the simple, clean lines of its upstairs dining room with its tatami floor, shoji screens, and artfully placed items of folk art and ceramics. Entrees are part of this pretty picture, carefully presented in handsome ceramics and lacquerware.

The kitchen excels at light, crisp tempuras and other traditional dishes of Nippon. It also likes to experiment, offering such curiosities as a dinner of shrimp prepared in seven different styles. And it features skewered delicacies called yakitori, common in Japan but not always available here. Unlike the larger Middle Eastern style kebabs, yakitori is rather delicate: small, tender bits of marinated meat, seafood, and vegetables threaded onto slim bamboo skewers and broiled over a charcoal fire.

A final touch: the tea that accompanies meals has a rich, nutlike flavor, accomplished by mixing browned rice with the tea leaves.

In addition to the traditional tatami room, the restaurant offers conventional seating for those unwilling—or unable—to enjoy leisurely dining with their legs rumpled beneath them. And it offers a sleekly modern sushi and appetizer bar downstairs.

7   **The Best Mandarin Restaurant: BRANDY HO'S**   *217 Columbus Avenue (at Pacific), 788-7527; also at 450 Broadway, 362-6268. Inexpensive to moderate; wine and beer (full bar at Broadway location). Open 11:30 a.m. to 11 p.m. daily (to midnight Friday and Saturday). MC, VISA, AMEX.* Can a noisy place plastered with "NO MSG" signs really be the best Hunan-style restaurant in the city? It's certainly one of the liveliest, and we like the fact that Brandy S.C. Ho's spicy entrees are free of that cloying monosodium glutamate. We also like the hustle, rustle, and clatter of this place.

This is a raucous marriage of Chinese cuisine and American marketing; the food is excellent and the waiters are unusually helpful at steering Caucasians through the menu. But this is no Chinatown tourist trap; the place brims daily with local Chinese and office workers from the nearby Financial District.

Although the well-prepared dishes are amply laced with those mouth-searing bits of dried red peppers, you can ask your waiter to go easy on the hot stuff. And the menu offers milder dishes, including some excellent steamed fish and a really fine sizzling rice soup.

If the clamor is too much, try the new, more sedate, and classy place on Broadway. "Spent lots of money, but I'm keeping prices within reason," Brandy tells us.

8   **The Best Mexican Restaurant: LAS MANANITAS**   *850 Montgomery Street (at Pacific), 434-2088. Moderate to moderately expensive; full bar. Open from 11 a.m. to 1 a.m. daily. Reservations advised; major credit cards.* Dozens of Mexican restaurants scattered along Mission Street and elsewhere in the city serve acceptable tacos and refritos, but each seems pretty much like the other. Any Latin food authority will point out that these are *Mexican-American* dishes, considerably altered from the original cuisine. To experience authentic Old Mexico fare—the sort of food you would enjoy at a better restaurant in Mexico City or a coastal town—try

51

Las Mañanitas. Seafood, grilled meats and fowl are more typical of south of the border haute cuisine, and Las Mañanitas (which means "morning song") excels at these offerings.

Try the chilled lobster, chicken in mole sauce, pork loin with avocado, the catch of the day grilled in a light lime sauce, or prawns in garlic. A special lunch menu offers a choice of authentic "Mexico City originals" and the more familiar California-Mexican enchiladas and fajitas.

The restaurant's elegant Latin decor of painted tile, wrought iron, brass, and hand-hewn ceiling beams enhances the dining experience. During balmy weather, you can adjourn to a garden patio graced by a gurgling fountain.

The check for a complete meal will average $20 or more, but then, this isn't Taco Bell.

9 **The Best Mideastern Cafe: THE GRAPELEAF**   *4031 Balboa Street (at 41st Avenue), 668-1515. Moderate; full bar. Dinner 6:30 to 10:30 p.m. Wednesday–Saturday; 5:30 to 9:30 p.m. Sunday. Reservations accepted; MC, VISA, AMEX.* When we feel the need to party, we gather a group of friends, adjourn to the Grapeleaf, and put ourselves in the capable hands of Gabe and Suzy Michael.

They cover our table with spicy Lebanese and other Mideastern delicacies and keep the wine flowing. They'll begin the banquet with a *mezza* appetizer tray of tiny dolmas, chick-peas, and spicy bits of meat and vegetables, then follow with kebabs of seasoned lamb or spiced fish, accompanied with marinated vegetables rich enough to serve as entrees. Between bites, we pause to study the aerobics of the resident belly dancer as she squiggles past, inviting us to tuck dollar bills into her skimpy waistband.

Diners can enjoy quiet evenings here as well; dancers don't perform every night, and the lantern-lit courtyard can be quite cozy and intimate. Incidentally, the Grapeleaf is one of the least expensive Mideastern restaurants in the city.

We once spent a month traveling through Turkey and came away delighted by the good-natured, warm-hearted people and their great array of rich foods. The Grapeleaf, with its Mediterranean courtyard decor and great Middle Eastern ambiance, beams us right back there.

10 **The Best Vietnamese Restaurant: THE GOLDEN TURTLE**   *2211 Van Ness Avenue (at Broadway), 441-4419; also at 308 Fifth Avenue (at Clement), 221-5285. Inexpensive to moderate; wine and beer. Lunch from 11:30 a.m. to 3 p.m. and dinner from 5 to 11 p.m. Tuesday–Sunday (dinner only at the Fifth Avenue location). Reservations accepted; MC, VISA, AMEX.* The Tran family earned quick critical raves when it opened the Golden Turtle on Fifth Avenue in the Richmond District in 1976; it followed that ten years later with a larger clone on Van Ness.

Although they're housed in conventional structures, each cafe captures the aura of Vietnam with the effective use of bamboo, tropical plants and native artifacts. A *koi* pond graces the portal to the larger Van Ness branch.

The Vietnamese community, with its distinctive cooking style, is a welcome addition to the local dining scene. It's livelier than most Asian cuisines, featuring several spicy kebab-type dishes suggestive of the Middle East. Peanuts and peanut sauces are used, along with a curious tuberous plant called lemon grass, whose thin leaves give dishes a ginger-citrus flavor. Among the two Turtles' specialties are lemon grass beef or chicken, pork kebabs, and Seven Jewel Beef, featuring beef in seven different presentations, from soup to peanuts.

Savoring Something Special

THE TEN BEST SPECIALTY AND CURIOSITY RESTAURANTS

Eat, drink and be merry, for tomorrow ye diet.
— William Gilmore Beymer

THE TEN BEST SPECIALTY RESTAURANTS

The selections below were compiled from extensive personal taste-testing and from nominations made by others in our *San Francisco's Ultimate Dining Guide.* They are listed alphabetically.

1 **The Best Breakfast Cafe: DOIDGE'S KITCHEN** *2217 Union (at Fillmore), 921-2149. Moderate; wine and beer. Open 8 a.m. to 1:45 p.m. Monday–Friday and 8 a.m. to 3 p.m. Saturday–Sunday. Reservations advised; MC, VISA.* Doidge's starts your morning like no other place in the city, with rich, bountiful, and sometimes innovative breakfasts. Although food is served through lunch, the menu is basically breakfast, featuring honey-cured ham, cinnamon French toast, buttermilk pancakes, and our favorite: a tasty "Breakfast Casserole" of diced new potatoes, green onions, spicy Italian sausage, and fresh-cooked tomatoes, topped with a dollop of sour cream or a poached egg.

You can pick from an assortment of omelets, including a peach-and-walnut-chutney number that tastes as good as it sounds. A soup of the day is added to give the egg-oriented menu a noontime tilt, and you can order a beer or select from a small list of wines by the glass.

It's a simply decorated little storefront cafe with seasonal prints lining white walls, captain's chairs pushed under burgundy tablecloths, and classical music sighing in the background. You can sit at a counter and watch breakfast happen or retire to a small non-smokers' dining room.

2 **The Best San Francisco Sunday Brunch: THE GARDEN COURT AT THE SHERATON PALACE HOTEL** *639 Market Street (at New Montgomery), 392-8600. Moderate; full bar. Sunday brunch 10:30* *a.m. to 2 p.m.; regular meal service the rest of the week. All major credit cards.* Other hotel brunches are equally lavish and tempting, but none is offered in a more handsome setting than the Garden Court, with its soaring spaces beneath a domed skylight. White-clothed tables are arrayed with tempting displays of goodies, all bathed under warm amber light from the dome.

This opulent room, known as the Grand Court when the hotel opened in 1875, was described by one critic as the world's most beautiful restaurant. It's a study in Victorian opulence with its great glass dome, marble Ionic columns, elaborate chandeliers, and statues in scalloped corner niches. At this writing, the Sheraton was closed for complete renovation, and was set to reopen in mid-1990. The Garden Court, according to the hotel's publicity firm, was to undergo "cosmetic cleaning and refurbishing," but would remain essentially unchanged. So we can assume that the bountiful brunches will be served in an even more splendid space.

3 **The Best Dim Sum Restaurant: KING OF CHINA** *939 Clement Street (at 11th Avenue), 668-2618. Inexpensive to moderate; full bar. Dim sum 9 a.m. to 3 p.m. daily; regular food service 3 to 10 p.m. daily. MC, VISA.* Dim sum means "little hearts" in Chinese. That's a nice way of describing an array of tasty morsels, usually three to a plate, served by waiters and waitresses who hurry by your table with temptingly laden carts.

The city's dim sum restaurants rival its sushi bars in number, and we've tried nearly all of them. For freshness, variety, and taste, King of China in the new "Asian Restaurant Row" along Clement Street is the best. Every item we tried — from spicy meat dumplings to ground taro topped with minced shrimp, herbs, and vegetables — was excellent. None was too greasy, a problem we have encountered in many dim sum parlors.

The restaurant is on the second floor; a take-out offering many dim sum selections occupies the ground level. During afternoons and evenings, the restaurant serves a variety of conventional Chinese dinners. Complete one-dish meals also can be ordered during dim sum hours, for those not tempted by broiled chicken feet or rubbery jellyfish noodles.

As you approach King of China, it becomes obvious that the cooks have better taste than the architect. The garish exterior — a glass and stainless steel collision between art deco and Tokyoesque excess — is exceeded only by the interior, a mélange of glossy red columns and panels and glaring golden dragons. Like most dim sum parlors, the main dining room is barnlike, but the lofty ceiling helps absorb the chatter of hundreds of hungry diners on a busy weekend. Get there before 10 a.m. on Saturday or Sunday to avoid a long wait. Another dim sum tip: If the approaching cart is nearly empty, its offerings probably have cooled, so wait for the next one.

4 **The Best Japanese-California Restaurant: ASUKA BRAS-SERIE AT THE MIYAKO** *1625 Post Street (in the Miyako Hotel), 922-3200, ext. 7223. Moderate; full bar. Breakfast 6:30 to 10 a.m. Monday–Saturday; Sunday brunch 10:30 a.m. to 2:20 p.m.; lunch 11:30 a.m. to 2:30 p.m. daily; dinner 5:30 to 10:30 p.m. daily. Major credit cards; reservations advised.* The menu here is an interesting blend of traditional Japanese and California cuisine, and the results are excellent. We think it's one of the most underrated restaurants in the city. Try such goodies as fillet of sea bass with seafood won ton, fettuccine Alfredo with smoked salmon, or the traditional Imperial Miyako Dinner with flying fish rolls, sashimi, and prawn-vegetable tempura. One of our favorites is Spicy Oriental Chicken done in teriyaki sauce with ginger, bell pepper strips, shiitake mushrooms, and cooked onions, topped with paper-thin scallions.

Meals begin Japanese style with the presentation of hot, steaming hand towels. They're served in a pleasant East-meets-West environment; the high-ceilinged room is predominately soft pink, brightened by anthurium blooms on linen napery, Japanese artifacts, and Japanese prints in contemporary frames. Chairs are softly cushioned, but with frames of polished barkwood. The restaurant's street side is a window wall, filling the place with warm light.

5 **The Best Pan-Mediterranean Restaurant: ARAM'S AT ORIENT EXPRESS** *50 Steuart Street (in No. 1 Market Plaza), 957-1776. Moderate; full bar. Lunch from 11 a.m. to 2:30 p.m. Monday–Friday; dinner 5 to 10 p.m. Tuesday–Friday. MC, VISA; reservations advised.* Pan-Mediterranean cuisine, should you wonder, is a spicy blend of ethnic foods of the Mediterranean, including Greek, Turkish, and Armenian, with hints of Italian and Spanish. It's remarkably healthy fare, since the cuisine is built around whole grains, fresh vegetables, and olive oil, with lamb, fish, and chicken. No one serves tastier Pan-Med fare than Khajag Sarkissian's Orient Express.

Dinners begin with the traditional *meza* tray of spicy hummus (pureed chick-peas), dolmas (stuffed grape leaves), cheese spinach puffs, and such. Chef Setrak Injian, working in his open kitchen, prepares such savory entrees as chicken *tamar* with Black Forest ham and fontina cheese in a port wine fig sauce; fish and shellfish Plaki in white wine with tomatoes, onions, garlic, and shallots; and rack of lamb marinated in pomegranate juice. Or you can build a complete meal around the *meza* offerings. Lunches are a mix of Pan-Mediterranean and American dishes, including Reuben and hamburger sandwiches.

The decor is a bright, intriguing blend of Mideastern and modern, with shallow Moorish arches, blonde woods, and Eastern tapestries.

6 **The Best Fifties Drive-in: MEL'S** *2165 Lombard (at Fillmore),* *WA 1-3039; also at 3355 Geary Boulevard (at Parker), EV 7-2244. In-* *expensive; wine and beer. Open 6 a.m. to 1 a.m. Sunday–Thursday and 6* *a.m. to 3 a.m. Friday–Saturday. No credit cards.* The current fifties-sixties wave has swept a pair of *American Graffiti* drive-ins back into San Francisco. Steven Weiss, whose father created the original Mel's, opened a shiny new version on Lombard in 1986, followed by another on Geary the next year.

These aren't done to decorators' excess, like many of the new, nostalgia-ridden diners. They're reasonable facsimiles of Dad's original, with jukebox outlets on Formica tables and green-trimmed vinyl booths. They return me to the fifties, when I tooled around Southern California in my pre-war Chevy, flirting with carhops in their doily-sized aprons. Unfortunately, with parking at a premium, the new versions don't offer carhop service.

The menu is from my past, too (but not the prices), offering lemon Cokes, banana splits, Mel Burgers, of course, and — good grief — they even brought back the fried egg sandwich. Will chicken-fried steak and lime phosphates be next?

7 **The Best Pizza Parlor: PIZZERIA UNO** *2200 Lombard (at* *Steiner), 563-3144; also at 2323 Powell (near Fisherman's Wharf),* *788-4055. Inexpensive; full bar. Open 10 a.m. to 12:30 a.m. Monday–* *Thursday, 10:30 a.m. to 1:30 a.m. Friday–Saturday, and noon to 12:30* *a.m. Sunday. MC, VISA.* Hard choices faced us here; we've had excellent pizzas at Vicolo Pizzeria (Ghirardelli Square, and 201 Ivy near the Civic Center), Calzone (430 Columbus), and Tommaso (1042 Kearny). But after a thorough taste-testing, Uno was our repeat winner, with its deep-dish "Chicago-style" pizza.

Our victor was the Uno Special; we were impressed by its rich herbal flavor and thick thatch of fresh melted cheese, tomatoes, onions, green peppers, and mushrooms over the pepperoni-sausage-tomato sauce filling. The crust is wonderfully crunchy. With its thick topping, you get about twice the mileage from an Uno as from a conventional pizza. The pizza for one is really sufficient for two. It's served steaming hot from the oven in its own cast-iron skillet. These are handmade pizzas, so plan on a 15- to 20-minute wait.

We also like the cheerful decor of this place and its completely isolated no-smoking section. Uno is one of the rare restaurants that make a point of offering a smoking or no-smoking choice as you enter.

8 **The Best Vegetarian Restaurant: GREENS AT FORT MASON** *Building A, Fort Mason Center, 771-6222. Moderate; wine. Lunch 11:30 a.m. to 2:30 p.m. Tuesday–Saturday; Sunday brunch 10:30 a.m. to 2 p.m.; dinner 6 to 9 p.m. Tuesday–Saturday and 6 to 8:15 p.m. Sunday. Reservations accepted; MC, VISA.* Wasn't it just a few months ago that Greens was the new rage in vegetarian restaurants? Actually, it's been around for more than a decade. When it opened in 1979, weeks were required for reservations, even for lunch; a day or so is sufficient today, although it still gets crowded on weekends.

The food quality hasn't suffered in those ten years; perhaps it has even improved. This is an "only in San Francisco" place: a Zen Buddhist restaurant serving vegetarian dishes in a former U.S. Army supply depot. The chefs do a remarkable job of showcasing their culinary talents. When their ragouts, pastas, and mesquite-grilled brochettes emerge from the kitchen, you'll swear they aren't vegetarian dishes. Entrees are so hearty and full-flavored that you'll forget they're meatless, fishless, and chickenless.

This former cargo shed is eye-appealing, with natural wood partitions, risers, and potted plants to offset the warehouse look of its 30-foot ceilings. And the view across the bay is awesome. The Zen Center also operates an outlet of its Tassajara bakery and take-out counter here, offering wonderfully tasty breads, muffins, and desserts.

9 **The Best San Francisco Hofbrau: HARVEY'S MAIN STEM** *No. 2 Turk Street (at Market), 776-3330. Inexpensive; full bar. Open 10 a.m. to 11 p.m. daily; no credit cards.* Old-fashioned hofbraus are part of the city's dining tradition, offering hearty "hand-carved" corned beef and pastrami sandwiches served cafeteria style. Most have disappeared to make room for fast-food parlors and "modern" cafeterias, but Harvey's Main Stem survives. The sight of that leg of beef in the window, slowly turning under its heat lamps and dripping savory juices, has been drawing people in for decades.

Nothing much has changed in this venerable, high-ceilinged brauhaus except the name, as succeeding generations of the same family take over the reins, from Tommy's to Sam's Original and now Harvey's. I've been looking at the same black and white photos of old San Francisco since the 1950s; the thick square columns have been holding up the heavy paneled ceiling for as long as I can remember.

The food isn't nouvelle, but neither are the prices. Lavish dinner plates with perfectly juicy meats and over-cooked veggies go for under $6, and sandwiches are around $3, with the usual side orders of baked beans, mashed potatoes, or sauerkraut. This is beer food, not wine cuisine, and diners can select from 85 varieties, with nine on tap. Wine is available, if you must.

10 **The Best Place for Dessert: JUST DESSERTS** *248 Church Street (at Market), 626-5774; No. 3 Embarcadero Center (Davis and Sacramento), 421-1609; 836 Irving Street (at Tenth Avenue), 681-1277; 3735 Buchanan Street (at Marina Boulevard), 922-8675. Moderate; no alcohol. Hours vary, but are generally from 8 a.m. to midnight. MC, VISA.* Save room for dessert at Just Desserts; these are pleasant little cafes specializing in wonderfully rich pies, cakes, pastries, cookies, and muffins, accompanied with teas and assorted espresso drinks.

Quality is not compromised, yet a slice of decadently rich pecan pie or chocolate fudge cake, accompanied by cinnamon-dusted caffè latte, is less expensive than dessert and coffee in a fine restaurant. Goodies range from $1.25 to $3 a serving. Also, the pies, cakes, and cheesecakes can be purchased en toto. The little cafes are cheerful and upbeat, popular with breakfast crowds and night owls. Our favorite is the 248 Church Street outlet just off upper Market, with a landscaped patio out back.

THE CITY'S TEN MOST UNUSUAL RESTAURANTS

San Francisco has never been short on the curious and the cutesy, and that's certainly reflected in its restaurants. Blessed with an excess of individualists and interior decorators, the city offers a good assortment of unusual places to eat. Want to dine beside an outlaw motorcycle or in a greenhouse? How about aboard a ship that doesn't go anywhere, or would you prefer one that does?

This is the place.

1 **CITY OF SAN FRANCISCO** *Pier 33, The Embarcadero (near Sansome), 434-0300. Continental cuisine on a floating restaurant yacht; expensive; full bar. Nightly dinner cruises depart at 7; weekday lunch cruises at 11:30 a.m.; and Sunday champagne brunch cruises at 10:30 a.m. Reservations essential; MC, VISA, AMEX.* What could be more unusual — and romantic — than a candlelit dinner while cruising about the bay? Hornblower Yachts' *City of San Francisco,* a luxury restaurant ship built specifically for on-the-bay dining, easily tops our list as the city's most unusual restaurant.

It's a handsome craft, built in the 1980s but fashioned after steam-powered passenger ferries that chugged around San Francisco Bay at the turn of the century.

As you sip your champagne and nibble your entree, the ship offers an ever-changing view, never following the same itinerary twice. The main dining salon is as posh as a luxury liner's, with fine china, crystal, and silver set on crisp white linen. Before and after your meal, you can wander about the ship and perhaps stop by the wheelhouse to watch the skipper guide his craft through Raccoon Strait or perhaps up the Oakland Estuary. Or linger in the dining room, where a combo plays dancing music.

We've taken the dinner cruise several times through the years, and felt it was worth the price: around $50 a person (more on weekends), including a multi-course meal, hors d'oeuvres, and entertainment. The food has been uneven; we've had excellent tournedos of beef, and bland, overdone fish. Our recommendation: Stay away from the seafood, settle back, and enjoy your cruise.

2 **CALIFORNIA CULINARY ACADEMY** *625 Polk Street (at Turk), 771-3500. Continental; moderate; full bar. Open weekdays only; main dining room: lunch sittings at noon and 12:30 p.m. and dinner sittings at 6, 6:45, and 7:30 p.m.; Brasserie: lunch 11:45 a.m. to 1:15 p.m.; Academy Grill: lunch 11:30 a.m. to 2 p.m. and appetizers 3 to 9 p.m. Reservations essential for dinner; no reservations for lunch. Major credit cards.* Dining at the California Culinary Academy can be a bit of a gamble, since you're relying on the skills of students to create a properly prepared breast of pheasant. All preparation, cooking, and serving are done by pupils.

Of course, they work under the watchful eyes of master chef-instructors, so most of our experiences here have been rewarding. And the setting is certainly impressive. Several years ago, the school moved from limited quarters on Fremont Street to the great open spaces of old Germania Hall (renamed California Hall during World War II), a historic-landmark building at Polk and Turk.

Three restaurants are operated by the Academy in the vintage structure. The main dining room occupies the lofty Grand Hall, where students serve a la carte lunches and prix fixe full-course dinners; expanses of glass allow guests to watch the students stirring their sauces in the kitchens. The Brasserie offers international lunches, and the Academy Grill, a comfortable old basement bar, serves light lunches and evening appetizers.

The focus here—particularly in the main dining room—is on the classic cuisines of Europe, and the prestigious cooking school has graduated some of the country's leading chefs.

The Academy also operates a Culinary Shoppe and Cafe, selling the students' baked goods, pastries, salads, and pâtés; hours are 8:30 a.m. to 6 p.m.

3 **THE GOLD SPIKE**   *527 Columbus (at Green), 421-4591. Italian; inexpensive; full bar. Open 5 to 10 p.m. Sunday, Tuesday and Thursday; 5 to 10:30 p.m. Friday–Saturday. No reservations; no credit cards.* The wonderfully cluttered Gold Spike dates back to Prohibition, when the Mechetti family opened the Columbus Candy Store here. Natalina peddled licorice whips up front while Paul stirred up spaghetti sauce and bathtub gin in the back room.

The licorice whips are gone and gin comes from bottles lining the busy old bar, but not much else has changed. Walls and ceilings drip with war souvenirs (pick your war), corsets, moose heads, faded photos, and about 10,000 business cards. It looks like a pioneer museum that exploded. The menu is small, and the food's remarkably good; we've enjoyed such Italian standards as veal parmigiana and scampi, with lots of pasta and sourdough bread. The price for a full dinner is around $10.

I've eaten there a dozen or more times and have always waddled away happy. I recall one evening when service was unusually slow; it's usually moderately prompt. The waitress came over to apologize: "Sorry, but we had to redo your scampi. The cook dropped the first batch on the floor."

You have to like this place.

4 **HARD ROCK CAFE**   *1699 Van Ness Avenue (at Sacramento), 885-1699.* American Graffiti menu; moderate; full bar. Open 11:30 a.m. to 11:30 p.m. daily. No reservations; MC, VISA, AMEX. This certainly qualifies for our list of unusual restaurants; it's a wild and wacky melee of fifties and sixties excess. Like many of the city's overdone "nostalgia" cafes, the focus is more on freaky decor than on the menu. Perhaps the management should start charging admission and give the food away.

Actually, it's improved since we last reviewed the place, from ordinary to not bad. And generally, you *can* get inside these days, although crowds of eager teenagers sometimes spill onto Van Ness Avenue. But go for the decor more than the food. Struggle into your old letterman's jacket, pick up a two-dollar glass of ordinary wine at the island bar, and wander around saying things like: "Wow, catch this! Hey, neat, man!"

Study the candy-apple red 1959 Cadillac convertible emerging from a wall, the Elvis posters, the plastic dairy cow, Waylon Jennings's guitar, the outlaw motorcycle atop the bar, and the football helmets dangling from the high ceiling of this former auto dealership.

Like, you're really gonna dig it.

5 **ISOBUNE SUSHI** *1737 Post Street (in the Japan Center), 563-1030. Sushi and sashimi; moderate; beer, wine, and sake. Open 11:30 a.m. to 10 p.m. daily. No reservations; MC, VISA.* We were skeptical when we first tried this place. A restaurant that serves sushi by launching it on little boats that float past diners? A Tokyoesque tourist gimmick, right? But Betty, who has an excellent sushi palate, confirms that it's as tasty and fresh as most of the other sushi served in the city. Prices are comparable to most other places (which isn't cheap, if you can put away as much sushi as my wife can).

Actually, it's kind of fun, watching two sushi chefs deftly shaping bits of rice and seafood and setting them afloat in the narrow mini-moat that surrounds the oval seating counter. You merely pluck your selections from the little wooden barges as they pass. Pricing is simple, too, based on the design of the plates you've plucked; the waitress totals your stacked-up dishes and presents your bill.

6 **LEHR'S GREENHOUSE AND FLORIST** *750 Sutter (adjacent to the Canterbury Hotel, near Taylor), 474-6478. American; moderate; full bar. Lunch 10:30 a.m. to 3:30 p.m. Monday–Saturday; dinner 5 to 10 p.m. Sunday–Thursday and 5 to 11 p.m. Friday–Saturday; Sunday brunch 9:30 a.m. to 2:30 p.m.; Patio Cafe (474-5047) 6:30 a.m. to 10 p.m. daily. Reservations accepted; major credit cards.* Lehr's once was *the* place to take Mom on Mother's Day; she could dine on predictable American food under a canopy of Boston ferns, surrounded by assorted other potted plants.

Mom will still love the place, and you may like it, too. The menu has been updated and improved, with lighter fish, fowl, and chop entrees, augmented by a health-oriented Great American Soup and Salad Bar.

Originally called Lehr's Greenhouse and Potting Shed, it still operates a florist shop up front, and it has added a Patio Cafe, which serves lighter snacks for longer hours. When you arrive for lunch or dinner, ask to be seated in the front dining room; it's much more lush than the back room.

7 **MAXWELL'S OF SAN FRANCISCO** *Ghirardelli Square (900 North Point), 441-4140. American-Continental; moderate to moderately expensive; full bar. Open 11:30 a.m. to midnight daily. Reservations accepted; MC, VISA, AMEX.* After a decade, garish Maxwell's of San Francisco (originally called Maxwell's Plum) is running the risk of becoming a fixture. Built as one of the city's first novelty restaurants, it has settled in as a reliable dining establishment.

The large menu ranges from hamburgers for a few dollars to fresh seafood, steaks, chops, and Continental dishes for a few dollars more. We suspect people still go there mostly for the outlandish decor and the striking view of the bay. Patterned after the original Maxwell's Plum in New York, it is $7 million worth of glitter, stained glass, leaded glass, lavish chandeliers, brass, chrome, velvet, and more glitter. It's a vision of opulence gone mad, the effect you might get by peeping into a kaleidoscope after a bad martini.

When the place opened in 1981, some San Franciscans were embarrassed by its silly glitz. But now that the city brims with decorator-excess restaurants, Maxwell's seems right at home.

8   **SAILING SHIP DOLPH REMPP RESTAURANT**   *Pier 42, China Basin, 777-5771. Seafood; moderately expensive to expensive; full bar. Lunch 11 a.m. to 2 p.m. Wednesday–Friday; dinner 6 to 10 p.m. Tuesday– Saturday. Reservations advised; major credit cards.* Dolphin P. Rempp's Sailing Ship doesn't sail around the bay with the *City of San Francisco* restaurant yacht; it's firmly dry-docked at Pier 42. But it's equally opulent inside, and the food is generally better. It serves an assortment of seafood dishes, often with Continental accents.

Built in 1908 as a gaff-rigged three-masted schooner, it carried lumber and spices between the North Atlantic, Africa, and the South Seas. Now it carries a small cargo of diners through a very stylish lunch or dinner.

It never flew a *Dolphin P. Rempp* banner over the briny; that's the name of the co-owner and current restaurant manager. A few years ago, Dolph converted the menu from seafood modest to Continental Expensive, creating a stylish environment with tables set as elegantly as any of the city's other fine restaurants. The lower deck houses a lively disco.

9   **SAN FRANCISCO BREWING COMPANY**   *155 Columbus Avenue (at Pacific), 434-3344. Pub grub; inexpensive; wine and beer. Open 11:30 a.m. to 2:30 p.m. Monday–Friday, 5 to 9 p.m. Monday–Thursday, 5 to 10 p.m. Friday, and noon to 10 p.m. Saturday. MC, VISA, AMEX.* This is San Francisco's first "brew pub," a place that brews its own beer and offers suitable pub grub to match its frothy offerings.

Opened in 1986 by brewmaster Allan Paul, it's housed in the scruffy old Albatross Saloon space. Historians claim that Jack Dempsey was once a bouncer here and that Baby Face Nelson was nabbed in a back room by the Feds during Prohibition. Paul has refurbished the 1907 mahogany bar and retained much of the character of the old place. Think of it as a grand old saloon with the addition of gleaming copper brew kettles.

Paul serves home-brewed beers with names like Emperor Norton Lager and Albatross Lager, made with malted barley and whole-leaf hops in the hearty style of European beers. He offers other "boutique" brews, including San Francisco's Anchor Steam, of course. Accompaniments include grilled sausages, sandwiches, hot pastrami, assorted salads, and a chili with his special brew as one of the ingredients. Diners and quaffers also can arrange a tour through the copper kettle finery of his brewery.

10 **TOMMY'S JOYNT**   *1101 Geary (at Van Ness Avenue), 775-4216. Hofbrau; inexpensive to moderate; full bar. Open 11 a.m. to 2 a.m. daily. Major credit cards.* If you think this legendary place with its wonderful Old San Francisco murals is only a tourist trap, check the necktie-clad crowd of bureaucrats and businessmen at lunchtime. Locals have been crowding into Tommy's hofbrau for decades for his thick pastrami sandwiches, corned beef and cabbage, and buffalo stew.

Tourists love it too, of course; they're drawn here by the bright mural exterior, then they stand dutifully in the serving line with the rest of us. While the white-aproned cook is slicing pastrami and dipping your sourdough bun in its juices, examine the cluttered interior of this place. Like the Gold Spike, it's a scatter of old posters, curios, and artifacts. And like Harvey's Main Stem, it has a long carved-wood bar specializing in scores of international beers. So the Joynt is a blend of both, offering us the best of two Old San Francisco worlds.

The Lunch Bunch

LISTS OF THE TEN BEST PLACES TO ENJOY NOONTIME NIBBLES

Fry one, hold the mayo! — Any waitress in any Chicago diner

THE TEN BEST BURGER LUNCHES

If you were to pick the traditional All-American lunch, it probably would be the hamburger. So it's not unusual to find assorted publications in earnest search for the best burger in captivity. But what's the use of a wonderful hamburger if the accompanying shoestring potatoes have the consistency of shoelaces? Or if the wine you ordered to complement your noontime nibble is so tannic it could be used to preserve lab specimens?

What we seek, therefore, is the Ten Best burger *lunches*. And by burger, we mean a cheeseburger. A hamburger without cheese is incomplete, like a Manhattan without bitters. Our lunches also include fries, the condiments that accompany the burger and a glass of red: whatever the establishment pours as its basic house wine. (We didn't require that our field-tested restaurants serve wine, but all of the winners except one did.) We weren't looking for economy here, but for the best burger lunch that money could buy. Predictably, none of the fast-food heat-lamp places survived the cut, although we gave them a fair test.

Our burger standards — which may differ from yours — are unyielding. A patty must be cooked as ordered (medium-rare in our case), and the bun should be toasted inside to fend off the soggies. We like skins-on, thick-cut fries; shoestrings are acceptable if they're properly crisp and not greasy. The burger should be presented open-faced, with condiments on the side. This gives one the option of creating a gloppy Bumsteadburger or eating the lettuce, pickle, tomato, and whatever as a small salad. (That's our preference; why smother good, hot beef with clammy, cold lettuce?)

A 20-point system similar to the one used in wine tasting was devised to measure the key elements of a burger lunch: the patty and cheese, the bun within which they arrived, condiments and fries, wine, and finally the atmosphere of the place. We've listed winners in the order of finish.

65

1 **WHITE HORSE TAVERNE**   *637 Sutter Street (at Mason), 771-1708. Full bar. Lunch 11:30 a.m. to 2:15 p.m. Monday–Friday; 11 a.m. to 2 p.m. weekends; breakfast and dinner also served in the adjoining restaurant. All major credit cards. Total points: 18; burger lunch price: $5.70.* Fortunately, little has changed at this 30-year-old English-style pub since we declared it the surprise winner in our burger competition in the first edition of *The Best of San Francisco*. It again out-scored tasty competition to retain its top spot.

Its entry is called the Beresford Cheeseburger Delux (named for the adjoining Beresford Hotel); the half-pound patty arrived perfectly medium-rare, beautifully charred, with American cheese on a toasted sesame seed bun. Crisp-cut lettuce, tomato slices, dill chips, and a dollop of mayo were on the side; the fries were thick, crisp, and delicious wedges. The wine was full-bodied yet mellow, an ideal burger companion. This lunch would have scored even higher with a more imaginative cheese. Significantly, although price wasn't a factor in our burger competition, our winner was one of the least expensive of the lot. The cheeseburger is $4.20 and the wine is $1.50 in the pub itself; it's a dollar more in the adjacent — and fancier — restaurant.

The White Horse Taverne has the look and feel of a comfortable old English alehouse with white plaster, cross-timbered walls, and rough-hewn ceiling beams. It's a friendly and cozy environment for San Francisco's Best Burger Lunch.

2 **WASHINGTON SQUARE BAR & GRILL**   *1707 Powell Street (at Union), 982-8123. Full bar. Lunch 11:30 a.m. to 3 p.m. Monday–Saturday; dinner 5:30 to 11:30 p.m. Sunday–Thursday; to midnight Friday–Saturday. MC, VISA, AMEX, DC. Total points: 17; price: $10.25.* The lovable old Square does everything well, or in this case, medium-rare. It serves the best hamburger patty in the city; it's perfectly seared and wonderfully seasoned. (Most patties are just ground-up cow; why don't other restaurants use seasoning to make them more interesting?)

This savory patty arrived under a cap of melted jack cheese, tucked inside a sourdough roll. The fries were the thin, shoestring style; we prefer them thicker, but these were nicely crisp, tasty and not oily. The lettuce, tomato, and pickle chip condiments were joined by a chili pepper to enliven the lunch.

A good, hearty glass of red wine rounded out this burger feast, served in the affable ambiance of one of the city's favorite watering holes.

3 **THE HOLDING COMPANY**   *No. 2 Embarcadero Center, 986-0797. Full bar. Lunch 11 a.m. to 3:30 p.m. Monday–Friday; dinner 5 to 10 p.m. Monday–Thursday, 5 to 11 p.m. Friday. MC, VISA, AMEX, DC. Total points: 16; price: $9.45.* This popular lunch spot for the lower Market

Street white-collar crowd placed third in our competition. We like the selections here: a choice of jack, Cheddar, or Swiss cheese on sourdough, rye, sesame seed bun, or onion roll.

The thick, juicy patty arrived perfectly charred and medium-rare, with a nice smoky flavor, accompanied with medium-cut fries along with the usual lettuce, tomato, and dill pickle. The wine was a bit light yet hearty enough for the burger. The Holding Company is an attractive place with a upscale but comfortable look: dark paneling, beveled mirrors, and bentwood chairs; it offers the option of outdoor seating during warm weather.

4 **HOT AND HUNKY** *4039 Eighteenth Street (at Castro), 621-6365; also at 1305 Polk Street (at Bush), 931-1004; also at 1946 Market Street (at Duboce), 621-3622. Wine and beer; 11 a.m. to midnight Sunday through Thursday, 11 a.m. to 1 a.m. Friday and Saturday. No credit cards. Total points: 16; price: $6.54.* This is our first winner that specialized in hamburgers, and it serves a good one — juicy without being greasy. Although it offers seventeen "square meals in a round bun," we selected the Double Hot and Hunky cheeseburger, which most closely approximated the competition. The double patties were medium rare despite their thinness — the work of an extremely alert chef. Two slices of American cheese on a toasted bun, lettuce, tomato, and a thick slice of Bermuda onion completed the ensemble. Fries were cut thick with skins on, among the better we've found. The wine, while not awesome was adequte. Hot and Hunky is a basic place with a walk-up window service; decor consists primarily of Marilyn Monroe photos and posters.

5 **EDDIE RICKENBACKER'S** *133 Second Street (at Minna), 543-3498. Full bar. Lunch 11 a.m. to 3 p.m. daily; dinner 5 to 10 p.m. Tuesday–Thursday and 5 to 11 p.m. Friday–Saturday. MC, VISA, AMEX. Total points: 14.5; price: $9.75.* If we were voting for the most eye-appealing establishment, Rickenbacker's would win: it's a virtual museum of World War I flying regalia, including a full-sized Sopwith Camel biplane hanging from the ceiling, and uniformed mannequins in a loft above the dining area.

Its burger patty was quite thick, tasty, and properly seared, with a cap of jack cheese melted over. (Jack is our cheese of choice for burger lunches.) The fries were standard shoestring, but they were excellent: crisp, hot, and not greasy. The wine was quite acceptable, complementing the lunch nicely; the condiments were standard lettuce-pickle-onion. The only major minus: even though the patty was large, the bun was even larger; if we'd wanted that much bread, we'd have gone to a bakery.

6 **BULLSHEAD RESTAURANT** *3745 Geary Boulevard (at Second Avenue), 668-2323. Wine and beer. Open 4 to 10 p.m. Sunday, 11:30 a.m. to 10 p.m. Monday–Thursday, 11:30 a.m. to 11 p.m. Friday, and 3 to 11 p.m. Saturday; also at 840 Ulloa (in West Portal), 665-4350; open noon to 10 p.m. Sunday, 11:15 a.m. to 10 p.m. Monday–Thursday, and 11:15 a.m. to 11 p.m. Friday–Saturday. Major credit cards. Total points: 14; price: $6.40.* We keep wanting to call this place the Bull Shed; perhaps it's the meat display case out front. But it's "Bulls Head," and it grinds its own beef, so you're assured of a fresh patty.

Our Chuckburger with cheese was offered with a choice of American, Swiss, or mozzarella, and the burger arrived on a sizzle platter so it was nice and hot; a large dollop of mayo was offered on the side. Medium-thick fries were not awesome but well above average. However, the sesame-seed bun wasn't toasted, so it was rather soggy, and the red wine had a slightly sweet taste.

We liked the sauce assortment on the table: Heinz ketchup, A-1 and Lea & Perrins, Gulden's mustard, even Tabasco. So you know these are *serious* hamburger places. Decor at both locations is similar: a pleasant blend of walnut paneling with brick trim. Both feature the up-front butcher case.

7 **WHAT'S YOUR BEEF?** *759 Columbus Avenue (at Greenwich), 989-1852. Wine and beer. Open 11 a.m. to 8 p.m. Monday–Saturday. No credit cards. Total points: 13.5; price: $6.15.* This is the only restaurant in the city ending in a question mark; there's no question about its burgers and distinctive homemade potato chips, however. The burger lunch deserves a spot in our Ten Best.

In an interesting role switch, George Erman left his job as Fournou's Ovens maître d' to open What's Your Beef? in North Beach. It comes in two pieces, both tiny: a booth-sized take-out with a few stools, and a charming and cozy dining room with only five tables.

Burger aficionados have a choice of seven different cheeses and the bun is a soft and tasty egg bread sprinkled with poppy seeds. Erman serves "heremade" warm, thick Maui-style potato chips that are as crisp as autumn leaves. But the thick burger sandwich arrives preassembled, so the lettuce, tomato, onions and mayo cool off the rather thin patty before you get your teeth into it. The wine is a good buy: a 10-ounce glass of hearty red for $1.95.

8 **BILL'S PLACE** *2315 Clement Street (at 24th Avenue), 221-5262; also in the GET Shopping Mall at 34th Avenue (at Sloat), 556-1146. Wine and beer. Open 11 a.m. to 9 p.m. daily. No credit cards. Total points: 13; price: $5.30.* Bill's offers a series of "Celebrity Burgers," so we tried the "Herb Caen," which arrived with a patty of jack cheese and sautéed onions tucked into a sesame seed bun.

Herb should have finished higher than eighth in the competition, but the meat was bland with no seasoning, and the fries were limp little shoestrings. The wine was — well — drinkable. Bill does offer a good variety of things to dress up your burger: Lea & Perrins and A-1 sauce, the ubiquitous Heinz ketchup, hot sauce, and mustard.

The place looks rather austere, except that one wall is lined with prim little engravings of the American Presidents and examples of White House china — a nice effect. We like the Japanese-style garden at the Clement Street location, where you can enjoy lunch under the sun on those rare days when the Outer Richmond fog permits it to shine.

9 **THE ORIGINAL CLOWN ALLEY** *42 Columbus Avenue (at Jackson), 421-2540; also at 2499 Lombard (at Divisadero), 931-5890. Beer (no wine). Open 24 hours daily. No credit cards. Total points: 12.5; price (with a beer, since it doesn't serve wine): $5.40.* Although it's a bit short on ambiance, we liked the Columbus Avenue Clown Alley's glass-walled outdoor patio. We also liked the generous patties served on oversized toasted sesame seed buns. The shoestring fries were crisp and tasty, and the cheese — although it was merely American — was properly melted over the flame-broiled patty. Sadly, the place offers no wine with which to rinse this down, but there is an assortment of beers, soft drinks, and juices.

A longtime fixture between the Financial District and North Beach, Clown Alley is basically a walk-up place and barely a cut above the fast food parlors in appearance. But all burgers are cooked to order, and if you're alert, you can get one medium-rare. Once you pick up your fare, adjourn to a condiment table where you can busy your burger with dill pickle chips, relish, mustard, and onion.

10 **HAMBURGER MARY'S ORGANIC GRILL** *1582 Folsom (at 12th Street), 626-5767. Full bar. Open 10 a.m. to 1:30 a.m. daily. MC, VISA, AMEX. Total points: 12; price: $9.25.* Dead last but finished is Hamburger Mary's, whose organic "Maryburger" disintegrates in your hands, not in your mouth. A bit of fine-tuning could make this one of the city's better burgers, since the patty is generous and of good quality and the harmless punk-rocker fry cooks occasionally sear it properly. And the hearty whole-earth bread used for a wrapper isn't a bad idea.

But it arrived as a gooey preassembled blob of patty, cheese, sauce, tomatoes, and about a cubic foot of chopped salad. By the time it reached our table, the patty had died of exposure from its surrounding mass of cold and damp condiments. And the fries — at $1.75 extra — were sad, limp little things.

The burger lunch with fries and wine is not cheap, yet the place is always jammed; Mary must be laughing all the way to Bank of America. This *is* a fun place in which to attack this curious creation; it's a clutter of posters, pictures, doodads, curios, and knickknacks plastered over weathered wood. The music is predictably rock but not as loud as it was when we first ate there several years ago. We were almost able to conduct a conversation during our last visit.

THE TEN BEST SUN-LUNCH PLACES

We've always loved alfresco dining, enjoying a meal and a glass of wine under the sun, watching the passing parade of people. Outdoor cafes have been popular for centuries in European cities, despite unpredictable weather. We're pleased that they're becoming more prevalent in San Francisco, despite *its* unpredictable weather.

We offer here a mix of places with views, heart-of-the-city restaurants with eyes to the sky and sidewalk cafes *a la Europa*.

1 **EMBARCADERO CENTER** *Above the Embarcadero near the foot of Market (between Clay and Sacramento), 772-0500.* Our clear winner isn't an outdoor cafe: it's a huge *collection* of outdoor cafes. The Embarcadero Center is a complex of four sky-rise office buildings with ground-floor and podium-level (whatever that means) shopping areas.

Many of its restaurants—the Holding Company, Scott's Seafood, La Fuente, Pasta Bella, Enzo's, and others—serve both outdoors and in. The shopping plazas are generously sprinkled with tables, chairs, and benches for the brown-bag set.

Nearly a dozen take-out cafes and food stalls are clustered around the base of Embarcadero Four beside the Hyatt Regency, just off the Embarcadero. Dozens of tables and chairs are a few steps away, bolted to the concrete deck of spacious Justin Herman Plaza. The assorted take-outs offer hot dogs, sushi, deli items, pizza, ice cream, fruit salads and designer cookies.

2 **BULL'S TEXAS CAFE** *25 Van Ness Avenue (at Market), 864-4288. Texas barbecue and Tex-Mex; open 11:30 a.m. to 10:30 p.m. Sunday–Thursday, and 11:30 a.m. to 11 p.m. Friday–Saturday. Major credit cards.* Bull's is what would happen if a Hard Rock Cafe opened in Luckenbach, Texas; it's a noisy, upbeat Western-style bar and restaurant that looks like it was decorated by Waylon, Willie and the boys. And if that blaring Country-Western jukebox withers your frijoles, you can take a powder to a semi-quiet patio. It's tucked behind the building, offering shelter from city sounds and the chronic Van Ness Avenue breeze.

Serving inexpensive barbecue and Mexican fare, it's a popular lunch stop for the Civic Center crowd. Among its notable dishes are excellent nachos, a serious Texas-style chili with no beans, fajita steak, and assorted things barbecued.

3 **COMPADRES MEXICAN BAR & GRILL** *Ghirardelli Square (at North Point and Polk), 885-2266. Mexican-American; full bar. Open 10 a.m. to 10 p.m. Sunday, 11 a.m. to 10 p.m. Monday–Thursday and 11 a.m. to 11 p.m. Friday–Saturday. Reservations advised on weekends; major credit cards.* Compadres, a brightly decorated Mexican-American restaurant, spills its camaraderie onto a terrace and along the outdoor walkway of the 1899 Mustard Building in Ghirardelli Square.

From its second-floor vantage point, it offers a visual sweep of Aquatic Park, the Hyde Street Pier, Alcatraz, and sailboats at play on the bay. Mexican handicrafts, tropical plants, and a couple of macaws named Syd and Cesar give the place a proper Latin atmosphere, and the place jumps with *pan hana*, a Mexican happy hour on Fridays, with live music.

Ghirardelli has several smaller sun-lunch places as well: Dixie Yacht Club is a soup and sandwich place occupying part of the former Modesto Lanzone restaurant site; La Nouvelle Pâtisserie is a breakfast and lunch pastry and espresso cafe with patio seating and a glass-roofed dining room; and Vicolo Pizzeria offers a few outdoor tables.

4 **LA TRATTORIA** *1507 Polk Street (at California), 771-6363. Full bar. Open 11:30 a.m. to 11:30 p.m. Monday–Saturday; 11:30 a.m. to 10:30 p.m. Sunday. MC, VISA, AMEX.* This place more closely suggests a European sidewalk cafe than any other in the city, with its wrought-iron trim and neat little tables open to the street life of Polk Gulch. It's roofed over, but the side is open to the street, and heat lamps keep things cozy in winter.

The Trattoria has been one of our favorite lunch spots for years, serving inexpensive lasagnas, tortellinis, and other Italian-American fare. Traffic noise sometimes intrudes into conversation, but that isn't La Trattoria's fault. In a civilized European city, Polk Street would have been converted into a pedestrian *Shoppingstrasse* by now. If you find the growl of the 19 Polk buses too noisy, you can retreat to an inside table.

5 **MISSION ROCK RESORT** *817 China Basin (at Mariposa), 621-5538. Full bar. Open 8 a.m. to 3 p.m. Monday–Friday; 8 a.m. to 4 p.m. Saturday–Sunday (the bar and a snack bar keep longer hours). MC, VISA.* The first trick is to find this place, and don't look for a mission, a resort, or a rock. Mission Rock is a funky, weathered cafe and bar at the waterfront on China Basin, just north of the foot of Mariposa Street.

On a windless day with a high blue sky, herds of white-collar types from the Financial District crowd onto the Rock's rustic outdoor dining area on an elevated dock. They prop their elbows on weathered wooden tables, eat hearty hamburgers and assorted fish fare, and absorb views of the waterfront at work. At a large dry-dock nearby, you may watch a fancy cruise ship or rusting freighter being overhauled.

Owners Robert and Norma Wahl also whip up great breakfasts, including a hefty eggs Benedict Sunday brunch that'll sink your schooner.

6 **CITY PICNIC** *384 Hayes Street (at Franklin), 431-8814. Wine and beer. Open 8 a.m. to 4 p.m. Monday–Friday, 10 a.m. to 2:30 p.m. Saturday. No credit cards.* The pleasant little City Picnic deli-cafe lures the Civic Center lunch bunch with an out-back garden patio offering a few tables, benches, and risers. It's a quiet spot, sheltered from street noise by surrounding buildings.

The "Picnic" specializes in generously sized sandwiches on Italian focaccia bread, which looks like it started out to be a pizza, then changed its mind. Assorted salads and sandwiches on conventional breads also are available.

7 **NOSHERIA** *Maiden Lane (at Grant), 398-3557. Wine and beer. Open 7 a.m. to 5:30 p.m. Monday–Saturday. No credit cards.* Six days a week, the folks at the Nosheria pull a few gold and blue umbrella tables into the middle of traffic-free Maiden Lane. Hungry downtowners quickly start lining up for some of the thickest pastrami and corned beef sandwiches in the city.

The Nosh also serves an assortment of salads and quiches. The sandwiches are so large that you may wind up brown-bagging *from* these outdoor tables.

8 **OLIVE OIL'S BAR & GRILL** *295 China Basin Way (at Pier 50), 495-3099. Full bar. Open 6 a.m. to 3 p.m. Monday–Friday; 10 a.m. to 3 p.m. weekends. No credit cards.* This is another South of Market waterfront place with indoor-outdoor dining. Like Mission Rock, it's popular with the North of Market lunch crowd, as well as waterfront workers. Fresh-air diners sit around old wooden cable spools on a deck just above water level, with a view of downtown Oakland across the way. If the weather's chilly, you can retreat to glossy bartop tables inside and admire pinups of Popeye's girlfriend. There's also a pool table to help pass the time.

The lunch crowd can choose from hamburgers, grilled sandwiches, and fish and chips. Olive's popular for breakfast as well, and serves good old-fashioned baking powder biscuits.

9   **RISTORANTE LA STROMA**   *The Cannery Courtyard (at Leaven-worth and Columbus), 776-6100. Italian; full bar. Open 11:30 a.m. to 9:30 p.m. daily. Reservations accepted; MC, VISA, AMEX.* Occupying one end of the Cannery Courtyard, this modestly priced trattoria with red-checked tablecloths serves hearty Italian fare on its patio and in a glass-roofed dining room.

The Courtyard was a railroad siding for the old Del Monte peach cannery before it was fashioned into an attractively landscaped patio for the Cannery shopping complex in the 1960s. Another restaurant, Cafe Zero, serves soups, salads, and sandwiches on its dining patio. The Courtyard's benches invite al-fresco brown-bagging as well, and two take-outs provide the fare: Emigre's sells skewered chicken and teriyaki, and Delizia provides ice cream, shakes, and juices. A nearby stage sometimes offers free entertainments, or you can step indoors for a fee and chuckle at Cobb's Comedy Club.

10   **SUISSE ITALIA CAFE**   *101 California Plaza (California at Drumm), 362-4454. Wine and beer. Open 5:30 a.m. to 6 p.m. Monday–Friday. No credit cards.* This large, contemporary deli serves an amazing assortment of lunchtime goodies from the ground floor of the 101 California high-rise. Sandwiches, quiches, salads, and cold pastas are dispensed efficiently, then carried by hungry Financial District folks to outside tables on the spacious 101 California Plaza.

It's a handsome wedge of open space with potted plants, a spillover foun-tain, and multilevel granite risers for additional seating. The recently opened Atrium Restaurant next door, with its large greenhouse front, offers sunny sit-down service. The 101 California complex qualifies, incidentally, for our list of the ten most attractive buildings in Chapter 20.

Biting the Budget Bullet

THE TEN BEST PLACES TO DINE INEXPENSIVELY

The most remarkable thing about my mother is that for thirty years
she served the family nothing but leftovers.
The original meal has never been found. — Calvin Trillin

There will be times when you don't want your mother's leftovers, but you're between paydays and you'd like to avoid the price of a restaurant meal. Fortunately, the city brims with inexpensive, informal restaurants serving hearty meals for about the price of a Stouffer's Lean Cuisine and deli salad: around $6.

We aren't talking about those awful fast-food places that are proliferating around San Francisco. (They multiplied so fast, in fact, that a temporary moratorium was placed on them in the mid-1980s.)

Hundreds of Asian cafes can offer a bowl of something-over-rice or stir-fried whatever for under $6. But to qualify for our list, the restaurants must offer a tasty, filling meal with a main course, side dish or veggie, and a drink for $6 or less. And they must be open for both lunch and dinner — at least until 8 p.m.

You won't need much money at these places, but take along a little; most don't accept credit cards. Not surprisingly, many of our winners are ethnic restaurants. The Chinese, Japanese, Vietnamese, Italians, Thais, and others who have enriched us with their bounty have done so at remarkably little cost. That's part of the adventure of San Francisco budget dining. You can eat cheaply and send your tummy on an around-the-world excursion.

1   **MAY SUN RESTAURANT**   *1740 Fillmore Street (at Post), 567-7789. Mandarin-teriyaki; wine and beer. Open 11:30 a.m. to 9 p.m. Monday–Saturday. MC, VISA, AMEX.* May Sun is more than our favorite inexpensive restaurant in San Francisco; it's one of our favorite restaurants at *any* price.

Not only are prices remarkably reasonable, but the food is consistently excellent, and it's served in a pleasant atmosphere; May Sun definitely is a cut above the typical ethnic Formica food stall. And it offers intriguing variety, since it serves both Japanese teriyaki and Chinese dishes.

We don't know how Jim Lam Ngo and his family hold the prices down, but you can buy a full teriyaki dinner with won ton, salad, rice, tea, and a cookie for $5.95. He also does the best *kung pao* prawns in the city, as part of a complete lunch for under $4. It's rich with succulent and tender prawns, bamboo shoots, bell pepper wedges and crunchy peanuts, accompanied with rice, a Japanese-style broth, and fruit. In fact, he features 20 different lunches for under $4! The lunch and dinner menu is surprisingly varied for such a small place, with a mix of spicy Mandarin and more subtly flavored Cantonese dishes, plus the featured Japanese teriyaki dinner.

May Sun is a prim little cafe with white-clothed tables over a burgundy carpet. A seascape painting fills one wall; coolers of chilled wines, beers, and soft drinks occupy another. Jim provides his patrons with a rack of newspapers — an implied invitation to enjoy an unhurried dinner, then relax over tea. And — always a plus for us — it has non-smoking areas. The restaurant is in the newly gentrified area of Fillmore Street, tucked under the bay window of an attractive blue, gray, white, and brown Victorian.

2 | **THE BAGEL DELI AND RESTAURANT** *1300 Polk Street (at Bush), 441-2212. Jewish-American deli cafe; wine and beer. Open from 8:30 a.m. to 11 p.m. daily. No credit cards.* This place is easy to spot; just look for the huge "AGEL" painted on the Bush Street side of the building; the "B" is on Polk. The Bagel is strong on hearty kosher dishes, and it offers a good selection of basic meat-veggie-rice entrees, dished up from an old-fashioned serving bar. It's popular with Polk Gulch and Russian Hill regulars and neighborhood beat cops.

Some under-budget examples: "hot dish of the day" (meat or fowl with veggies or rice and roll), $4.50; sweet and sour stuffed cabbage, $5.10; roast chicken, $4.75.

3 | **CORDON BLEU** *1574 California Street (at Polk), 673-5637. Vietnamese; wine and beer. Lunch 11:30 a.m. to 2:30 p.m. Tuesday– Saturday; dinner 5 to 10 p.m. Tuesday–Thursday, 5 to 11 p.m. Friday–Saturday, 4 to 10 p.m. Sunday. No credit cards.* Although most of the city's Vietnamese restaurants have opened within the past decade, Cordon Bleu has been around since 1972. From the day it opened, critics have been raving about its delicious, low-cost food. The little restaurant, tucked under the marquee of the Lumiere Theatre, specializes in a succulent five spice chicken.

A couple of low-budget examples: five spice chicken with a shish kebab, curry salad, and roll, $5.50; or how about chicken curry salad with an imperial roll for $4.20?

4 **GOLDEN BOY PIZZA** *542 Green Street (at Columbus), 982-9738. American-Italian; wine and beer. Open noon to 11:30 p.m. Monday– Thursday, noon to midnight Friday–Saturday, noon to 8 p.m. Sunday. No credit cards.* Well, of course you can get pizza-by-the-slice in lots of places for well under $6. But three things earn Golden Boy a spot on our list: a huge square of excellent pesto and meat pizza for $2, a chilled vegetable salad for $1.50, and a root beer mug full of drinkable red wine for another $1.50, for a total of $5.

This is not mass-produced pizza. Perched on your stool, listening to KJAZ jazz, you can watch the proprietor preparing the next deep-pan pizza, almost lovingly spreading the thick sauce and sprinkling the freshly shredded cheese and other ingredients by hand.

5 **IL POLLAIO** *555 Columbus Avenue (at Union), 362-7727. Italian; wine and beer. Open 11:30 a.m. to 9 p.m. Sunday, Monday, Wednesday and Thursday; 11:30 a.m. to 9 p.m. Friday–Saturday. No credit cards.* This tiny wedge of a place just off Washington Square will put three pieces of flame-broiled chicken, a generous salad, and two chunks of bread before you for $4.70. Half a chicken with salad still stays under our budget at $5.50; or you can savor two large Italian sausages with salad for $4.

Il Pollaio means "chicken coop," but it's much better than that; the place is neat as a pin and rather brightly decorated for a budget restaurant.

6 **KUM YUEN** *1247 Stockton Street (at Pacific), 434-1128. Chinese; no alcohol, but it can be brought in. Open 8 a.m. to 11 p.m. daily. No credit cards.* What distinguishes this place from dozens of other scruffy-but-clean little family-owned Chinese restaurants is the cost. Generally, you need to order at least two dishes in a small Chinese restaurant to build a properly balanced meal. Kum Yuen is one of the few places where you can get two items for less than $6, to qualify for our budget supper.

A couple of examples of dozens of dishes under $3: beef and tender greens over rice, $2.90; and barbecued spareribs, $2.80. Oyster and roast pork hot pot, adequate for a huge meal, is $5. And you get tea free with all of the above.

A final note on this small place: the food isn't average — it's excellent!

7 **LITTLE HENRY'S** *955 Larkin (corner of Post), 776-1757. Italian; wine and beer. Open from 11 a.m. to 10 p.m. daily. No credit cards.* Is it Henry Martinelli or Sorrento, perhaps? Nope. Henry Heng. Although the place is Italian, Henry and his prices are very Chinese. And you can get much more than a few raviolis here for under $6. A couple of suggestions: spicy chicken Creole with Italian hot sauce and bell peppers for $5.95, or spaghetti with ham, baby clams, and mushrooms for $4.95.

It's a simple-but-cute little corner cafe with simulated wood-grain wainscoting and real red and white checkered tablecloths.

8 **NIPPON SUSHI**   *314 Church Street (at 15th), no phone. Inexpensive; no alcohol. Open noon to 10 p.m. Monday–Saturday. No credit cards.* Nippon Sushi is a tiny restaurant jammed with tables and chairs a block and a half off Market; it has no identifying sign out front and no listed phone, so you can't call and ask how to get there. Just look for a nondescript storefront filled with people eagerly eating sushi.

What makes this place special is its amazingly cheap prices; sushi-lovers can get a complete meal here within our $6 range, and the food is quite good. The joint is rather basic: a few hard seats, an Oriental artifact or two. But at these prices, the hungry diners aren't sitting around admiring the decor.

9 **SIAM CAFE**   *807 Geary Street (at Hyde), 775-5821. Thai; wine and beer. Open 10 a.m. to 8 p.m. Monday–Saturday. MC, VISA.* If you order one of our favorites here — shrimp, bamboo shoots, onions, and red peppers — order a glass of water as well. This dish is so hot you'll be eating the onions to cool it down. All the entrees in this tiny Thai restaurant aren't firebrands, however; the menu offers an assortment of items mildly flavored with lemon grass.

The thing all dishes *do* have in common is a low price: pork, chicken, or beef with hot chili and mint, $4.50; special curry of the day, $3.95; ginger chicken with five spices, $3.95. Add dessert for $1.75 and coffee for 75 cents and you're still under budget with most of them.

10 **VIETNAM**   *620 Broadway (at Grant), 788-7034. Wine and beer. Open 8 a.m. to 3 a.m. daily. No credit cards.* This tiny place, not much wider than a hallway, serves excellent Vietnamese fare at remarkably low prices.

Customers crowd around a few small tables and perch at a narrow counter; some are served at a shelflike window table, perhaps so passersby can see them enjoying themselves. And they should be happy. They're getting spring rolls for $2, chopped pork with rice noodles for $2.75, spicy beef stew and noodles for $3, imperial rolls for $2.50, and meatball soup for $2.75. Any two of these will make a filling meal well within our budget.

Flushed with success, the owners opened a much classier Vietnam II at 701 Larkin (at Ellis) in late 1988; it specializes in Vietnamese and Chinese seafood. The hours are 10 a.m. to 10 p.m. daily, and it takes MasterCard and

VISA. But the prices aren't quite the bargain you'll find at the scruffy little original.

We have thus dined well — and stretched our budget to next payday. The check, please.

Run and Eat

THE TEN BEST TAKE-OUTS

Timid roach, why be so shy?
We are brothers, thou and I.
In the midnight, like thyself,
I explore the pantry shelf.
— Christopher Morley

But suppose there is nothing on that pantry shelf but a can of tuna, a bottle of soy sauce, and one forlorn cockroach, who looks as hungry as you feel?

It's 6 p.m. and you're not in a mood to cook, or you're stuck in a hotel room and weary of eating out. A TV re-run of "Star Trek: The Wrath of Kahn" starts in half an hour, and you have some sort of moral objection to fast-food places. What to do?

Fortunately, San Francisco brims with delicatessens and other intriguing take-outs. You never need be bored by their offerings, since they come in assorted nationalities. You can dine on anything from piroshki to quiche. What follows is a list of our ten favorite ethnic delis and other take-outs.

1 **VIVANDE PORTA VIA** *2125 Fillmore (at California), 346-4430. Italian. Open 11 a.m. to 7 p.m. Monday–Friday, 11 a.m. to 6 p.m. Saturday, and 11 a.m. to 5 p.m. Sunday.* An Italian cornucopia of cuisine, Vivande is the most beautifully appointed delicatessen-cafe in San Francisco. It features brim full cheese and deli cases, a large wine and gourmet cookbook section, and a trim little restaurant with white-clothed tables. It is indeed more than a deli, also functioning as a trattoria and *pasticceria* (pastry shop).

Vivande offers a startling variety of pâtés, cold meats, cheeses, salads — even items such as hickory-smoked ducks and chickens — as well as a line of Italian bakery goods. It offers fully prepared dishes to take home, such as cannelloni and gnocchi. If you choose to dine there, you can watch busy chefs and bakers preparing pleasing pastas and pastries in the sleek stainless-steel open kitchen.

2 **ACROPOLIS BAKERY AND DELI**   *5217 Geary Boulevard (at 16th Avenue), 751-9661. Greek and Russian. Open 8 a.m. to 7:30 p.m. Monday–Saturday.* This pleasant little Richmond District deli offers a wide range of take-home Mideastern specialties such as piroshkis, *spanakopita* (spinach pie), cheese blintzes, Greek meatballs, Russian honey cookies, baklava, and phyllo pastries. In addition to its delectable-looking and spicy smelling take-out counter, the Acropolis has a small dining area.

3 **THE CANNERY GOURMET MARKET**   *2801 Leavenworth (at Columbus), 673-0400. Open 10 a.m. to 6 p.m. Monday–Saturday, 11 a.m. to 6 p.m. Sunday; extended hours in summer and on holidays.* Several specialty shops make up this large ground-floor market in the Cannery shopping center: a bakery and deli, a candy shop called Confetti, a Ghirardelli chocolate shop, a picnic shop, a gourmet counter featuring imported foods, a large wine cellar, and a liquor store with a huge selection of miniature bottles. Oriented to the heavy Fisherman's Wharf tourist traffic, it's a handy place to pick up a piroshki, sandwiches, or some specialty meats and cheeses for an informal picnic.

4 **DAVID'S DELICATESSEN RESTAURANT**   *474 Geary Street (at Taylor), 771-1600. Jewish. Open 7 a.m. to 12:45 a.m. Monday– Saturday; 8 a.m. to 12:45 a.m. Sunday.* David's has been the ultimate Jewish deli and the late-night dining haven for after-theater crowds and other night owls since 1952. It's across the street from the Geary and Curran theaters and its walls are trimmed with framed photos of performers past and present.

The take-out section offers a large variety of kosher foods with a Chicago accent. Featured items include cheese blintzes, corned beef, pastrami, beef tongue, and, of course, matzoh ball soup. Desserts are a specialty, and David's Napoleons and rum balls are legendary.

5 **HOUSE OF PIROSHKI DELICATESSEN CAFE**   *1231 Ninth Avenue (at Lincoln), 661-1696. Russian-Mideastern, specializing in piroshkis. Open 11 a.m. to 6 p.m. Tuesday–Friday, 10 a.m. to 6 p.m. Saturday.* This place offers a curious mix for a deli. Stepping inside, you see a small candy case featuring truffles and pastries, several soft-drink coolers, and a rather sparsely furnished deli case. But the heart of this place is a vertical stainless steel heat cabinet behind the counter, from which emerges the best piroshkis in San Francisco. This Russian-Mideastern specialty comes in half a dozen varieties, with spicy fillings of cheese, beef, chicken, cabbage, and various combinations thereof.

Do your piroshki shopping early; they're made fresh daily, and by mid-afternoon, many varieties are sold out.

6 LA VICTORIA MEXICAN BAKERY AND GROCERY *2937 24th Street (at Alabama), 550-9292. Mexican. Open 11 a.m. to 10 p.m. daily.* Several Mexican delis and markets are clustered along 24th Street between Mission and Alabama, and La Victoria is perhaps the most versatile: it's a combined bakery, grocery, deli, and restaurant. The pleasant little restaurant is in the rear, reached by a mazelike corridor from the main store (or via an entrance on Alabama). Just about everything on its menu can go home with you: tasty homemade tamales, burritos, chiles rellenos and enchiladas. And don't forget a bag of homemade tortillas and tortilla chips.

On your way out, pass through the large bakery to pick up tasty pastries such as *cocadas* (macaroons) and *churros* (long and slender sugar-dusted Mexican doughnuts).

7 LUCCA DELICATESSEN *2120 Chestnut Street (at Steiner), 921-7873. Italian. Open 10 a.m. to 6:30 p.m. Monday–Friday, 9 a.m. to 6:30 p.m. Saturday, and 9 a.m. to 6 p.m. Sunday.* For more than 50 years, this tiny rosticceria and deli has dispensed its famous herb-flavored, vegetable-stuffed roast chicken to the Marina District faithful and to others lured from the city's farthest reaches. Roast beef and turkey also are featured, along with fritattas, salads and a fair assortment of cheeses, spiced meats, sausages, and wines.

The place has that special cluttered look of a good Italian deli, with overflowing food cases and counters, and fat sausages dangling from the ceiling. Lucca modestly calls itself "The tastiest little deli in the world." That may sound a bit brash, but withhold judgment until you savor the roast chicken.

8 MOLINARI DELICATESSEN *373 Columbus Avenue (at Vallejo), 421-2337. Italian. Open 8:30 a.m. to 5:30 p.m. Monday–Saturday.* In business since 1896, this cluttered North Beach deli is jammed to the rafters with sacks, cans, bags, bottles, and bins of just about everything that's edible, drinkable, and Italian. Large cans of olive oil are stacked on the floor, sausage ropes and garlic strings dangle from the ceiling, specialty foods fill floor-to-ceiling shelves, wine bottles crowd display racks, windows overflow with packages of pasta, and every thinkable type of spiced meat, fresh-cooked pasta, and pasta salad is stuffed into the deli case.

It is *the* unabridged Italian deli.

9   **SUNRISE DELI AND CAFE**   *2115 Irving Street (at 22nd Avenue),* *664-8210. Mideastern. Open 9 a.m. to 8 p.m. Monday–Saturday, and 9 a.m. to 5:30 p.m. Sunday.* This modestly decorated but cheerful little cafe serves shawarma, tasty thin-sliced marinated lamb roasted on a vertical spit — a rare treat that's difficult to find outside the Middle East. Also available to eat here or take for a walk are pita sandwiches and Mideastern specialities such as *falafel, dolmas* (stuffed grape leaves), *baba ganoush* (pureed eggplant), *tabouleh* (a minced salad made of bulgur wheat, mint, parsley, and tomato), and *hummus* (pureed chick-peas).

10   **YUEN'S GARDEN RESTAURANT**   *1131 Grant Avenue (at Pacific), 931-1132. Chinese. Open 7 a.m. to 6 p.m. daily.* Tucked under a large burgundy awning, Yuen's is the most versatile of Chinatown's many take-outs, with a complete deli, a large bakery, and a small sit-down restaurant. The deli offers assorted Asian items such as sweet and sour pork, glazed ducks, spicy Chinese sausage, soy sauce chicken, chicken wings, and an extensive selection of stir-fried and braised dishes. The bakery has both Chinese and American confections and pastries.

Typical of Asian take-outs, it is devoid of decor and almost always crowded. But the variety is good and the food is excellent. Be prepared to push your way to the front of the line on a busy morning. Chaos slows in the afternoon, but some items may be depleted by then.

Goodies

THE HIT PARADE OF SAN FRANCISCO DELICACIES

Part of the secret to success in life is to eat what you want and let the food fight it out inside. — Mark Twain

It's no secret, as we've established thus far, that San Franciscans love to eat. So it's hardly surprising that many specialty foods are either produced here or featured in the city's stores and restaurants.

San Francisco–style sourdough bread is legendary, and to a lesser degree, so is the salami produced in the Bay Area. With our large Chinese and Mexican populations, locally made take-home products such as pork buns and tamales are popular. Residents will pay outrageous prices for a single scoop of ice cream, so long as it's considered *gourmet,* and they get into serious cocktail party discussions about which bakery produces the flakiest croissant.

The San Francisco Seven and their palates were assembled in neutral territory one evening to conduct a serious series of tests. Several examples of the items below were subjected to their unforgiving taste buds, then scored and tallied on my Canon LS-31 solar calculator. It was a true blind tasting, with no labels showing. (Irish coffees were tasted and notes were made at the scene, since bartenders seemed reluctant to make us samples to go.)

To gain input from the innocence of youth, we also included my teenage son Dan in the panel; Elizabeth Martin, former wine and gourmet foods specialist for Macy's California, supervised the tasting and acted as referee.

Here are our results, listed in the order served. (Item No. 11 was Bromo-Seltzer.)

1 **The Best San Francisco–baked Croissant: BAKERS OF PARIS** *Outlets at 1605 Haight (626-4076); 3989 24th Street (863-8725); 449 Castro (863-9451); and 1101 Taraval (863-8726).* Bakers of Paris croissants exhibited a nice flaky crust and soft, fresh-tasting interior. It was a runaway winner, garnering six of eight first-place votes. (Five were sampled.)

2 **The Best San Francisco–style Sourdough Bread: COLOMBO**
Made by Colombo Baking Company of Oakland; available at various outlets. A good, crunchy crust and soft center with a tangy sourdough flavor gave Colombo the nod over some strong competition. For continuity, we used the extra-sour version of each bread tasted. (Four were sampled.)

3 **The Best Chinese Baked Pork Buns: LI JOHN DELICATESSEN**
1019 Grant Avenue (at Jackson), 982-1393. A Chinatown specialty, pork buns are large, doughy creations filled with a mixture of pork, onion, egg, and a sweet sauce. Li John's buns had the tastiest and most generous filling of all those sampled. (Eight varieties tasted.)

4 **The Best Bay Area Salami: GENOA STYLE BY COLUMBUS**
It's said that the San Francisco Bay Area's cool, damp climate nurtures natural mold on salami casings, which assists in proper aging. Whatever the reason, Bay Area salami is rated among the best in the country. A Genoa style — much larger around than the more familiar sausage-shaped salami — made by the San Francisco Sausage Company of South San Francisco (761-3944) won our nibble-off. Our victor was spicy and tangy, with a minimum of greasiness. The firm markets its products under the Columbus label. (Four were sampled.)

5 **The Best San Francisco–made Tamales: ROOSEVELT TAMALE PARLOR** *2817 24th Street (at Bryant), 550-9213. Open 9 a.m. to 10:30 p.m. Tuesday–Saturday and 9 a.m. to 9:30 p.m. Sunday. VISA, MC.* Several establishments in San Francisco's Mexican community make their own cornhusk-wrapped tamales, encased in *masa*. Most are along 24th between Folsom and Potrero, a region of Mexican shops, produce stores, small restaurants, and delis. Easily the best of our bunch were the huge, meat-filled creations of Roosevelt Tamale Parlor, a restaurant that does a busy take-out service. A nice feature of Roosevelt's take-out tamale is that it comes with a small container of zesty chili sauce, which can be heated and poured over once you get home. (Six sampled.)

6 **The Best San Francisco Ribs: HOG HEAVEN** *770 Stanyan (at Waller, beside Golden Gate Park), 668-2038. Open 5 to 9 p.m. Monday–Tuesday, and 11 a.m. to 10 p.m. Wednesday–Sunday. MC, VISA.* Despite strong competition from Firehouse Bar-B-Que (the place founded by a San Francisco firefighter at 501 Clement Street) and Bull's Texas Cafe (25

Van Ness Avenue), Hog Heaven won our barbecue competition. It produces tasty, smoky ribs, offered with a choice of regular or hot sauce.

Claiming to offer "Southern barbecue cooking in the Memphis tradition," the place serves filling and inexpensive meals built around its pork or beef ribs or barbecued chicken, with excellent baked beans, cole slaw or potato salad, and corn bread and plenty of napkins. It has a sense of humor in addition to tasty barbecue; walls are adorned with "historic" paintings of Albert Einswine, Porkahontas, and a touching scene from Swine Lake. And the menu advises patrons: "If God had meant man to use a knife and fork, He wouldn't have given him fingers. Do not allow previous table training to interfere with your enjoyment."

Oink!

7   **The Best San Francisco Irish Coffee: BUENA VISTA CAFE**
2765 Hyde Street (at Beach), 474-5044. Open 9 a.m. to 2 a.m. Monday–Friday and 8 a.m. to 2 a.m. weekends. San Francisco pubs have been noted for their Irish coffee since 1952, when the late *San Francisco Chronicle* columnist Stan Delaplane told Buena Vista owner Jack Koeppler of a tasty hot drink he'd enjoyed at Ireland's Shannon Airport. Koeppler experimented extensively to perfect this blend of whiskey, coffee, and thick cream; he even flew to Shannon to fine-tune the recipe.

Many places now serve Irish coffee, but the original Buena Vista version is still the best. It's made with Irish whiskey, a couple of cubes of sugar, and moderately strong coffee, topped with lightly frothed whipping cream. (Some pretenders use—good grief!—whipped cream from aerosol cans.) The Buena Vista imports and labels its own Irish whiskey (Tillimore Dew) and offers it to the faithful at $14.75 a liter, along with a free recipe folder. (Many Irish coffees sampled; many bars hopped.)

8   **The Best Designer Chocolate Chip Cookies: MRS. FIELD'S**
To find the chocolate chip nearest you, look in the Yellow Pages under Cookies. Competition from Famous Amos, Otis Spunkmeyer, Laura Todd, and Baker Street couldn't sway our panel's taste buds from the rich chocolate chip chewiness of the original designer cookie. You won't have a problem finding a sample of the winner; there seems to be a Mrs. Field's outlet on every other street corner. (Five sampled.)

9   **The Best Gourmet Ice-Cream: UNCLE GAYLORD'S**   *Ice-cream parlors at 1900 Market (864-1971) and 721 Irving (759-1614); also sold at various outlets.* A serious run by Double Rainbow failed to scoop Uncle Gaylord's out of first place. Our panel sampled ice-creams from six top Bay Area producers; for continuity, we offered them the same flavor:

strawberry. The smooth creaminess, good fruit presence, and richness of Gaylord swayed our sweet-toothed crew. Uncle Gaylord claims to use only cream, milk, strawberries, sugar, and egg yolks; that fresh, natural taste certainly is evident.

A sign at the 1900 Market Street outlet insists: "If you don't live near an Uncle Gaylord's…MOVE!" To save all that packing, call the main plant at (707) 778-6008 to find out where it's sold. That's in Petaluma, in the middle of Sonoma County dairy country. Could all those cows be wrong?

10 **The Most Decadent Sold-in-San Francisco Chocolates: MANON** *Available in Macy's Cellar and other outlets.* We end our Goodies chapter with an offering to the chocaholics among us. These seductively rich chocolates are hand-crafted in a small shop in Belgium, then flown to San Francisco. They come with a tasty variety of fillings, including some scrumptious fresh fruit versions. Sin, of course, has its price. Manon chocolates go for more than $25 a pound. (Too many sampled.)

Crawling Among the Best of Pubs

LISTS OF THE TEN BEST PLACES TO SIT AND SIP

A man's got to believe in something.
I believe I'll have another drink. — W.C. Fields

No, we didn't try to sample all 2,100 bars in San Francisco, or we would have been in no condition to complete this guide. But through the decades, we've paused in many of the city's popular watering holes. And in doing this revision of *The Best of San Francisco,* we initiated a serious study of its cocktail lounges and pubs, visiting old favorites and discovering some new ones.

Bars and the men and women who built them, drank in them, wrote books and poetry in their dark corners, and made love in their upper rooms are the fabric of San Francisco history. Researchers say a bar may have been the city's first business establishment, predating the 1849 Gold Rush by five years.

If your idea of a night out is to loaf in a grimy pool hall that smells of stale cigarette smoke and yesterday's spilled beer, you may disagree with many of our selections. We prefer brighter, livelier bars that appeal to couples. While we're certainly fond of comfortable old saloons with their mahogany planks and dusty moose heads, we're also drawn to some of the cheerful new watering holes, where drinking is more of a social exchange than a melancholy ritual.

THE CITY'S TEN BEST WATERING HOLES

The ultimate pub must fill several needs for those seeking solace or social contact. It should be a gathering place where people come not merely to drink, but to meet and mingle. It also should provide quiet corners for those wishing private conversation. Although the pub can be part of a restaurant, it must be a bar in its own right, and not merely a corner bar counter where you wait to be called to dinner.

Above all, the ultimate drinking establishment must be a place of good cheer.

1 **THE BANK EXCHANGE SALOON AND RESTAURANT** *600 Montgomery Street (at Clay), 983-4800.* When we first visited this place built into the thick concrete buttresses of the Transamerica Pyramid, we didn't expect to find the ultimate pub. It was interesting, but with a suspicious yuppie tilt. We kept returning, drawn by its camaraderie, its bright spaciousness, and its mix of clientele from gray-suited stockbrokers to cabbies to a sprinkle of singles.

It came to pass that the Bank Exchange was indeed our favorite watering hole. Its friendly atmosphere attracts an animated after-work crowd at the polished bar, yet it also provides high-backed booths and quiet corners for those seeking privacy. The open design and high ceilings permit hushed conversation even at the peak of TGIF conviviality. Prices are fair, and hot nibbles are offered during the early evening cocktail hour.

The decor is a pleasing brew of San Francisco's past and present. The blend isn't subtle, but neither is it jarringly abrupt. The heavy wooden bar and elegant back bar with elaborately carved columns and leaded glass insets speak of the past. Yet the place is upscale and modern: glass-roofed, bright, and ferny. The name, incidentally, was borrowed from an earlier pub established near here in 1853.

To round out its versatility, the Bank Exchange also functions as a restaurant and—several nights a week—as a disco called the Park Exchange.

2 **THE CARNELIAN ROOM** *Top floor of the Bank of America building, 55 California Street (at Montgomery), 433-7500.* In addition to offering the most stunning view of any bar in the city, the Carnelian Room cocktail lounge is handsome within, dressed up with fine old European paneling, chandeliers, and art objects. Although prices in most skyroom bars seem to increase with the elevation, the tariff here isn't unreasonable.

Incidentally, it's the private Bankers' Club during the daytime, so the bar isn't open to the public until 3 p.m. on weekdays and 4 p.m. on weekends. The adjacent restaurant, listed among our Ten Best dining spots, starts serving at 6 p.m.

3 **EDINBURGH CASTLE** *950 Geary Street (at Polk), 885-4074.* This spacious old Scottish pub offers noisy conviviality around its main downstairs bar and quiet retreats for couples on the mezzanine level. Naturally, there's a dartboard. The place also is a virtual museum of Scottish and

English lore, exhibiting everything from heraldic banners to World War II military mementos, both in the main lounge and in a storefront space that once held a tartan shop.

If that good British brew on tap or a strenuous game of darts works up an appetite, Old Chelsea Fish and Chips is close by, at 932 Larkin. The barkeep will arrange delivery, saving you the need to interrupt your beer. The pub doesn't open until late afternoon: usually around 5 p.m. Old Chelsea serves from 4 to 11 p.m.

4 **HARRINGTON'S**   *245 Front Street (at California), 392-7595.* It takes two large rooms, each with its own bar and a score or more tables, to hold a proper Irish drinking crowd, and that's what Harrington's has provided for as long as anyone can remember. This roomy, cheerful place is a lively stopover for homeward-bound Financial District commuters, and a late-hour refuge for city-dwelling night owls. Harrington's is more Irish in spirit and attitude than in decor; what little trim you see in this place is nautical, not Gaelic.

5 **THE HOUSE OF SHIELDS**   *39 New Montgomery (at Market),* *392-7732.* Good grief, they've put bar stools in the House of Shields! Even moved out a couple of spittoons to make room for them. Opened in 1908, the city's last standup bar sat down in the fall of 1986. But it remains a wonderful pub, rich with dark woods and camaraderie.

Situated across the street from the Sheraton-Palace, it is elemental old San Francisco, with heavy squared columns, walnut paneling, and a handsome back bar with shields carved into the woodwork. Tulip-glass chandeliers dangle from the high coffered ceiling; an elk head stares moodily from one wall and a Cape buffalo glares from another. High-backed booths are filled with a Financial District lunch crowd on weekdays. Like any proper San Francisco pub, Shields serves bar nibbles and puts out the dice cups during the evening cocktail hour.

6 **IRON HORSE**   *19 Maiden Lane (just off Kearny), 362-8133.* This pleasant cellar bar in the heart of the city provides a quiet, dimly lit refuge. Like most of our other selections, it offers both lively companionship at the bar, and booths and tables for gazing into the eyes of someone special. And it serves — hands down — the best hors d'oeuvres of any San Francisco pub. Stop by during happy hour for tasty meatballs and sausage links in spicy sauce, fresh-cut veggies with dip, even fresh fruit.

Bottoms up and bon appetit!

7 **LEFTY O'DOUL'S** *333 Geary Street (at Powell), 982-8900.* If there is such a thing as a family bar, the place built by the late Lefty O'Doul qualifies. It's not merely a pub but a deli and hofbrau dispensing some of the most inexpensive family fare in the city. But put the kids to bed by 9 p.m., when the piano is tuned up and Lefty's becomes a comfortable hangout for the downtown after-hours crowd.

O'Doul was a local baseball hero a few generations ago, first as a star with the minor league San Francisco Seals, then as a major leaguer, and finally as the Seals' manager. Walls brim with glossies of Lefty in action, or posing with other sports greats such as San Francisco's own Joe DiMaggio.

8 **PERRY'S** *1944 Union Street (at Laguna), 922-9022.* Perry Butler is back at his near-legendary Marina District saloon and restaurant, after abandoning it temporarily to focus on his two Marin County places, Perry's and Butler's. Back also is Michael McCourt, bartender extraordinaire, offering his big Irish grin and generous drinks to the regulars.

Tucked under the bay window of an old Victorian, Perry's is vintage San Francisco with its big mirrored back bar, warm woods, and embossed tile ceiling. Like the Washington Square Bar and Grill, it's something of a media hangout where the likes of radio's Scott Beach and *Sports Illustrated*'s Ron Fimrite play liars' dice and swap lies with the barkeeps.

9 **RAFFLES'** *In Fox Plaza at 1390 Market Street (at Polk), 621-8601.* Tourists and downtown crowds haven't discovered this friendly, roomy place with its South Seas decor, candlelit tables, reasonable prices, and tasty Oriental hors d'oeuvres. But it has a large following; the clientele is a mix of Civic Center bureaucrats, next-door Auto Club employees, and crowds bound for nearby Davies Symphony Hall, the Opera House, and Civic Auditorium.

It's also a rather good, moderately priced Polynesian-Oriental restaurant. The decor consists of the requisite fishnets, glass floats, and stuffed swordfish. The objects on the walls probably haven't been dusted in a decade, but fortunately, the lights are kept low.

10 **VESUVIO** *255 Columbus Avenue (at Broadway), 362-3370.* Jack Kerouac and the restless, rebellious Beat Generation are gone, replaced by bottom lines, BMWs, and upward mobility. But Vesuvio survives to remind us of that era when pondering over our reason for being was more significant than fretting over trickle-down economy and tax shelters.

It sits on its narrow corner in a pleasant state of arrested decay. It's still gaudy in a funky way, still displaying the works of North Beach artists, and still offering sanctuary and cheap wine to the writer, the disillusioned leftist, and the occasional curious tourist.

Incidentally, several small streets in North Beach and elsewhere in the city have been re-named for San Francisco writers and artists, at the suggestion of the City Lights bookstore folks across the alley from Vesuvio. That alley is now Jack Kerouac Street; nearby Adler Place, site of the neighboring Specs' 12 Adler Museum Cafe, has become Saroyan Street.

THE TEN BEST NEIGHBORHOOD PUBS

A proper neighborhood pub may differ somewhat from the ultimate watering hole. Size isn't significant as long as it offers adequate haven to area residents. Comfort, familiarity, and intimacy are important. The atmosphere should encourage relaxation and companionship, not raucous partying. One goes to the corner bar to unwind, not to refuel. Most neighborhood pubs reflect the lifestyle of the region, so our selections will differ from area to area.

1 **Chinatown: LI PO** *916 Grant Avenue (at Washington), 982-0072.* We begin with an exception. Li Po doesn't reflect the lifestyle of busy, industrious Chinatown; it's a haven *from* it. Most Asians, says my Chinese wife and co-author, are too industrious to waste time hanging around bars. Perhaps that's why Chinatown can support more than a hundred restaurants but only one real neighborhood pub.

Li Po has been a quiet retreat from the multicolored confusion of Chinatown for half a century. With its subdued lighting, the place has an almost grim look, except for a huge yellow and red lantern hanging from the ceiling. A bronze gong and brass Buddha occupy dusty niches behind the cluttered bar. Sitting on a worn stool, sipping Tsing Tao beer, you expect Charlie Chan to brush through the beaded curtain. Or at least Sydney Greenstreet.

Except there isn't a beaded curtain.

2 **Glen Park and Twin Peaks: GLEN PARK STATION** *2816 Diamond Street (near Glen Park Bart station), 333-4633.* This is the exemplary neighborhood pub: an honest working folks' saloon where denizens of Glen Park and the hills above gather to sip suds and swap shop talk and sports statistics. Three TV sets beam the latest ball game from any angle and Waylon Jennings wails from the jukebox. A much-used pool table occupies a back room, remote from the friendly commotion of the main bar, so players can concentrate on a serious game of eight ball.

3 **Haight-Ashbury and Sunset: ACHILLES HEEL** *1601 Haight Street (at Clayton), 626-1800.* In recent years, gentrification has reared its capitalistic head in the old neighborhood of the Flower Children, and Achilles Heel offers a suitable bridge between past and future. Its mix of Victorian chandeliers, ferns, old settees, and worn carpet speaks of earlier days, while the Baby Boomers can identify with its white-wine list and the selection of reading material, like *CitySports* and *New York Times Magazine,* which invites lounging.

The look is Victorian funk, but this is no punk rock hangout; the clientele is a blend of neighborhood white shirts and short skirts.

4 **The Marina: CHESTNUT STREET GRILL** *2231 Chestnut Street (at Scott), 922-5558.* The Marina District is second only to North Beach in its collection and selection of drinking establishments. What to choose here for the best neighborhood pub: the raucous Pierce Street Annex, upscale Perry's, the earthy Bus Stop, the trendy new brass-and-glass Golden Gate Grill? We settled on the Chestnut Street Grill, which *works* at being a neighborhood pub. Regulars are honored by special sandwiches bearing their names; patrons sign up for group outings to ball games or gather to scream themselves hoarse during Monday Night football.

Indeed, this place is noisy, but it's *gregarious* noise.

5 **The Mission: LA RONDALLA** *903 Valencia Street (at 20th Street), 550-9002.* For nearly four decades, this convivial Mission District Mexican restaurant and bar has encouraged the accumulation of clutter and Christmas decorations in its three oversized rooms. Festive garlands and tinsel go up each year, added to those remaining from the season before. Neighbors and curious outsiders gather nightly to sing with a mariachi band or relax and sip Corona Extra and Dos Equis in the shadow of a stuffed antelope head wearing a red Christmas ball.

6 **North Beach: SPECS' 12 ADLER MUSEUM CAFE** *12 Saroyan Street (off Columbus near Broadway), 421-4112.* Specs' 12 Adler Museum remains a haven for North Beach locals simply because most visitors can't find the place. It's tucked into a short alley across Columbus from Vesuvio's, with a small sign reluctantly confirming its presence. Those who do stumble on it discover a funky blend of bar and museum filled with sundry artifacts from assorted global corners. The regulars quaffing their beer and swapping familiar tales politely ignore outsiders, who lean over them to study African and New Guinea relics in the wall-mounted display cases.

7 **Pacific Heights and Fillmore: HARRY'S SALOON** *2020 Fillmore (at Pine), 921-1000.* Harry's is an upscale watering hole decorated mostly by noisy ambiance. Although it offers no specific attractions beyond friendly barkeeps, pretty waitresses, fair food, and honest drinks, it has found quick success where several others on the site have failed. Opened in the late 1980s, it is *the* watering hole for yuppies of Pacific Heights and the newly trendy upper Fillmore; it's currently in vogue as a singles bar.

Harry's is a classy-looking place and kind of clubby, decorated with half a million dollars worth of mahogany, brass, and mirrored walls opposite a mirrored back bar. Light meals are served on an elevation just above the plank.

8 **Richmond: CHURCHILL'S** *455 Clement Street (at Sixth Avenue), 752-0580.* With its dusky decor of wood-paneled walls and weathered tables and chairs, Churchill's is beginning to look out of place on a street now dominated by Asian restaurants, markets, and shops. This comfortable old corner saloon, stuck under a curiously pink Victorian, offers peaceful sanctuary in a neighborhood now invigorated by the ambitious new arrivals.

Although certainly open to all, the pub draws primarily from middle-class whites who seem more tempted by the gentle diversion of placing elbows on the well-worn bar, sipping something cool, nibbling from the snack bowls, and watching football on one of two ceiling-mounted tellies.

9 **South of Market: THE PARADISE LOUNGE** *1501 Folsom (at Tenth Street), 861-6906.* Since we wrote the original version of this book, South of Market has become *the* night life area of the city. But most of the new places—Juke Box Saturday Night, DV8, and City Nights—are too contrived or dance-oriented to qualify as local pubs. But the Paradise Lounge fits that role nicely. It's a properly funky corner bar with a main lounge, a cozy little back room offering live rock and jazz sessions and even a smoky old poolroom called Above Paradise among the rafters upstairs. A disco, Never Was Paradise, opened in late 1988.

This place may be a bit upbeat for a neighborhood pub, but then, SOMA is a rather upbeat area. Between shows and discos— listed on psychedelic colored posters outside—you can find quiet retreat at the back room tables. And yes, the main lounge does offer bar nibblies, an essential for a neighborly saloon.

10 **Upper Market and Castro: METRO BAR AND RESTAURANT** *3600 16th Street (at Market), 431-1655.* This darkly contemporary lounge done in purple and gray with touches of violet neon is haven for both the gays and straights of Upper Market and the Castro District. It's a handsome second-floor place, with window-walls looking over busy Market Street. A large oval bar dominates the room, and small tables line the walls. A restaurant is adjacent.

Unlike the intense heavy-leather aura of some Castro Street bars, the scene here is a bit more mellow. A straight couple would not feel ill at ease, unless he or she is bothered by loud music.

THE TEN BEST BARS OF A SPECIFIC SORT

Like people, saloons can have distinct characteristics. What follows is the Ten Best bars with the most interesting personalities.

1 **The Best Singles Bar: PIERCE STREET ANNEX**   *3138 Fillmore (at Greenwich), 567-1400.* We must point out that the Annex is not primarily a singles bar. It is the definitive barfly's bar, the ultimate pub for those seeking the noisy intimacy that only a good saloon can provide. A huge island bar dominates the barnlike interior, although regulars tend to wedge themselves around a smaller plank near the entrance, clutching sweating bottles of Beck's and Corona Extra. Live entertainment emanates from a small stage, including amateur "Starmaker" shows twice weekly; several TV sets hang from the high ceiling to draw the sports crowd. Cartoon sketches of regulars — some dating back a couple of decades — fill one wall.

The singles scene is mellow but not subtle. A set of "rules" printed on a wall suggests the proper procedure for approaching someone, and the bar's matchbooks provide space for a name and phone number.

2 **The Most Elegant Bar: THE COMPASS ROSE**   *In the Westin St. Francis Hotel, Powell at Geary, 774-0167.* Amidst the splendor of fluted Greek columns and scalloped drapes in this exquisite bar off the St. Francis Hotel lobby, you can enjoy a $56 snack of Beluga caviar, carefully rinsed down with a $30 glass of Dom Perignon. Settle back in your plushly upholstered chair and sip slowly while listening to the delicate strains of a cello and piano duet during evening cocktail hour. Or go for lunch or mid-afternoon high tea. It's all pure elegance. Sorry, Redwood Room.

3 **The Noisiest Bar: CADILLAC BAR AND GRILL**   *No. 1 Holland Court (off Howard, between Fourth and Fifth streets), 543-8226.* Behind an innocent-looking red and green sign in an alley off Fourth Street lurks the Fourth of July, New Year's Eve, and Cinco de Mayo. The friendly chaos is jammed between four walls decorated with Mexican flags, a highway-sized Dos Equis billboard, and cactus, both potted and painted.

Amazingly, an excellent Mexican restaurant manages to function right beside the incredibly noisy bar, fenced off from the chaos but not from the roar of the crowd. The only way to carry on a conversation is to get within two inches of the listener's ear, so go with someone with attractive lobes.

4 | **The Quietest Bar: PIAZZA LOUNGE** *In the main lobby of the Ramada Renaissance, 55 Cyril Magnin Street, 392-8000.* What a wonderful place to go for Cadillac Bar burnout! Lean back in an overstuffed chair, admire the artworks around you and listen to the pleasant tinkle of a grand piano. Sounds drift upward to be absorbed by crystal chandeliers hung from the four-story atrium ceiling of this spacious lobby bar. The bar service area is off to one side; even the slosh and tinkle of drink preparation are remote. Here, you lean toward your partner's ear only to whisper.

5 | **The Best Sports Bar: PAT O'SHEA'S MAD HATTER** *3754 Geary Boulevard (at Arguello), 752-3148.* Any pub posting a sign proclaiming: "We cheat drunks and tourists" is all right in our book. The Mad Hatter is a favorite Richmond District hangout that serves good food along with good cheer. It's also the consummate sports bar, with half a dozen TV sets posted around the walls and a blackboard listing upcoming jock telecasts.

Naturally, O'Shea's cables in the special sports channels; on a given autumn Sunday, one can watch two or more football games concurrently. Heads swivel left to cheer the 49ers, then swing right to boo the Rams. And of course, the decor includes a scatter of sports regalia.

6 | **The Best Tourist Bar: THE BUENA VISTA CAFE** *2765 Hyde Street (at Beach), 474-5044.* The weathered old Buena Vista, housed in a landmark Victorian near Fisherman's Wharf, has been a haven for locals and a magnet for tourists for decades. It is not a tourist trap, but an honest pub where visitors often get their first sample of San Francisco togetherness: the oversized tables beneath the high windows are expected to be shared. Incidentally, the place also functions as a fine little cafe, particularly noted for its hearty breakfasts.

Of course, the Buena Vista is famous for its Irish coffee, introduced here in 1952 by the late Stan Delaplane. We discussed this in greater detail in the previous chapter.

7 | **The Best Lobby Bar: THE OTHER TRELLIS** *In the Hyatt Regency, No. 5 Embarcadero Center (foot of Market Street), 788-1234.* How can any other lobby bar compete with a soaring 16-story atrium ceiling, a massive circular sculpture suspended above a spill-over fountain and the "Star Trek" look of missile-shaped elevators shooting up and down the inside walls? The Other Trellis tempts you further with live music and hors d'oeuvres weeknights. On Friday, become part of a more genteel era with the weekly Hyatt Tea Dance.

8 **The Best Wine Bar: LONDON WINE BAR** *415 Sansome Street (at Sacramento), 788-4811.* It was San Francisco's first, and it's still the best bar for wine aficionados. You can choose from a variety of vintages at a stand-up tasting plank or at a more intimate sit-down bar, or retire to a table or cozy booth. Wine, wine, everywhere and every drop to drink. The essence of the grape lines the back bar, decorates high shelves around the wall (empty bottles, actually), and boxes of wine are stacked near the entrance.

If you descend to the little basement cafe, where these civilized folk forbid smoking, you'll find — what else? — a wine cellar.

9 **The Best Bar for Intellectual Conversation: CAFFE TRIESTE** *601 Vallejo Street (at Grant), 392-6739.* In this survivor of the Beat Generation, you can sit in the same seats warmed by Jack Kerouac and Allen Ginsberg and ponder the state of society with an understanding friend. Like other coffeehouse survivors of the sixties, it has no hard liquor but offers espresso, wine, beer and sundry aperitifs.

Although the service bar looks suspiciously like a deli, Caffé Trieste is still a pub of sorts. It offers sanctuary for seekers of quiet conversation beneath walls cluttered with scenes of old North Beach, intermixed with glossies of opera stars, film stars, and snapshots of Trieste regulars, past and present.

10 **The Most Historic Bar: THE SALOON** *1232 Grant Avenue (at Fresno Alley), 989-7666.* This cranky old man of a bar stands stubbornly on upper Grant Avenue, where it has stood for well over a century. Housed in a rust-colored Victorian (or is that just rust?), it may be the oldest saloon still active in San Francisco. The Saloon was constructed in 1861 as the Fresno Hotel Bar, and it has survived a tempestuous life as a whorehouse and Prohibition speakeasy. It even survived the great 1906 earthquake and fire. Navy firefighters, perhaps recalling fond memories of a night with one of the upstairs ladies, rushed with fire hoses to drench the tough old bar, saving it from approaching flames.

The place has a achieved a measure of respectability of late as a blues bar, but it's a raucous respectability that the ghosts of the old saloon probably enjoy. Every Monday through Saturday evening (and sometimes Sunday), the ancient pub rattles to the sounds of a blues band that keeps slipping into hard rock, stopping just short of heavy metal. Herds of celebrants crowd into a small space before the band to dance and stomp up a storm. The ancient floorboards shudder and sway; you can't help thinking that the ghosts are dancing, too.

It seems appropriate to end our bar chapter in the old Fresno Hotel Bar, raising a little hell with the spirits of the San Francisco that was, and sometimes, still is.

Nights on the Town

LISTS OF THE TEN BEST WAYS TO ENJOY AN EVENING OUT

They talk of the dignity of work. Bosh. The dignity is in leisure.
— Herman Melville

We've dined, wined, and even stocked the refrigerator. Now it's time to get out on the town. Anyone who can't find entertainment in this city just isn't paying attention to the pink section that appears in the Sunday *Chronicle-Examiner,* which, incidentally, is the best available guide to what's happening here and in the greater Bay Area.

ALIVE AND ONSTAGE

As the only West Coast city with a major symphony, ballet, *and* opera company, along with several resident theater groups, San Francisco is the leading performing arts center west of the Rockies. (Los Angeles may have its Music Center, but the city often borrows our ballet and opera.)

Some words about getting ticketed: BASS and Ticketron are the two major Bay Area ticket agencies for the arts and sporting events. Both have several outlets and charge-by-phone numbers: 762-2277 for BASS tickets and 835-3849 for a recorded events calendar; and 392-SHOW for Ticketron. Downtown Center Box Office in the parking garage of the same name at 325 Mason (between Geary and O'Farrell) is a good ticket source, too. STBS, tucked into an alcove on the Stockton Street side of Union Square, offers discounts on unsold day-of-performance tickets, up to half off. It's also a regular full-service ticket agency; call 433-STBS.

1 **SAN FRANCISCO SYMPHONY** *Davies Symphony Hall, Van Ness at Grove. Call 864-6000 between 9 a.m. and 5 p.m. weekdays for season ticket information or 431-5400 for individual tickets. For a list of upcoming performances, write: San Francisco Symphony, Davies Symphony Hall, San Francisco, CA 94102.*

"Music is a constantly developing form," San Francisco Symphony Director Herbert Blomstedt once commented. "We discover something new every day, not only in the new music, but also in the old."

This best sums up the success story of the San Francisco Symphony, rated as one of the top civic orchestras in America. With each season, it wins new audiences in Northern California and around the world. And it wins accolades and awards both for its classic works and for innovation.

The symphony was established in 1911, the descendant of small ensembles that had been performing in the city since the Gold Rush. Now permanently based in the Louise M. Davies Symphony Hall, it offers a rich and varied September-through-June schedule of more than 200 programs, performing classics, pops and youth concerts. It features guest performers the likes of Michael Tilson Thomas, Isaac Stern and—to exhibit its sense of humor—Victor Borge. Blomstedt's group also has taken several world tours, most recently to Asia, and it records under exclusive contract with London/Decca records.

You will understand why we placed the symphony atop our list if you witness a performance in the elegantly coiffed Davies Hall, with its 8,000-pipe Ruffatti organ. *That* is a sight to hear!

2 **AMERICAN CONSERVATORY THEATRE** *Geary Theatre, 415 Geary Street (at Mason). For show information, dial 749-2228 or 749-2200 or write ACT Subscriptions Office, 450 Geary Street, San Francisco, CA 94102.* Originally founded in Pittsburgh, ACT was brought to San Francisco lock, stock, and backdrop by William Ball in 1967. It has since established itself as the Bay Area's leading resident theater group; it won a Tony Award for excellence in repertory theater and actor training in 1979.

The ACT season consists of eight classic and contemporary plays, including an occasional premiere. Both season subscriptions and individual performance tickets are available. The group performs from September through May at the Geary Theatre.

3 **CURRAN, GOLDEN GATE, AND ORPHEUM THEATRE SERIES** *For schedule and ticket information, call 243-9001 for the Curran (445 Geary) and 474-3800 for the Golden Gate (No. 1 Taylor at Market) and the Orpheum (1192 Market). Individual performance tickets on sale at the three box offices.* Three venerable San Francisco theaters have fallen under the wing of Carole Shorenstein Hays and James M. Nederlander, who present an ongoing series of "Best of Broadway" comedies, dramas, and musicals, dance revues, and individual performers.

Such stars as Rex Harrison, the late Richard Burton, and Claudette Colbert have trod the boards in these old playhouses. Although most of their productions are prepackaged, Ms. Hays has produced her own shows, such as *Fences,* which won a Pulitzer Prize on Broadway.

4 **EUREKA THEATRE** *2730 16th Street (at Harrison); phone 558-9898 for ticket information.* This resident professional drama group, operating out of a new state-of-the-art complex south of Market, presents a season of innovative theater, ranging from serious drama to slapstick comedy. Founded in 1972, it moved to permanent quarters in 1985 after a disastrous fire destroyed its temporary home on Market Street. It has earned national recognition for fostering young writers and for seeking out and premiering new plays that focus on contemporary social issues.

5 **THE MAGIC THEATRE** *Fort Mason Center, Building D; call 441-8822 for tickets and show information.* This highly acclaimed resident company seeks out and produces works of contemporary American playwrights, both established and emerging. It has premiered notable works such as Sam Shepard's Pulitzer Prize-winning *Buried Child.* The Magic has earned both drama awards and critical praise and was described by critic John Roszak as "the most adventuresome company in the West."

6 **MARINE'S MEMORIAL THEATRE** *In the Marines Memorial Association building, 609 Sutter Street (at Mason). For ticket information, call 771-6900.* Charles H. Duggan presents an assortment of shows, usually prepackaged, that range from Broadway musicals to one-man specialty acts and dance recitals. Recent examples were George Peppard in a one-man Hemingway show and Phyllis Diller in a farce called *Nunsense.* (The shows have nothing to do with the USMC; the theater and Duggan's offices just happen to be in a building owned by an association of former Leathernecks.)

7 **SAN FRANCISCO BALLET** *Performances at the War Memorial Opera House, 401 Van Ness Avenue (at Grove); offices at 455 Franklin (at Fulton). For schedule and ticket information, call the box office at 621-3838.* One of America's three largest ballet companies and certainly one of its best, the San Francisco Ballet schedules an ambitious season of classical dance at the Opera House.

Established in 1933 to provide dancers for the San Francisco Opera, it became an independent company in 1942. During its half century of excellence, the ballet has gained international acclaim. It was the first American ballet troupe to tour the Orient (in 1957), and it has won two Emmies for TV performances.

Currently, the company begins its season with a fall tour of major American cities. It then opens at home in mid-December with its annual presentation of *The Nutcracker,* which has become as much a part of the city's Christmas as the lighted trees in Union Square. The company also operates a highly respected ballet school out of its elegant $13.8 million permanent home on Franklin Street.

8 SAN FRANCISCO OPERA *For schedule and ticket information, call 864-3330 or stop by the box office, or write: San Francisco Opera, War Memorial Opera House, San Francisco, CA 94102. Tickets go very quickly, so inquire as early as possible.* For decades, one of America's most honored opera companies has dazzled local audiences with its lavish and splendidly staged productions at the historic Opera House. It won national plaudits for its ambitious *Ring of the Nibelung* in 1985 and scheduled the Wagner *Ring* cycle again in 1990.

Operas generally are presented in two seasons: from May to June and from early September to mid-December, although the spring season is sometimes dropped to permit a more ambitious fall schedule. The opera's fall opening is perhaps the leading social event of the San Francisco cultural season. The company also operates a nationally recognized training program for young singers.

Established in 1923, it has presented more than 150 major operas, including 21 American premieres. Unafraid of innovation, the company features "supertitles" for those who want to hear the operas in their original language instead of a stilted English translation, but who still want to understand what the soprano is shrieking.

9 LORRAINE HANSBERRY THEATER *620 Sutter Street (in the Sheehan Hotel, near Mason); phone 474-8800 for show schedules and ticket information.* This award-winning Black drama group found a permanent home in a theater off the lobby of the Sheehan Hotel in 1988. Its focus is on contemporary drama, special adaptations from Black literature, and musical revues featuring the works of musicians such as Duke Ellington.

In addition to functioning in its 300-seat theater, it sometimes joins forces with the American Conservatory Theatre for special projects in ACT's Geary showplace.

10 THEATRE ON THE SQUARE *450 Post Street (in the Kensington Park Hotel, near Powell). Call 433-9500 for schedules and ticket information.* This second-floor theater in the refurbished Kensington Park Hotel is the city's off-Broadway showplace, hosting comedies, dramas, and musicals particularly suited to small houses. Primarily, it offers shows produced by others. The theater is in an intriguing 1924 Mediterranean-Gothic hall that has been remodeled into a modular theater with flexible seating.

THE TEN BEST CLUBS AND PUBS WITH LIVE AMUSEMENTS

San Francisco's list of nightspots offering live entertainment is longer than a Sunday morning hangover, and with the rapid growth of South of Market dance clubs, it's getting longer. We're not big fans of the glitzy SOMA discos where rock music is blasted over speakers the size of mini-vans, but we do like the flash and excitement of some of the new nightclubs opening in that area.

What follows is a Ten Best mix of some of the cabarets, clubs, and cocktail lounges offering live and hopefully lively entertainment.

1 **THE GREAT AMERICAN MUSIC HALL**   859 O'Farrell Street (at Polk), 885-0750. Supper club; cover. Tickets at BASS agencies and Tower Records. Call for a schedule of performers or write c/o 859 O'Farrell, San Francisco, CA 94109. This classy little hall earns our number one spot for its selection of consistently good entertainers and its appealing old music hall decor. The city's most charming small supper club, it features a family oriented mix of old favorites and rising new stars.

The Hall's eclectic blend ranges through folk, light rock, comedy, and jazz. Through the years, we've enjoyed everything from a revival of the Limelighters to a Zasu Pitts Memorial Orchestra concert-dance. The acoustics are excellent, the baroque gold-leaf, red velvet trim is pleasing, food and drink prices are reasonable, and kids over six are allowed.

2 **BEACH BLANKET BABYLON SERIES**   *Club Fugazi, 678 Green Street (at Powell); cabaret theater. Call 421-4222 for show times and tickets, or write the club at 678 Green Street, San Francisco, CA 94133.* This zany musical review has been makin' whoopee at Club Fugazi for well over a decade; it hit its 5,000th performance in late 1988.

A wildly paced blend of comedy, song and dance routines, and character impersonations, the shows are generated by the fertile brain of Steve Silver. Just about the time the current production begins to slow down, he conjures another, with a new variation on the *Beach Blanket* theme and title. One local critic calls the show "a delightful 90-minute giggle."

3 **COMEDY CLUBS**   Cobb's, *in the Cannery at 2801 Leavenworth (at Columbus), 928-4320;* **Holy City Zoo,** *408 Clement Street (at 15th Avenue), 386-4242;* **Other Cafe,** *100 Carl Street (at Cole), 681-0748;* **The Punch Line,** *444 Battery Street (at Washington), 397-7573.*

Feel the need to giggle your cares away? San Francisco offers four major comedy clubs — listed above — and 20 or so minor ones. Considered the stand-up comic capital of the world, it launched the likes of Phyllis Diller, the Smothers Brothers, and Pat Paulson. Today's future stars are featured on a weekly cable TV show, and the city hosts an international comedy competition every fall. Stand-up comics tend to rotate among the major clubs, so call to find out who's dropping one-liners where. Some of the country's top new comics currently work here, including Rita Rudner and *Police Academy's* Bob Goldthwait. Robin Williams once finished second in the city's annual comedy competition and went on to major stardom; nobody remembers who finished first.

Clubs charge a cover ranging from $2 to $7. Most shows start at 9 p.m., with a second one at 11 on Friday and Saturday. Of the "majors," the Punch Line is the largest and is owned by rock promoter Bill Graham; Cobbs is frequently the highest rated and draws heavily from tourist traffic around Fisherman's Wharf; the Other Cafe is a small and comfortable room in the Haight-Ashbury; and the Holy City Zoo is the father of them all, dating back over a decade.

4 **FAIRMONT HOTEL**   *950 Mason Street (at California), 772-5000. Live music in several lounges; modest cover in New Orleans Room.* The Fairmont extensively renovated — and enlivened — many of its lounges and restaurants following the closing of the venerable Venetian Room supper club. The New Orleans Room features live music nightly from 9:30; there's a modest entertainment charge. In the Bella Voce Ristorante, the Bella Voce Singers serve up popular show tunes and bits from operas and operettas while the waitstaff serves seafood, pasta, and pizza; serenading begins at 6:30 nightly. Near-legendary Peter Minton tickles the 88s at Mason's. Brightened but unchanged is the Tonga Room with its wonderful Polynesian excess; patrons can dance nightly in this jungled haven to a live band and to the periodic rumble of tropic storms.

5 **KIMBALL'S**   *300 Grove Street (at Franklin), 861-5555. Restaurant-jazz club; modest cover and food or drink minimum.* This cheerful, airy restaurant with light woods and old brick has become one of the city's leading jazz clubs, where the likes of Ahmad Jamal, the Hi-Lo's, and Buddy Collette perform. Live music is featured Friday, Saturday, and sometimes Sunday nights, with shows generally at 9 and 11 p.m. Located near Davies Symphony Hall, the Opera, and Civic Auditorium, it's also a popular pretheater restaurant, so dinner reservations are essential.

6 **PAUL'S SALOON**   *3251 Scott Street (between Lombard and Chestnut); 922-2456. Country-western-bluegrass music nightly, starting around 9; no cover or minimum.* Paul's Saloon has been hosting live country and western music for more than 20 years, featuring some of the best darn toe-tappin' bluegrass this side of the Great Smokies. Several bands rotate through the week; our longtime favorite is a group called High Country. There's no cover or minimum and drink prices are surprisingly moderate for a place with live music.

The saloon itself isn't one of those slick designer cowboy bars, but a comfortable old San Francisco watering hole with the requisite weathered wooden bar, ceiling fans, and an eclectic photo collection on the walls.

7 **PIER 23 CAFE**   *On the Embarcadero at Pier 23, 362-5125. Jazz club–bar–restaurant; modest cover.* Despite a new paint job after a recent fire, Pier 23 retains its 1930s funk; it's a pleasant setting for a mix of jazz, soul, blues, and Dixieland music. Different groups perform Tuesday through Saturday starting from 9 to 10 p.m.; there's also a Sunday afternoon set.

Although it's still a popular waterfront bar, Pier 23 is gaining stature as an excellent, moderately priced restaurant featuring light lunches and dinners, done in the American nouvelle style. We dined there recently on a curious but wonderful lasagna made with polenta and Italian sausage.

8 **THE PLUSH ROOM**   *In the York Hotel at 940 Sutter (at Hyde), 885-6800. Cabaret; cover charge.* Think of the Plush Room as a mini-Venetian Room, without the restaurant. Beautifully refurbished a few years ago, this cozy 150-seat show club features lounge-type acts ranging from impressionists to Margaret Whiting to small musical revues. With its art deco elegance, the room is described by local critics as the most inviting small show lounge in the city.

9 **SLIM'S**   *333 11th Street (at Folsom), 621-3330. Nightclub-restaurant; tickets through normal outlets or at the door an hour before show time.* Co-owned by Boz Skaggs, Slim's is one of the spiffiest new South of Market clubs. The facade is old New Orleans, with plantation porch columns, chandeliers, and wrought iron, behind which lurk state-of-the-art sound and lighting systems. Opened in late 1988, it offers a mix of American-roots musical groups, ranging from jazz to rock to rhythm and blues, including guest appearances by the Boz himself (in the guise of Presidio Slim).

Slim's also features a full-service restaurant specializing in California and American regional cuisine.

10 **THE WARFIELD/DOWNTOWN**   *982 Market Street (near Taylor and Golden Gate), 775-7722. Nightclub-dance club-disco; cover charge.* Refurbished in late 1988 by rock impresario Bill Graham, the old

Warfield on Market Street was reborn as a glitzy Manhattan-style showplace with the requisite mix of track lighting, graffiti graphics, and gilt-edged curlicues.

It functions in a dual role, as the Warfield Theater with live entertainment and, Thursday through Saturday, as a yuppie-oriented disco called Downtown. Guests can dine at a sleek tiered restaurant and catch a variety of acts ranging from stand-up comics to rock to upbeat combos. During disco nights, it becomes a glitter of flashing lights, and the disc jockey rules from a wall-mounted opera box uncovered during renovation.

THE TEN BEST PLACES TO DANCE YOUR SOX OFF

Dancing — dirty and otherwise — is experiencing a major comeback in the city, particularly South of Market. Not since John Travolta tried to dislocate his left hip in *Saturday Night Fever* have so many wriggled so furiously to such loud music.

We don't frequent these places, since the median age is somewhere between puberty and 30; also, we prefer to preserve our eardrums for Bach and bluegrass. But in the interest of democracy, we list the ten most popular dance clubs. We do think Jukebox Saturday Night is cleverly done, and we've voted it the best on our list. Most of these establishments are discos, but a few feature live bands.

A note about South of Market: Don't expect SOMA to be a wall-to-wall glitter of night life, like the original Soho in London. The area is still mostly dingy warehouses and dimly lit alleys where you might hesitate to venture unaccompanied. The nightspots are widely spaced and some are poorly marked, as if challenging you to find them. Others, like Slim's and Jukebox Saturday Night, are glittery and inviting. And since dance clubs are a rising new fad, expect some of them to be out of business by the time you read this.

1 **JUKEBOX SATURDAY NIGHT**   *650 Howard Street (at Second),* *495-5853.* When I first stepped into JBSN, a recorded Debbie Reynolds was singing the theme from *Tammy;* it took me back farther than I wanted to go. Think of Jukebox Saturday Night as the Hard Rock Cafe of discos. The walls are splashed with excellent graphics ranging from Marilyn Monroe and Mighty Mouse to Joe Montana completing a pass to Jerry Rice. Mostly, it's strictly Dick Clarksville, with a glittering 1957 Chevy as a DJ booth from which emerges rock, folk, and pop music of the fifties, sixties and seventies.

A diner fills one end of the large main room. JBSN also is a sports bar with more TV monitors than Macy's video department; between games, they show TV nostalgia. The place is easy to find; look for the nose of an old Chevy plunging through the wall. The age limit is 21.

2 **CITY NIGHTS** *715 Harrison (at Third)*, *546-7774*. This big club with a cavernous dance floor features a mix of modern, top 40, and rock music. The age limit is 18, and the crowd ranges up to mid-twenties.

3 **DNA LOUNGE** *375 11th Street (at Harrison)*, *626-1409*. Live groups are followed by a disco DJ in this upscale SOMA cabaret lounge. The music is essential rock, the age limit is 21, and the clientele extends into the Baby Boomer generation.

4 **DV8** *540 Howard (at First Street)*, *777-1419*. Another large SOMA establishment — this one with two dance floors — DV8 is geared to the Travolta fans of the seventies, with music to match. The age limit is 21, and the crowd doesn't go much beyond that.

5 **I-BEAM** *1748 Haight (at Cole)*, *668-6006*. An industrial-strength club with decor to match, Haight-Ashbury's I-Beam offers an assortment of live band and DJ shows, mostly heavy rock at shingle-shaking volume. It also features teen and tea dances; the age limit varies, depending on the event.

6 **THE PARK EXCHANGE** *600 Montgomery Street (at Clay)*, *983-4800*. The Bank Exchange, built into the concrete legs of the Financial District's Transamerica Pyramid, is our favorite cocktail-hour pub, but we depart around 9 p.m. when the lights go down and the volume goes up. It then becomes the Park Exchange, a yuppie-oriented disco with two dance floors. The age limit is 21.

7 **SOUTHSIDE** *1190 Folsom (at Seventh)*, *431-3332*. Trendy and slick, with an accompanying restaurant, Southside draws an upwardly mobile crowd; it's one of the city's most popular clubs, so expect mobs on weekends. Live rock Wednesdays, recorded music Thursday through Saturday. The age limit is 21.

8 **THE SPECTRUM** *No. 1 Embarcadero Center (at Battery)*, *956-8768*. Recently changed from Channel's, this small and attractive disco done up in mirrored neon draws primarily from the yuppie set. It's on the podium level of the upscale Embarcadero Center shopping complex. Mostly rock; no live music; the age limit is 21.

9 **TROCADERO TRANSFER** *520 Fourth Street (at Bryant), 495-0185.* The first SOMA dance club and one of the oldest in the city, the Troc now functions in a dual role: as "X," a Friday-night disco appealing primarily to teenagers, and as Red Square on Saturdays, with rock music aimed at the 21-plus crowd. The original Troc nightclub now opens only for special events, although the recently remodeled Troc Cafe next door was functioning at this writing.

10 **UNDERGROUND** *201 Ninth Street (at Howard), 552-3466.* Most of the time, this is Lipps, a SOMA corner bar. It transforms into the Underground on Friday and Saturday nights. One of the city's few all-night discos, it keeps the platters spinning until 8 a.m. for the slumming yuppie set. The age limit is 21.

THE TEN BEST PLACES TO CATCH A MOVIE

Instead of shaking your sox at the Troc, perhaps you'd prefer a quiet movie. Sadly, many of the city's grand old art deco theaters have been redeveloped out of existence or have taken on new roles; one is a glitzy nightclub, another a Korean church. But many survive, along with some newer showcases.

1 **NORTHPOINT** *2290 Powell Street (at Bay), 989-6060.* The Northpoint is our favorite movie palace, offering the largest screen and one of the most sophisticated Dolby sound systems in the city. Built in the early 1970s, this modern film house features major first-run movies. It's one of the few big houses that hasn't been chopped up into mini-theaters with small screens in narrow halls.

2 **BALBOA** *3634 Balboa Street (at 38th Avenue), 221-8184.* A venerable movie house with art deco trim, the Balboa has been showing first-run films in the Richmond District since 1926; it's still operated by the Levins, the family who built it. It offers a double bill of first-run features on each of two screens. We love its rocking-chair loges.

3 **CASTRO** *429 Castro Street (at Market), 621-6120.* The Castro is another grand old film palace that has escaped the redeveloper's wrecking ball. The big screen in this large theater shows oldies and goodies, a range of foreign and American classics. It features film star retrospectives or movies with common themes, and it hosts occasional film festivals. Between shows, patrons can listen to sonorous notes of the theater's huge Wurlitzer pipe organ.

4 **CLAY** *2261 Fillmore (at Clay), 346-1123.* The oldest continuously operating movie theater in the city, the Clay opened in 1910. Preceding the art deco period, its look is more turn-of-the-century neoclassic. The relatively small 400-seat auditorium is filled with Dolby stereo and shows first-run foreign films.

5 **CORONET** *3575 Geary (at Arguello), 752-4400.* Built in 1949, the Coronet is another San Francisco movie house that still retains its big screen. Remember the days of CinemaScope? They're still here, along with Dolby stereo, of course. This and the Northpoint are *the* theaters of choice for comfort and big-screen productions.

6 **GALAXY** *1285 Sutter (at Van Ness), 474-8700.* We make fun of the startling glass box architecture of this new wave multiscreen theater in Chapter 20. But the slick lobby is worth a look, and the theater's four viewing rooms are comfortable, if small. The Galaxy features first-run films, and it hosted the world premiere of the Oscar-winning *Amadeus* in 1984.

7 **GATEWAY CINEMA** *215 Jackson Street (at Battery), 421-3353.* Since its completion in 1967, this theater in the Golden Gateway Center has been *the* San Francisco art film center. When not hosting a premiere, benefit, or film festival, it shows major foreign and art movies.

8 **RED VIC MOVIE HOUSE** *1659 Haight Street (at Cole), 863-3994.* This cozy little theater built into the ground floor of an old red Victorian shows a mix of current American and foreign classics, plus occasional cult films and some local independent productions. The theater is known for its funky, comfortable atmosphere; many of its seats are couches and loveseats. The Red Vic even exhibits a culinary concern for its patrons, selling popcorn with nutritional yeast, served in wooden bowls, and home-baked goods. Not a Milk Dud in sight.

9 **REGENCY III** *420 Mason Street (at Geary), 397-8414.* This downtown theater has survived by modernizing, yet it still reveals glimpses of its past. Built in the early 1900s, it's now a contemporary showplace with first-run films. But you should pause with your popcorn to study the lobby murals, depicting Chinese legends, that were brought here for the 1939 Golden Gate Exposition. They were considered so bizarre for their day that they were never exhibited at the fair.

10 **VOGUE** *3290 Sacramento Street (at Presidio), 221-8183.* The focus here is on classic foreign and domestic art films; the theater sometimes screens an important movie for several months. Built in 1910 (the same year as the Clay), this pre–art deco house originally was called La Petite, certainly appropriate, since it seats only 316. It's noted for its friendly, sometimes amusing staff, and it's a stopover for stars such as Cloris Leachman, Robin Williams, Elizabeth Ashley, Carol Channing, and Mary Martin when they're in town.

For Mature Adults Only

THE TEN NAUGHTIEST THINGS TO DO IN SAN FRANCISCO

The most romantic thing any woman ever said to me in bed was:
'Are you sure you're not a cop?' — Larry Brown

Perhaps grown weary of the erotic overkill of the 1960s and 1970s, San Francisco is no longer America's sexual freedom center as it moves into the 1990s. Most of the topless-bottomless shows along Broadway have been called on account of disinterest; fear of AIDS has muted the gay community; swingers' clubs are going out of fashion.

But the permissiveness that brought America topless dancing and bawdy movies still survives. Here are ten harmless ways to pursue naughtiness in San Francisco.

1 **CATCH A PAIR OF LEGENDS AT THE CONDOR** *300 Columbus Avenue (at Broadway), 392-4443.* Business was slow at the Condor Club on the opening night of the Republican National Convention in 1964. It got brisk when a waitress-turned-dancer named Carol Doda donned a topless bathing suit and stepped onstage.

The DA's staff thumbed nervously through the law books and it took the police several days to bust (pardon the expression) Ms. Doda. Then the courts ruled that nudity of itself was not pornographic, and the topless revolution was in — uh — full swing. Carol has retired her silicone assets, but other more or less endowed women dance and prance at the Condor and the other surviving nude parlors along Broadway.

Topless dancing has been an on-again, off-again affair in recent years at the Condor. During your next visit, you might find the bikini-clad dancers ignoring the bald-headed conventioneer's pleas to "Take it off."

The Condor heads our list because of its important place in history. Seriously. Next time you're in the neighborhood, look for a marker bearing an odd likeness to historical landmark plaques. (You need a sense of humor in the topless-bottomless business.) It reads:

The Condor, where it all began. The birthplace of the world's first topless and bottomless entertainment. Topless, June 19, 1964; bottomless, September 3, 1969, starring Ms. Carol Doda. San Francisco, California.

See? History in the making.

2 **SAY IT WITH FLASH INSTEAD OF FLOWERS**   FTD was never like this! Instead of sending flowers or candy, you can now send a striptease artist to the boys and girls at the office, or to the bachelor or bachelorette party. These swinging telegrams are co-ed and this is not an endorsement, but I love the name of one outfit: Bouncing Buns and Baubles.

How far will these take-out strippers peel? That's up to you to negotiate. Several such places do business in San Francisco, listed under "Singing" in the Yellow Pages. (We looked under "Stripping" and wound up reading about paint remover.)

3 **TAKE A PEEK AT A NAUGHTY MOVIE**   *Mitchell Brothers' O'Farrell Theater, 895 O'Farrell Street (at Polk), 776-6686.* While Carol Doda was shaking things up at the Condor, the Mitchell Brothers pursued pornographic breakthroughs in the naughty film business. We don't go in for this sort of thing, but we understand that two or more of their reels of raunch are showing on any given day in their O'Farrell Street theater. The place also features live-and-onstage topless dancers and something called the Ultra Room, whatever that is.

The brothers of porn apparently are on the leading edge of the industry, since their place has been busted a few times in the past. And it all happens behind a rather dramatic facade; the building is covered with an aquatic mural of whales, dolphins, and other sea creatures.

4 **SKINNY-DIP WITH SOMEONE SPECIAL**   *Baker Beach, off Lincoln Boulevard in the Presidio.* Rangers of the Golden Gate National Recreation Area are faced with a curious dilemma. While the National Park Service does not encourage skinny-dipping, much of the city's beach front is part of the GGNRA, and there's nothing in federal law prohibiting nudity.

"If we hauled a nude sunbather before a federal magistrate, we'd be laughed out of court," a ranger told us. "So we ask them to limit themselves to particular areas."

Essentially, those areas consist of the northern end of Baker Beach and several small rock-sheltered coves between there and the Golden Gate Bridge. Most of the skinny-dippers are slender young men, but I've noticed some remarkable exceptions.

5 **READ ALL ABOUT IT IN A NAUGHTY NEWSPAPER** Have you ever wondered what was inside the pages of those provocative-looking one-dollar tabloids in the news racks? Most are published in Los Angeles, but at least one, *The Pleasure Guide,* is a local product.

The inside pages are full of what's left of the sexual revolution: classified ads for swing parties, escort service, phone sex, outcall massage and lots of bosomy photos. It also features some badly written porn stories and it discusses your erogenous zones. Actually, the entire publication is an erogenous zone.

If you're too embarrassed to pull one of these tawdry tabloids from a news rack in public, you might drop a line to *The Pleasure Guide,* P.O. Box 1892, San Francisco, CA 94101.

6 **GET RUBBED – SOMETIMES THE WRONG WAY – AT A MASSAGE PARLOR** There are two kinds of masseuses in San Francisco: those who do shiatsu massage and those who can't even pronounce it. You can get massaged by the second variety, but mostly in the wallet. Police no longer license massage parlors, but they keep careful tabs on them to discourage prostitution. The odds are that when you pay for a massage in this town, that's all you'll get.

Of course, many legitimate places are in business to give you a skilled, professional rubdown. The tone of their ads will reveal if a particular place is more serious about rubbing your body than your wallet.

During a special—uh—investigative trip to one of the bawdier parlors, I was was rubbed every way imaginable for $50, then the masseuse offered to "fulfill all my fantasies" for a mere $200 more. She clicked a hand-held imprinter expertly across my VISA card, then led me into a "special room." But the only thing special there, other than a red-tasseled canopy over the massage table, was the price. I did get rubbed with palm oil, but for $200, I could have bought my own palm tree.

7 **NIBBLE A LITTLE SIN** *The Cake Gallery, 290 Ninth (at Folsom), 861-CAKE and 1045 Polk Street (at Post), 775-CAKE.* Put down the phone, lady, we're talking about *food.* The Cake Gallery's two outlets will bake you an X-rated cake or other naughty nibbles. They can be as anatomically complete as you wish. The firm also has a full line of G, PG, and R-rated pastries.

Mee Mee Bakery, 1328 Stockton Street (at Broadway), sells X-rated fortune cookies but they're not really very naughty. Fortunately, they're good fortune cookies.

8 **GIGGLE WITH THE GENTLEMEN OF THE CHORUS AT FINOC-CHIO'S** *506 Broadway (at Kearny); 982-9388. Show times vary with the seasons; the minimum age is 21.* After more than half a century, Finocchio's has become San Francisco's institution of harmless naughtiness. Its small, lively cast of female impersonators prances and dances about convincingly, to the applause of the tour bus crowd, conventioneers, and every Bay Area resident's cousin who ever visited this city.

In these jaded times, the show is no longer shocking, and only barely naughty. It's a harmless satire of a striptease that is neither bawdy nor off-color; a film version probably would get no worse than a PG rating. We think it's kind of cute.

9 **SPEND A LITTLE FOR EVEN LESS AT MIDSUMMER NIGHTS LINGERIE** *Pier 39, second level (on the Embarcadero), 788-0992. Open 10:30 a.m. to 8:30 p.m. daily. Major credit cards.* This Pier 39 lingerie shop offers tasteful little bits of sensual fluff for m'lady. It's a refined place; you'll find none of the tawdry peek-a-boo attire featured in the Frederick's of Hollywood type shops. The selection ranges from filmy nighties to Kama Sutra Oil of Love. So if you're a sensuous lady seeking something silky, or a gentleman seeking to impress such a lady, this place is very nice. The naughty comes later.

10 **SHOP FOR SOMETHING SEXY WHILE SIPPING SCOTCH** *Megatrends Entertainment X-Change, 752-2957.* This firm has an eye-catching method of marketing its fragile fragments of fluff. Instead of displaying provocatively attired mannequins in store windows, it takes its show on the road. Live models wear feathery fashions before lunch and cocktail hour crowds at various San Francisco restaurants and pubs.

Fetching young women sashay among the diners and sippers, showing off the latest filmy creations. They offer tickets for a series of drawings and some lucky customer gets to take home the prize. (No, silly, the lingerie!) Schedules change frequently, so call the number above to learn which cafes or saloons are hosting the sensual shows.

A City Celebrates

THE TEN BEST SAN FRANCISCO FESTIVALS

Make the coming hour o'erflow with joy
And pleasure drown the brim.
— Shakespeare, *All's Well that Ends Well*

San Franciscans not only like to party individually and with consenting friends, they also enjoy it with organized groups. Any excuse is a good reason for a celebration in this city, and the rich legacy of our ethnic groups adds to the festivities. The San Francisco Visitor Information Center in Hallidie Plaza at Market and Powell (391-2000) will have specifics on these celebrations.

1 **THE SAN FRANCISCO FAIR** *Fort Mason Center in early September; call 392-FAIR for specifics.* There isn't a cantaloupe patch in sight, but San Francisco's county fair is one of the city's most popular celebrations — and it's our favorite festival. This is an urban-style county fair, with popular restaurants setting up food booths, wineries offering tastings and more than 600 performers, from jugglers to stand-up comics to operatic divas. And the street artists are here, carving their sculptures, weaving their macrame, and potting their pots.

This delightfully San Franciscanized version of a fair offers events such as a fog-calling contest, landlord-tenant tug-of-war, and the Impossible Parking Space Race.

2 **BLACK AND WHITE BALL** *Late May in the Civic Center; call 431-5400 for ticket information.* Can a formal ball really be worth $150 per ticket? Only in San Francisco, and only if it involves a dozen orchestras playing everything from waltz to rock in five major Civic Center buildings, while dozens of merchants and wineries offer free food and drink.

Possibly the world's largest ball, the Black and White is the annual fundraiser for the San Francisco Symphony. In a good year, more than 7,000 attend. They trip the light fantastic — sometimes over one another — in Davies

Symphony Hall, the Opera House, Veterans Memorial, City Hall, and the Civic Auditorium. Outside, streets are blocked off, and a giant rotating mirror ball dangling from a crane casts a fantasy of moving light throughout the Civic Center.

The idea here is to limit your attire to various combinations of black and white. The gents usually are stuck with the tux, but the ladies go to town conjuring original and unusual ballgowns. It's a Day at Ascot turned into night and multiplied a hundredfold. Even if you can't spare the price of admission, pause a few moments on the sidelines to watch the spectacle of thousands of Ascot-themed celebrants moving around the Civic Center, bathed in a twinkle of revolving lights.

3 **CHERRY BLOSSOM FESTIVAL**   *Middle to late April in Japantown and Japan Center, Post and Webster; 922-6776.* In Japan, where space is precious, thousands of acres are given over to a cherry tree that bears only blossoms. The Japanese honor the brief two-week spring bloom with a celebration called *Sakura Matsuri*. The tradition has come to Nihonmachi, the Japanese community in the Western Addition.

Activities include classic Japanese theater, folk dances, flower arranging, bonsai demonstrations, and other things Japanese. Most events occur in and about Japan Center and the adjacent Buchanan Street mall. In the festival's climactic parade, sweating youths carry portable shrines through the streets while *taiko* drummers pound out their thunder.

4 **CHINESE NEW YEAR'S CELEBRATION**   *February to March in Chinatown and downtown San Francisco; Chinese Chamber of Commerce, 730 Sacramento Street, San Francisco, CA 94108; 982-3000.* Don't even try to figure out the day on which Chinese New Year falls. Just check the local papers or call the Chinese chamber or San Francisco Visitor Bureau (974-6900). New Year's Day itself is celebrated quietly in Chinese homes. The holiday goes public a bit later — usually late February to early March — with a Miss Chinatown USA pageant, the explosions of thousands of ear-jarring little red firecrackers, lion dancers, folk dancing, martial arts demonstrations, crafts exhibits, and such.

As with the Japanese festival, the climax is a parade, one of the city's largest. The star of the procession is the block-long *gum lung*, the glittering golden dragon that snakes and snorts along the parade route, held aloft by dozens of dragon-bearers.

5 **LATIN FESTIVALS**   *During May in the Mission District; 826-1401.* San Francisco's Latin neighborhood sponsors two major springtime festivals.

115

Cinco de Mayo is celebrated during the week including May 5 with folk dancing, art exhibits, guided tours past the neighborhood's 200 murals, special food shows, and the like. There's a parade, of course, usually scheduled on the Sunday closest to May 5. For information, call 826-1401. In case you wondered, Cinco de Mayo marks the Battle of Puebla on May 5, 1862, in which a group of greatly outnumbered Mexican forces defeated the invading armies of Napoleon III.

Carnaval is the Latin community's version of Mardi Gras, but it's held the last weekend of May rather than during the pre-Lenten period. Festivities represent the cultures of Mexico, Central and South America, and the Caribbean. Activities include costumed dancing, street parties, live bands, arts, crafts, international foods, a parade, and the world's longest conga line, which — in a good year — stretches for more than several blocks. For information, call the Mission Economic and Cultural Association at 826-1401.

6 **COLUMBUS DAY FESTIVITIES** *The week including Columbus's birthday (October 12); 434-6440 or 391-2000.* Old Chris never got this far, but thousands of other Italians have settled here, and they celebrate his birthday with festivities from late September through his birthday. It begins quietly with the blessing of the fleet at Fisherman's Wharf. Later, old Chris finally arrives in California with a reenactment of his landing, at Aquatic Park.

Festa Italiana, centered around the wharf and North Beach, is a three-day revel with ethnic food fairs, street dances, live entertainers, a bocce ball tournament, and nightly fireworks. The Columbus Day Parade proceeds from the foot of Market up — where else? — Columbus Avenue.

7 **FESTIVALS OF THE FEET** *Bay to Breakers, third Sunday in May, San Francisco Examiner Promotions Department at 777-7770; San Francisco Marathon, mid-July, Pamakid Runners Club, 681-2322; San Francisco Stride, late August, CitySports magazine, 546-6150.* A fitness-oriented city, San Francisco sponsors three major foot-races every year, and you can win one of them in a walk.

The famous Bay to Breakers, attracting tens of thousands of runners, dashes from the edge of the bay at the Ferry Building to the ocean on the Great Highway, about 7.5 miles away. Fewer but more serious runners show up for the San Francisco Marathon, a grueling, gasping, and groaning 26.2 miles through the streets of the city.

The newest foot festival, begun here in 1985 and now spread to several other cities, is called the City Stride, a walking race that rivals the Bay to Breakers in attendance. Sponsored by *CitySports* magazine as the country's first major walking race, it takes power striders over some of the city's steepest hills.

8 **FOURTH OF JULY**   *July 4 at Crissy Field, sponsored by the* San Francisco Chronicle; *556-0560.* The old small-plane field along the Presidio waterfront is the Fourth of July focal point in San Francisco. All-day festivities include a 50-cannon salute to the states, comedy shows, bluegrass music, kids' games, band concerts, and other folksy stuff to keep the crowd amused until fireworks light up the sky starting at 9 p.m. The rockets' red glare, glimmering off the Golden Gate Bridge and reflecting colored ripples in the bay, is a sight to see.

The idea is to get there early and walk — don't drive. The pre- and post-fireworks traffic jams are awesome.

9 **OPENING DAY OF THE YACHTING SEASON**   *The last Saturday in April on San Francisco Bay.* You don't have to own a yacht or even a dingy to enjoy this aquatic spectacle. Virtually every sailboat in the greater Bay Area takes to the waters, filling the bay with glittering white triangles and brilliant billows of spinnakers. The best viewing points are from Fisherman's Wharf, the Golden Gate Promenade between Fort Mason and the Golden Gate Bridge, the bridge itself, Fort Point, and Marin Headlands above the bridge. Pray for sunshine and take your camera.

10 **SAN FRANCISCO BLUES FESTIVAL**   *Mid-September on the Great Meadow at Fort Mason; 826-6837. Tickets at all regular outlets.* The San Francisco Blues Festival is a huge outdoor concert held over a weekend in September, from 11:30 a.m. to 6 p.m. Dozens of local and national blues artists perform in these two marathon concerts. Look for folks like Elvin Bishop, C.J. Chenier and his Red Hot Louisiana Band, Johnny Copeland, and something called the SuperHarps. One magazine called this "*the* blues event of the year on the West Coast."

117

The Cultural and the Curious

LISTS OF ART MUSEUMS, SPECIALTY MUSEUMS, AND GALLERIES

The Devil whispered behind the leaves, 'It's pretty, but is it art?'
— Rudyard Kipling

We counted 50 museums in the San Francisco Yellow Pages, celebrating everything from Turkish art to tattoos. Some are world class, others virtually unknown. We offer herewith our lists of the Ten Best museums, first large and then small. We conclude with the city's Ten Best galleries, where you can buy something from the art world for your very own.

You'll note that nominees in the first two lists aren't all art museums; they fit the broader classification of places that preserve for future generations the things of the past. (Other specialized museums are listed under attractions in Chapter 2.)

Admission charges are modest, and some museums are free; those that do charge often have free days, so call ahead if you're short on cash.

Note: For recorded information concerning hours and current exhibits at the M.H. de Young Memorial Museum, Asian Art Museum, and California Palace of the Legion of Honor, call 750-3659.

SAN FRANCISCO'S TEN BEST MAJOR MUSEUMS

1 **M. H. de YOUNG MEMORIAL MUSEUM**   *Golden Gate Park, just off John F. Kennedy Drive; 750-3600. Open 10 a.m. to 4:45 p.m. Wednesday–Sunday; closed Monday and Tuesday. Admission $4 for adults, less for juniors 12–17 and seniors, kids free; ticket is good the same day for the Asian Art Museum in the same building and the Palace of the Legion of Honor Museum in Lincoln Park (see listings below). Free all day the first Wednesday of each month and from 10 a.m. to noon the first Saturday of each month.*

Our favorite San Francisco museum is the oldest, largest and one of the most honored municipal museums in the West. It traces the cultural development of Western man from the pharaohs to America's greatest artists. Exhibits include European and American sculptures and paintings, tribal and folk arts of Asia and the Americas, and an outstanding collection of textiles. It also hosts major traveling exhibits.

2 **ASIAN ART MUSEUM** *Golden Gate Park, occupying a wing of the de Young Memorial Museum building; 668-8921. Open 10 a.m. to 5 p.m. Wednesday–Sunday (to 8:45 p.m. the first Wednesday of each month); free days are the same as the de Young. Admission is $4 for adults, $2 for juniors 12–17 and seniors, kids free; ticket is good the same day for the de Young and the Palace of the Legion of Honor.* Although it shares the de Young building, the Asian Art Museum is a separate entity. It exhibits the priceless Avery Brundage collection of 10,000 Oriental objets d'art, plus other sculptures, paintings, jades, bronzes, and ceramics from 40 Asian countries. It hosts traveling exhibitions and offers periodic thematic exhibits from its permanent collections.

3 **CALIFORNIA ACADEMY OF SCIENCES** *Golden Gate Park, 750-7145. Open 10 a.m. to 5 p.m. daily, longer in summer. Admission $3 for adults; $2 for students and seniors; free day is first Wednesday of month. Admission includes Natural History Museum and Steinhart Aquarium; Alexander Morrison Planetarium extra.* The Academy is just possibly the greatest science facility complex in the West, with its combined life-sciences museum, aquarium, and planetarium. See Chapter 1 for more enthusiastic detail.

4 **CALIFORNIA PALACE OF THE LEGION OF HONOR** *In Lincoln Park, 750-3600. Open 10 a.m. to 4:45 p.m. Wednesday–Sunday. Adults $4, $2 for seniors; same-day tickets good at de Young and Asian Art museums; Saturdays (except during special shows) and the first Wednesday of the month are free days.* This splendid building, fashioned after the original in Paris, stresses European art, including a major Rodin sculpture collection, paintings, tapestries, furniture, prints, drawings, and porcelains. Light nibbles are available at the museum's Cafe Chanticleer.

5 **THE MEXICAN MUSEUM** *Fort Mason Center, Building D, 441-0404. Open noon to 5 p.m. Wednesday–Sunday. Adults $3, students and seniors $2, kids under 10 free; Wednesdays are free days.* Permanent and changing exhibits focus on the art of the Latin community, particularly here in San Francisco. The facility also has a small but interesting book and gift shop with Mexican folk crafts for sale.

6 **THE PRESIDIO ARMY MUSEUM** *Lincoln Boulevard (at Funston Avenue) in the Presidio, 561-4115; for guided tours, call 921-8193. Open 10 a.m. to 4 p.m. Tuesday–Sunday; free.* The facility focuses on the military history of San Francisco, going back more than two centuries when the Presidio housed the Spanish garrison that accompanied the first padres to this area. (Note: the status of this museum may change following the deactivation of the Presidio as a military base in 1990; call to ensure that it's still open.)

7 **OLD U.S. MINT MUSEUM** *88 Fifth Street (at Mission), 974-0788. Open 10 a.m. to 4 p.m. Monday–Friday; free.* Have you ever stared at a million dollars in gold bars and coins? You can do so in this museum, which functioned as the San Francisco Mint from 1874 until 1937. It has been restored to its original 19th century appearance, offering an intriguing museum of coinage and mining equipment, with hourly tours.

8 **NATIONAL MARITIME MUSEUM** *Fisherman's Wharf (part of the GGNRA), Beach and Polk streets, 556-8177. Open 10 a.m. to 6 p.m. daily in summer, 10 a.m. to 5 p.m. rest of the year; free.* This facility is housed in a unique building that looks like the Art Deco superstructure of a ship. Inside are ship models and other historic mementos of the shipping trade, particularly as it relates to the Bay Area. Hyde Street Pier (556-6435), also part of the Maritime Museum, features several walk-aboard ships at anchor at the foot of Hyde Street, including the 19th-century British square-rigged *Balclutha* and a retired San Francisco Bay ferryboat.

9 **SAN FRANCISCO MUSEUM OF MODERN ART** *Veterans Memorial, Van Ness Avenue at McAllister, 863-8800. Open 10 a.m. to 5 p.m. Tuesday–Friday (until 9 Thursday); 11 a.m. to 5 p.m. weekends. Adults $3.50, seniors and kids $1.50; free on Tuesday.* San Francisco's fascinating contemporary art museum challenges your perception of art. It's one of the country's leading exponents of the leading edge of the modern movement.

Is some of this stuff art? Is it even pretty? Go decide for yourself. The museum also has a fine little cafe and an excellent art bookstore. A privately endowed facility, it is set to move to larger quarters in the early 1990s.

10 **TREASURE ISLAND MUSEUM** *Just inside the Treasure Island gate; park outside and walk in; 765-6182. Open 10 a.m. to 3:30 p.m. daily except Thanksgiving, Christmas, New Year's, and Easter; free.* The TI museum is concerned with our sea services — Navy, Marine Corps, and Coast Guard — with exhibits relating to their worldwide exploits. It also

120

tells the story of Treasure Island's 1939–40 Golden Gate International Exposition and the China Clipper seaplanes that flew from here between 1939 and 1946.

SAN FRANCISCO'S TEN BEST SMALL MUSEUMS

We won't try to pick a favorite here because each of these facilities is different in character and subject; they're all listed alphabetically.

1 **CARTOON ART MUSEUM**   *665 Third Street (at Brannan), 546-3922. Open noon to 6 p.m. Thursday and Friday; 10 a.m. to 5 p.m. Saturday; $1 for adults, 50 cents for pre-teens.* Located on the fifth floor of the Northern California Print Center, this little-known facility features art, books, and figures from the world of cartooning, ranging from original comic strip panels to self-portraits of noted cartoonists. Exhibits change periodically.

2 **JEWISH COMMUNITY MUSEUM**   *121 Steuart Street (at Mission), 543-8880. Open 10 a.m. to 4 p.m. Sunday–Friday; free.* San Francisco's only Jewish museum offers a fresh perspective on contemporary and traditional Jewish art and artifacts. There's a small shop in the facility, featuring Jewish arts and crafts.

3 **MUSEO ITALO AMERICANO**   *Building C, Fort Mason Center, 673-2200. Open noon to 5 p.m. Wednesday–Sunday; free.* The museum features exhibitions of works by Italian and Italian-American artists; it also sponsors programs concerning Italian language, literature, music, and art.

4 **MUSEUM OF MODERN MYTHOLOGY**   *693 Mission, ninth floor (at Third Street), 546-0202. Open noon to 5 p.m. Wednesday–Sunday; $2 for adults, $1.50 for teens and seniors, $1 for kids 6 to 12.* The only museum of its kind in the world, this archive focuses on American advertising characters, other media phenomena, and mass-produced commodity folk art. Rotating exhibits draw from its collections of cloth and vinyl dolls, print ads, point-of-sale displays, and other artifacts featuring the likes of Mr. Peanut, the Jolly Green Giant, and Speedy Alka-Seltzer.

5 **THE OCTAGON HOUSE**   *2645 Gough Street (at Union), 441-7512. Open noon to 3 p.m. on the second Sunday and second and fourth Thursdays of the month (closed during January); free, donations ac-*

cepted. The Octagon House displays furniture, silver, lacquerware, and pewter from America's Colonial and Federal periods, plus documents of those eras. If you can't catch the exhibits because of the facility's limited hours, the building itself is worth a look. It's a curious octagonal-shaped structure with a turret on top, resembling a fortress or perhaps a lighthouse.

6 **SAN FRANCISCO CRAFT AND FOLK ART MUSEUM** *Fort Mason Center, Building A, 775-0990. Open 11 a.m. to 5 p.m. Tuesday–Sunday, 10 a.m. to 5 p.m. Saturday; adults $1, seniors and youths 50 cents, kids under 12 and groups free.* Exhibits range from elegant to witty in this museum featuring American folk art, contemporary jewelry, and ethnic arts from the United States and other countries. Exhibits change frequently.

7 **SAN FRANCISCO FIRE DEPARTMENT MUSEUM** *655 Presidio Avenue (at Bush), 861-8000, ext. 365. Open 1 a.m. to 4 p.m. Thursday–Sunday; free.* Trace the history of San Francisco firefighting action from the Gold Rush to the present in this small facility. Exhibits include one of the city's first fire engines and old firefighting regalia; it's the largest such collection in the west.

8 **THE SAN FRANCISCO ROOM** *Third floor of the main library, Larkin at McAllister (in the Civic Center), 558-3949. Open noon to 6 p.m. Tuesday and Friday; 1 to 6 p.m. Wednesday, 10 a.m. to 6 p.m. Thursday and Saturday; free.* This little-known mini-museum in the archive room of the San Francisco Public Library features early-day memorabilia such as old keys to the city, artifacts unearthed from the 1906 earthquake and fire, and a silver shovel used by Mayor "Sunny Jim" Rolf in Civic Center groundbreaking ceremonies in 1913. It also has an extensive collection of books on San Francisco, the Bay Area, and the west; it's a great hangout for serious scholars and historians.

9 **TATTOO ART MUSEUM** *30 Seventh Street (at Market), 775-4991. Open noon to 6 p.m. daily; $1 donation.* You can go for a tattoo or view the world's only tattoo museum, next to the shop of famous tattooist Lyle Tuttle. Elaborate Oriental "skin art" and primitive tattoo implements are on display.

10 **WELLS FARGO HISTORY ROOM** *420 Montgomery Street (at California), 396-2619. Open banking days from 9 a.m. to 5 p.m.; free.* An original Concord stagecoach, Gold Rush memorabilia, and a large collection of Western postage stamps and franks are featured in this attractive bank museum. Visitors can take an imaginary ride in the "Stagecoach Under Construction" exhibit on the mezzanine.

SAN FRANCISCO'S TEN BEST ART GALLERIES

What follows are the Ten Best places in the city to go art shopping or browsing. *Bay Area Gallery Guide,* published by the San Francisco Art Dealers Association (485-8323), lists addresses and hours of dozens of Bay Area galleries. Another booklet, *San Francisco Gallery Guide,* offers similar listings and is produced by the William Sawyer Gallery, 3045 Clay Street (921-1600). Both guides are available at many hotels and galleries.

Our good friend "Von" Von Schlafke, recently retired from the San Francisco Museum of Modern Art and much a part of the contemporary art scene, guided us in our gallery selections.

1 **HANK BAUM GALLERY** *2140 Bush (at Webster), 752-4336. Call for hours and exhibits.* The upstairs Baum gallery features contemporary works by established artists from California and elsewhere. Exhibits run the gamut from prints to collages and paintings. Some of the brightest and most innovative contemporary art in town can be found here.

2 **CHARLES CAMPBELL GALLERY** *647 Chestnut Street (at Columbus), 441-8680. Open 11 a.m. to 5:30 p.m. Tuesday–Friday, from noon to 4 p.m. Saturday.* Campbell's eclectic gallery specializes in intimate representational art, everything from 18th-century Indonesian puppets and modern American coffee-can art to the etchings of contemporary California artist Wayne Thiebaud.

3 **GUMP'S GALLERY** *250 Post Street (at Stockton), 982-1616. Open 9:30 a.m. to 5:30 p.m. Monday–Saturday.* In business since 1891, this gallery offers contemporary paintings, sculptures, drawings, and artistic works on paper. Its Oriental Gallery specializes in antique and contemporary Asian art and furniture.

4 **HARCOURTS GALLERY** *460 Bush Street, 421-3428. Open 10 a.m. to 5:30 p.m. Monday–Saturday.* Paintings, sculptures, and graphics by major 19th- and 20th-century artists are exhibited; included are works by Picasso, Chagall, Matisse, and Renoir. Also shown are contemporary American and European works by artists such as R. Lee White, Sylvia Glass, and Jeffery Laudenslager.

5   **KABUTOYA GALLERIES**   *In Ghirardelli Square (North Point at Polk), 776-2800; also 454 Sutter (at Stockton). Open 10 a.m. to 6 p.m. Sunday–Thursday, 10 a.m. to 9 p.m. Friday–Saturday.* Kabutoya offers works of both traditional and modern Japanese artists, including the legendary Hiroshige. More than a hundred artists are represented in this large collection of woodblock prints, silk screens, and watercolors.

6   **SAN FRANCISCO ART EXCHANGE**   *458 Geary Street (at Taylor), 441-8840. Open at 9 a.m. daily; various closing hours.* Paintings and prints of the "perfect women" from the estate of Alberto Vargas are available here, along with works by hyper-realist Charles Becker, Rolling Stones guitarist Ron Wood, and other contemporary American artists.

7   **SAN FRANCISCO ART INSTITUTE GALLERIES**   *800 Chestnut (at Jones), 771-7020. Open 8 a.m. to 5 p.m. Monday–Saturday.* The Art Institute, housed in an old Spanish-style structure, has three public galleries. The most famous is the Diego Rivera Gallery with an original Rivera mural; contemporary works are exhibited in the Emanual Walter and Atholl McBean galleries. Student works, which are for sale, are on display in the courtyard and sometimes in the Rivera gallery.

8   **VORPAL GALLERY**   *393 Grove (at Gough), 397-9200. Open 11 a.m. to 6 p.m. Monday–Friday, noon to 5 p.m. Sunday.* The sleek Vorpal Gallery focuses on post-modern painting, drawing, and sculpture. Its two floors offer an extensive survey of recent works by artists of California and the west. It also has a large collection of graphic arts, including works by M.C. Escher and Yozo Hamaguchi.

9   **WILLIAM SAWYER GALLERY**   *3045 Clay (at Broderick), 921-1600. Open 11 a.m. to 6 p.m. Tuesday–Saturday.* Sawyer's long-established gallery specializes in original sculptures and paintings by emerging and established contemporary American artists. The emphasis is on landscape and realism, with a number of abstract artists also represented.

10   **XANADU GALLERY**   *Ghirardelli Square (North Point and Polk), 441-5211. Open 10 a.m. to 6 p.m. Monday–Thursday, 10 a.m. to 9 p.m. Friday–Saturday and 11 a.m. to 6 p.m. Sunday.* Is it an art gallery or an import shop? We think it's a balance of both. Xanadu features tribal art and artifacts from assorted Asian, African, and South Pacific island tribes. Included in the collection are tribal objects from Papua New Guinea, and fine Asian textiles.

Browsing and Buying

A SHOPPER'S TEN BEST

Whoever said money can't buy happiness didn't know where to shop.
— Author unknown

In addition to its many other attributes, San Francisco is the premier shopping center for Northern California. Its shopping complexes, department stores, and upscale boutiques offer everything except enough chairs for weary, package-toting husbands.

1 **The Best Shopping Complex: THE EMBARCADERO CENTER**
At the foot of Market Street (at Drumm). Nearly 200 shops and restaurants occupy four open-air plazas at the base of the high-rise Embarcadero Center complex. With its open breezeways, monumental works of art, outdoor cafes, and sunny patios, this upscale center offers a wide range of stores, from trendy boutiques to affordable clothiers to specialty shops. Concerts and seasonal activities add to the interest here.

2 **The Best Themed Shopping Center: GHIRARDELLI SQUARE**
900 North Point. The first is still the best. William Matson Roth saved this collection of fine old brick buildings from redevelopers and opened the city's first themed shopping center in 1962. Originally housing a chocolate factory and several light industries, the fine brickwork now shelters 80 shops and restaurants, focused around plazas and a wonderful Ruth Asawa fountain. Ghirardelli avoids the gimmickry to which many tourist-oriented shopping complexes fall victim.

3 **The Best Urban Shopping Center: SAN FRANCISCO CENTRE**
865 Market Street (at Powell and Fifth). Perhaps we're stretching a point with this category, but the impressive new San Francisco Centre deserves a place in our book. Dozens of upscale shops line mezzanine floors of a dramatic eight-story atrium, linked by a fascinating architectural lacework

of *curving* escalators—the only such devices on the continent.

The most striking occupant in this architectural drama is Nordstrom, filling the four top floors beneath a bold oval dome. In addition to the usual departments, Nordstrom has a spa, a pub, five restaurants, and a concierge. Independent shops and boutiques occupy several floors below the big department store, and the Emporium—a longtime Market Street fixture—is dovetailed into the new complex. When you've finished shopping, return to the patio level and call for your car, because, of course, San Francisco Centre offers valet parking.

Of course.

4 **The Best Shopping District: UNION SQUARE** A few years ago, as veteran downtown stores began closing, we feared that the shopping focus would shift to parking lot suburbs, a fate undeserved by a cosmopolitan city. Then the stores began returning, and new ones arrived, including such prestigious retailers as Neiman-Marcus, Nordstrom, and Saks Fifth Avenue. The opening of San Francisco Centre just across Market in late 1988 was a major coup for downtown.

Now more than ever, this area—including the nearby Crocker Galleria at Post and Montgomery—offers the most complete shopping facilities in northern California.

5 **The Best Shopping Street: UNION** *Three blocks up and parallel to Lombard's "motel row."* This handsome street in the Marina District has come a long way from its Cow Hollow days, when the area was the site of several dairies. It's now lined with trendy shops, boutiques, galleries, and restaurants, many of them in fine old Victorians. It's the proper promenade for crystal, upscale clothing, artworks, antiques, and home decorator items. You can find everything along Union Street except a place to park.

6 **The Best Ethnic Shopping Area: THE RICHMOND DISTRICT** *Outer Geary Boulevard and Clement Street.* The Richmond is the neighborhood of Asian restaurants we mentioned in Chapter 7. It also offers a fine international mix of shops, specialty stores, and foreign grocers. You can find Chinese, Vietnamese, Russian, and other ethnic stores and restaurants along Clement Street, and several Korean shops line Balboa Street. Japanese artworks, foods, and souvenirs spill from Japan Center at Geary Boulevard and Buchanan Street, in the Western Addition just outside the Richmond District.

7 **The Best Department Store: MACY'S** *Stockton at O'Farrell,* *397-3333.* The largest department store in San Francisco has gotten even larger, with the addition of the former Liberty House across the street. Although the newer Nordstrom gets a lot of press these days, Macy's is still *the* place to shop in the city.

As you push through one of its many doors onto the huge main floor, you're offered a perfume sample; down in Macy's Cellar, someone in a chef's hat demonstrates cookware by stirring up something that smells wonderful; up in the toy department, a clerk is toying with a new electronic game. The maze of aisles brim with the tempting products of our consumer society. With its Easter floral extravaganza and elaborate Christmas window displays, Macy's has been woven into the fabric of San Francisco. What a wonderful place in which to mistreat your credit card!

8 **The Best Import Store: COST PLUS** *2552 Taylor Street (at* *Bay), 928-6200.* Want a Tijuana taxi horn, Moroccan goat bells, a batik shirt, Mexican paper flowers, a pound of Kona coffee, or a teak coffee table? Cost Plus isn't an import store; it's an import empire that scatters over thousands of square feet in several buildings. If you can't find a particular import item here, no one anywhere has made it yet.

9 **The Best Discount Store: WHOLE EARTH ACCESS** *401* *Bayshore Boulevard (at Courtland; take Army Street exit from* *Bayshore and go east), 285-5244.* Despite the funky name, Whole Earth Access isn't a Haight-Ashbury health food store; it's a fast-growing discount chain that stacks merchandise to the rafters. These are stark, barnlike places devoid of all decor, but they offer a wide range of merchandise, and we like the price tags. When we shopped recently for new kitchen appliances, Whole Earth's prices were lowest, and the follow-up service was surprisingly responsive for a discount place. (Like everything else in our book, this is an unsolicited testimonial.)

10 **The Best Supermarket: PETRINI'S** *Petrini Plaza, Fulton at* *Masonic; individual departments listed in the white pages.* Why can't all supermarkets be like this? Petrini's resembles a friendly corner market that multiplied; it has a huge meat department, an equally large fish and deli section, tangy-smelling take-home things cooking in roasters, a flower stand, and a bakery.

I recall Petrini's when I lived in a shabby Victorian flat across the street three decades ago. The store was always crowded, noisy, busy with the smelling and selling of good things to eat. It hasn't changed a bit. Fortunately.

THE TEN BEST STORES OF A SPECIFIC SORT

Where do you go when you need a pound of Kona-Moroccan coffee, a star map, or the tastiest truffles this side of a weight-loss clinic? We'll tell you where:

1 **The Best Bakery: FANTASIA CONFECTIONS** *3465 California Street (at Laurel Street, in Laurel Village), 752-0825.* The Weil family's Fantasia bakery has been luring people away from diets since 1948, offering a savory array of cakes, pies, cookies, and other sweets. A specialty is European cookies and pastries; Fantasia makes the best Linzertorte west of Vienna, plus a tasty assortment of stollens and petits fours. A few small tables occupy one corner, and you can order coffee, tea, or chocolate with your goodies, in case you can't wait to get them home.

2 **The Best Camera Store: ADOLPH GASSER** *181 Second Street (at Howard), 495-3852; 750 Bryant Street (at Fifth), 543-3888; and 5733 Geary Boulevard (at 22nd Avenue), 751-0145.* Although popular Brooks Cameras has more outlets, Gasser is *the* camera store for professionals and serious amateurs. Adolph's crew invariably has that hard-to-find piece of equipment as well as examples of virtually every photographic brand on the market.

Gasser also rents camera and video equipment for pros and people who want to take home images of their San Francisco visit.

3 **The Best Coffee Stop: SPINELLI COFFEE COMPANY** *2455 Fillmore (at Jackson), 929-8808; 3966 24th (at Sanchez), 550-7416; and 1257 Folsom (at Eighth), 862-2272.* That's right, coffee stop, not coffee shop. Spinelli's offers one of the largest selections of gourmet coffees in the city. Shoppers can step to gleaming coffee grinders to create their own special blends from whole beans. Fresh-brewed coffee also is sold by the cup, and a couple of window seats invite patrons to linger a while.

The Folsom Street store is a combined retail-wholesale outlet.

4 **The Best Life-Sciences Store: THE NATURE COMPANY** *No. 4 Four Embarcadero Center, 956-4911; Ghirardelli Square, 776-0724.* Intrigued by lofty stars or lowly bugs? The Nature Company specializes in the world around us. Offerings include telescopes, star maps, sundials, wildlife guides and other nature books, wall prints, nature toys, and such. For those on your Christmas list who have everything, how about sending them a cassette recording of whale sounds? (*That* should get them off your list.)

5 **The Best Record Store: TOWER RECORDS** *2525 Jones Street (at Columbus), 885-0500.* Listen, you want the latest on the charts? Some funky oldies, classics, elevator music? Tower Records probably has the largest selection in the city. Busy, narrow corridors are filled with records, cassettes, compact disks, noise, and finger-snapping teenagers; it's the way a record store should be.

6 **The Best Sweet Shop: JOSEPH SCHMIDT CONFECTIONS** *3489 16th Street (at Sanchez), 861-8682.* Joe does some of the best truffles and chocolate sculptures in town. The expression "sinfully rich" comes to mind when we browse his shop, eyeing elegant little creations that rival the finest crafted chocolates from Switzerland. What a way to ruin a diet.

7 **The Best Toy Store: F A O SCHWARZ FIFTH AVENUE** *Corner of Stockton and O'Farrell, 391-0100.* In this huge children's paradise with its chugging choo-choos, wind-up toys that are always wound up and cute things dangling from the ceiling, *everyone's* still a child. Recently relocated from smaller Post Street quarters, Schwarz's new home at Stockton and O'Farrell is even more delightfully cluttered with children's dreams.

8 **The Best Travel Store: TRAVEL MARKET** *130 Pacific Avenue Mall (at Front Street), 421-4080.* The ideal shop for the wayfarer, Travel Market is abrim with travel books, directories, and maps, luggage ranging from upscale Ciao suitcases to simple nylon backpacks, plus sundry other travel accessories, ranging from globes to hand-held translator-calculators.

9 **The Best Video Cassette Shop: CAPTAIN VIDEO** *141 Columbus Avenue (at Kearny), 788-1414.* Although the city has many video outlets, Captain Video is special because of its location: on the ground floor of the skinny old Sentinel office building on a wedge of Columbus Avenue. (We also nominated it as part of a photo angle in Chapter 4.) After you've finished admiring this green architectural curiosity, you'll find a good video cassette selection inside. Incidentally, Francis Coppola owns the building, and his Zoetrope Studios occupy the upper floors.

10 **The Best Wine Shop: CONNOISSEUR WINES** *462 Bryant Street (at Second Street), 433-0825.* It's in a warehouse but it has the ambiance and aroma of an ancient French wine château. Thousands of vintages fill Connoisseur's coffers; the place offers one of the city's largest selections of imports, along with an extensive domestic assortment and several wine books.

Connoisseur sells six- and 12-bottle samplers of similar wines, handy for vertical or horizontal tastings. And for the serious aficionado of the grape, the firm rents temperature-controlled storage bins for wine collections. For a catalog of wine selections, write Connoisseur Wines, 462 Bryant Street, San Francisco, CA 94107.

Pillow Talk

LISTS OF SPECIAL PLACES TO REST YOUR HEAD

A great hotel is like a duck swimming — composed and serene above the water, but paddling like hell underneath. — Hotel executive Tim Carlson

Finding a place to stay in San Francisco is no clever trick — unless there's a major convention in town. The city brims with world-class hotels, and Van Ness Avenue and Lombard Street are rimmed with motels. But suppose you're tired of look-alike motels, and you want something more intriguing than a $150-a-night hotel room with a view of the adjacent hotel?

In recent years, many venerable Victorians, scruffy small hotels, and even tired old apartment houses have been converted into bed and breakfast inns or smart new mid-sized hotels. This book isn't intended as a budget guide, but we will point out that, in most cases, these smaller places are considerably less expensive than the major hotels.

For knee-jerk preservationists such as ourselves, the nicest thing about this trend is that it results in the redemption of many older buildings that otherwise would have been reduced to parking lots.

The rates were current at the time we compiled this guide but, of course, they're subject to change, invariably upward. All rates listed are for doubles.

SAN FRANCISCO'S TEN BEST BED AND BREAKFAST INNS

The bed and breakfast "movement" began in California about a decade ago, and San Francisco, with its hundreds of Victorians, was a natural growth area. A visit to a B&B is — forgive us, Mr. Bush — a journey back to a kinder and gentler time, be it Victorian San Francisco, rural England, or provincial France. Or perhaps a visit to Grandmother's house, assuming the old lady was loaded and could afford her own interior decorator.

1 **SPRECKELS MANSION**   *737 Buena Vista West (at Masonic), 861-3008. Doubles from $88 to $190; MC, VISA, AMEX. Ten rooms, eight with private baths; TV and phones in rooms, some fireplaces. Large Continental breakfast; ample street parking.* Adolph Spreckels lived in baronial splendor in this 1887 Victorian mansion overlooking Buena Vista Park. For less than the price of an ordinary hotel room, you can experience the sweet life of the sugar king: the lush opulence of crystal chandeliers, antiques, fireplaces, leather couches, and clawfoot tubs with brass fittings.

The Spreckels Mansion is easily the most opulent of the city's bed and breakfast inns. The pillared Victorian sits on a quiet, little-known street about 15 minutes by car from downtown. An adjoining mansion with an elaborate wrought-iron gate is part of the complex. Although most rooms are furnished with period antiques, the San Francisco and Star-Gazer suites are modern with Oriental accents.

2 **THE BED AND BREAKFAST INN**   *No. 4 Charlton Court (off Union, between Laguna and Buchanan), 921-9784. Doubles from $68 to $184; no credit cards. Ten rooms, six with private baths; TV and phones in most rooms. Large Continental breakfast; street parking, public garages nearby.* The first bed and breakfast in the city, it remains one of the most charming. The look is cheery colonial English, with grass cloth, bamboo, louvered window shutters, and ceiling fans. The rooms are bright, airy and comfortable, with none of the somberness of some Victorian inns.

The location is excellent: within a few steps of the Union Street shopping area and a short drive from downtown. Tucked into the end of a short street, it's a surprisingly quiet refuge within the busy city.

3 **DOLORES PARK INN**   *3641 17th Street (at Dolores), 621-0482. Doubles from $50 to $75; no credit cards. Six rooms, two with private baths; TV in rooms; some fireplaces. "Extended Continental" breakfast; off-street parking.* This 1874 Italianate Victorian inn offers quiet sanctuary from the busy city, with a garden, patio, and spa. Although not lavish, the rooms are handsomely appointed, with antiques, ceiling fans, and ceramic fireplaces. Considering the high quality of accommodation, it's one of the city's best B&B bargains.

It's located in the Mission District, less than a block from Mission Dolores and a few minutes from downtown.

4 **HERMITAGE HOUSE**   *2224 Sacramento Street (at Buchanan), 921-5515. Doubles from $80 to $120; MC, VISA, AMEX. Six rooms, all with private baths, TV, and room phones; some fireplaces. Full breakfast; off-street parking.* A turn-of-the-century manor house with a bold curving two-story bay window, the Hermitage is one of the city's most impeccably furnished inns. It's a pleasant mix of antique and modern, accented by leaded glass, crystal chandeliers and redwood wainscoting. Despite the use of warm woods and antiques, the rooms are bright and cheery.

A sunny sitting room and a formal English garden offer quiet retreats from the city. The inn is located in Pacific Heights, handy to Fillmore Street restaurants and Union Street shops.

5 **INN SAN FRANCISCO** *943 South Van Ness Avenue (at 20th Street), 641-0188. Doubles from $64 to $180; MC, VISA, AMEX. Fifteen rooms with TV, refrigerators, and room phones; 13 with private baths. Large Continental breakfast; some off-street parking spaces.* This handsomely restored 1870s Italianate, once the home of a city commissioner, is tucked into a row of old mansions in a little-known Victorian area of South Van Ness. Room decor is true to the period, with Oriental carpets, fainting couches, decorative borders on print wallpaper, and big poofy bedspreads.

A garden, sun deck, and hot tubs make this a particularly appealing haven. For total privacy, you can rent a garden cottage with a separate sitting room.

6 **JACKSON COURT** *2198 Jackson Street (at Buchanan), 929-7670. From $88 to $140; MC, VISA, AMEX. Ten rooms with private baths, TV, and phones, some fireplaces. Continental breakfast; street parking.* A square-shouldered brick mansion with a mansard roof, Jackson Court has more the look of a New England townhouse than a Victorian. The opulent interior is a tasteful blend of modern and antique. Dark woods accent a bright, rather cheerful decor of textured wallpaper, lace, and brass. One room has its own patio garden.

The Court is situated in Pacific Heights, handy to Fillmore and Union street restaurant and shopping areas.

7 **PETITE AUBERGE and WHITE SWAN** *863 and 845 Bush Street (at Mason), 928-6000 (Auberge) and 775-1755 (Swan). From $106 to $250; MC, VISA, AMEX. Each has 26 rooms with private baths, TV, and phones; most have fireplaces. Full breakfast; valet parking.* We've grouped these together because they're practically next door and owned by the same family; services and amenities are similar.

Beautifully fashioned from two old bay-windowed row-house hotels, the inns have a pleasing European country look, with print wallpaper, armoires, and fireplaces. Petite Auberge is done in French country fashion; the Swan is described as "English garden style." Both have exceptionally pretty breakfast rooms. We like their location: within a short walk of Union Square and all that is happening in downtown San Francisco.

8 **THE SPENCER HOUSE**   *1080 Haight Street (at Baker), 626-9205. From $95 to $150; no credit cards. Six rooms, three with private baths, some with fireplaces. Full breakfast; street parking.* One of the most charming attractions of this elegant Victorian is hostess Barbara Chambers; she'll greet you with a warm smile — and possibly in her bare feet — then invite you into the kitchen to chat while she prepares a tea-time snack.

The house is an 1890 Queen Anne; the rooms are spacious and beautifully furnished with antiques, poofy coverlets, and hand-carved armoires. Padded fabric wall covering and thick theatrical curtains complete the feel of opulence. The Spencer House is in a neighborhood of Victorian mansions in the Haight-Ashbury, across from Buena Vista Park.

9 **UNION STREET INN**   *2229 Union Street (at Fillmore), 346-0424. From $75 to $195; MC, VISA, AMEX. Six rooms, all with private baths, TV, and room phones. Continental breakfast; limited street parking; public garages nearby.* It's a pleasant surprise to step off busy Union Street and into the large, beautifully landscaped garden that frames this 1904 Edwardian home. The interior look is 19th-century European-American, with hand-woven rugs, wood paneling and beamed ceilings. The furnishings are a mix of antique and contemporary.

The inn is located in the heart of the Union Street shopping district.

10 **VICTORIAN INN ON THE PARK**   *301 Lyon Street (at Fell), 931-1830. From $78 to $125; MC, VISA, AMEX. Twelve rooms, all with private baths, TV, and phones; some fireplaces. Large Continental breakfast; ample street parking.* One of the most impeccably restored inns we visited, this 1897 Victorian is a study in European splendor, with coffered ceilings, carved wood paneling, velvet drapes, and bordered print wallpaper. The large rooms have antique furnishings, armoires, and queen-size beds. The third-floor rooms are charmingly cozy little retreats shaped by cupolas and gabled roofs.

The Victorian Inn sits across Fell Street from the Golden Gate Park panhandle, a short drive to the Civic Center and downtown.

THE CITY'S TEN BEST BOUTIQUE HOTELS

Concurrent with the recent growth of bed and breakfast inns has been the arrival of many new boutique hotels. For lack of a better measure, we define boutique hotels as small inns with fewer than 90 rooms, generally done in an old world style. Many on our list are reincarnations of older hotels, so again the new innkeepers function as preservationists.

Although the line separating a B&B from a boutique hotel is sometimes fuzzy, the latter invariably has room phones, private baths, color TV, and other hotel-like amenities. A B&B always serves some sort of breakfast. Some of our boutique inns do; others do not. Many offer free limo service.

1 **THE ARCHBISHOP'S MANSION** *1000 Fulton Street (at Steiner), 563-7872 or (800) 533-4668. From $100 to $250; MC, VISA, AMEX. Fifteen rooms, ten with fireplaces. Large Continental breakfast; off-street parking.* A decade ago, John Shannon and Jeffery Ross purchased one of San Francisco's landmark mansions and fashioned it into Northern California's most luxurious small hotel. The former residence of the archbishop of San Francisco, this French Empire–style manor is regally costumed with canopied beds, carved armoires, embroidered linens, and valanced drapes. Crystal chandeliers grace coffered ceilings, tapestries adorn the walls, and a great oval leaded-glass dome glitters above a three-story grand stairway.

Appropriately, the mansion is on the edge of Alamo Square, in the heart of the city's finest collection of 19th-century homes. Not surprisingly, it has been designated as a San Francisco historic landmark.

2 **ASTON REGIS HOTEL** *490 Geary Street (at Taylor), 928-7900; or (800) 854-0011 in California and (800) 354-4443 outside. From $92 to $225; major credit cards; 86 rooms. Honor bars; some fireplaces. Regina's Restaurant adjacent; valet parking.* Aston Hotels and Resorts of Hawaii, generally noted for palm-fringed hideaways, has come to town to create a stylish 19th-century hotel. The rooms are furnished with Louis XVI-period French and English antiques, half-canopied beds, and scalloped drapes. The bathrooms are Italian marble with brass fixtures.

The Regis is in the downtown area, a short walk from theaters and restaurants, and a few minutes from the Financial District. The adjoining Regina's Restaurant specializes in French Creole fare.

3 **THE ELLES'MERE ON NOB HILL** *655 Powell Street (at Pine), 477-4600; or (800) 334-6966 in California and (800) 426-6161 outside. From $125 to $250; major credit cards; 48 rooms. Full kitchens; office desks, entertainment centers with TV, VCR, and AM-FM. Garage parking nearby.* The Elles'mere is one of a growing number of "suite hotels"; think of it as an upscale condo. It features a full kitchen, a large desk with a dual phone link for your laptop, free movies on VCR, and a library with current best-sellers. Furnishings are contemporary and rather exquisite, set off by thick decorative rugs and scalloped drapes.

The hotel's Nob Hill location is handy to Union Square and the rest of downtown.

4 HYDE PARK SUITES *2655 Hyde Street (at North Point), 771-0200; or (800) 227-3608. From $165 to $220; all major credit cards; 24 rooms. Full kitchens, honor bars, two TVs in each room; Continental breakfast; parking available.* Another suite hotel, Hyde Park offers a pleasant mix of old world and modern decor, with terrazzo tile floors, pastel colors, and contemporary furnishings. Each unit has a separate sitting room and bedroom. Two particularly pleasing features are a landscaped atrium courtyard and a roof garden with a view of San Francisco Bay.

Hyde Park Suites is on the edge of Fisherman's Wharf.

5 INN AT THE OPERA *333 Fulton Street (at Franklin), 863-8400; or (800) 423-9610 in California and (800) 325-2708 outside. From $99 to $180; MC, VISA, AMEX; 48 rooms. Wet bars, microwaves, and honor bars in rooms; Continental breakfast. ACT IV lounge and restaurant; garage parking across the street.* Once a retreat for visiting opera stars, the Inn at the Opera has been transformed into a sophisticated little boutique hotel. The furnishings are a balance of European and contemporary American, set off by pastel colors, with coordinated drapes and spreads.

On the edge of the Civic Center a few steps from the Opera House, Davies Symphony Hall and Civic Auditorium, the hotel still attracts a theatrical crowd, both performers and patrons. Recent guests have included such luminaries as Placido Domingo and Mikhail Baryshnikov. Act IV is a popular and handsomely styled California-Continental restaurant.

6 KENSINGTON PARK HOTEL *450 Post Street (at Mason), 788-6400 or (800) 553-1900. From $89 to $109; Royal Suite with fireplace $350. Major credit cards; 83 rooms. All have desks and dual phones; morning coffee and pastries. Valet parking.* Highlighted by an Old English–style lobby with 20-foot coffered ceilings and a grand piano, the Kensington blends old world decor with corporate conveniences such as dual phone outlets for computer-packing executives. The look is Queen Anne, but with a light touch and cheerful colors, and no Victorian clutter.

The Kensington is on the edge of downtown. Theatre on the Square (see Chapter 14) is located in the building.

7 THE MAJESTIC *1500 Sutter Street (at Gough), 441-1100; or (800) 252-1155 in California and (800) 824-0094 outside. From $95 to $200; major credit cards; 60 rooms. Four-poster canopied beds; writing desks; fireplaces in most rooms; refrigerators in suites. Cafe Majestic and* *cocktail lounge off lobby; valet parking and street parking.* Restored "beyond its original elegance," the Majestic rivals the Archbishop's Mansion and the Mansion Hotel (below) as the most lavishly attired boutique hotel in the city. Built in 1902 as a luxury hotel, the Majestic has retained its posh Edwardian look, with canopied beds and a mix of 18th- and 19th-century museum-quality antiques and artworks.

The lobby is an opulent study in gilt-edge mirrors, crystal chandeliers, and valanced drapes. Cafe Majestic continues this European elegance with bentwood chairs, wainscoting and crisp white linens, and with a menu based on updated Old San Francisco recipes; the adjoining bar has a stately men's club look. Sitting just off Van Ness Avenue, the Majestic is minutes from the Civic Center and downtown.

8   **THE MANSION HOTEL**   *2220 Sacramento Street (at Laguna), 929-9444. From $74 to $150; major credit cards; 20 rooms. Billiard and game room; sculpture gardens. Restaurant; full breakfast; parking available nearby.* Who says elegance can't be fun? Certainly not Robert Pritikin, who fashioned this 1887 twin-turreted Queen Anne mansion into a plush hotel and furnished it with museum-worthy antiques and paintings. Then, to reinforce his sense of humor, he added a macaw (alive), a chirping monkey (stuffed), a Lawrence Welk bubble machine, and other bits of whimsy. A surrounding garden contains an awesome collection of Benny Bufano sculptures.

Guests in the hotel's opulent Mansion Restaurant sit down to the tasty and beautifully presented European fare of David Coyle, once personal chef to the Duke and Duchess of Bedford. Weekend dinners are preceded by delightfully madcap music and magic shows. They feature the irrepressible Pritikin, who serenades guests on his musical saw and performs such magic feats as the "incredible Peking snow duck double transfer." Weeknight concerts spotlight resident ghost Claudia Chambers, who plays invisibly at a very visible piano.

The guest list at the Pacific Heights hotel-restaurant has included Barbara Streisand, Joel Grey, George McGovern, Paul Simon, and even Alan Funt, who must have thought he'd stumbled into a gag set for "Candid Camera."

9   **NOB HILL INN**   *1000 Pine Street (at Taylor), 673-6080. From $85 to $225; MC, VISA; 21 rooms. Fireplaces in many rooms; some kitchen units. Continental breakfast; garage parking available nearby.* The Nob Hill is an exquisite boutique hotel with a *very* European feel: floral wallpaper, brass beds, and elaborately carved armoires. A fascinating focal point in the nicely appointed lobby is a glassed-in European-style lift.

137

Located atop Nob Hill, it's handy to downtown and the Financial District.

10 **QUEEN ANNE HOTEL** *1590 Sutter Street (at Octavia), 441-2828; or (800) 262-2663 in California and (800) 227-3970 elsewhere. From $94 to $125; major credit cards; 49 rooms. Fireplaces and wet bars in some rooms. Continental breakfast; off-street parking.* The Queen Anne began life in 1890 as a boarding school for proper young ladies, built by Senator James G. Fair (of the Fairmont Hotel). It's an attractive boutique hotel today, with a mix of European and American antiques in color-coordinated rooms. The grand parlor is particularly impressive, with its thick red carpet, fluted columns, tulip chandeliers, and scalloped drapes.

The Queen Anne is in Pacific Heights, at the opposite end of the block from the Majestic.

THE CITY'S TEN BEST MID-SIZED HOTELS

Candidates for this category are larger than the boutiques: up to 160 rooms, but substantially smaller than the major hostelries of Nob Hill and Union Square. Many offer amenities similar to those in the big houses and generally at a much lower price. Many appeal to corporate travelers who don't have unlimited expense accounts, and most have corporate rates.

Our winner is not inexpensive, but it rivals — and perhaps excels — the city's largest hotels in service and ambiance.

1 **THE MANDARIN ORIENTAL** *222 Sansome Street (at Pine), 885-0999; or (800) 622-0404. From $230 to $900 (lower weekend rates); major credit cards; 158 rooms. All rooms with city view, mini-bar refrigerators, three phones, modem terminals, large desks. Silks Restaurant and Mandarin Bar; valet parking.* The newest small hotel in San Francisco is also the most stunning. Opened in 1987 and managed by the prestigious Mandarin Oriental group of Hong Kong, it's a flawlessly beautiful creation built into the top 11 floors of the twin-towered First Interstate Center. It's the city's third tallest building, and every room offers striking aerial views. Glass catwalks connect the two hotel towers, providing more awesome vistas.

The circular ground-level lobby is done in glossy marble; Oriental art objects and a huge beaded chandelier provide touches of elegance. The comfortable and quiet Mandarin cocktail lounge is off the lobby. A stairway leads to Silks, an exquisitely designed restaurant featuring creative California cuisine and some of the most sinfully delicious deserts we've ever tasted. The dining room is a serene creation in soft peach and brass trim, with pastel harbor scenes painted on silk panels.

The rooms are what you'd expect for $230 and up: bright, modern, and spacious, with an almost sinful opulence. Amenities range from remote-controlled entertainment centers to hair dryers, robes, and Thai-silk slippers. Guests can soak away their cares while absorbing the scenery; the tubs in the Italian marble bathrooms offer picture-window views of the city.

2 **CAMPTON PLACE**   *340 Stockton Street (at Post), 781-5555; or (800) 235-4300 in California and (800) 647-4007 outside. From $180 to $250; major credit cards; 126 rooms. Writing desks; dual phones for computer use; roof garden. Campton Place Restaurant off lobby; valet parking.* Campton Place rivals the larger world-class hotels in its guest-pampering service. Valets accompany patrons to their rooms, offering to unpack their luggage, then repack when they depart; an in-house laundry can have a bit of stray ketchup removed from your jacket before you've finished dinner.

All this coddling occurs in an atmosphere of cool elegance. Rooms are done in taupe and apricot, with English antique reproductions and contemporary artworks.

The adjoining Campton Place Restaurant is one of the city's finest, featuring excellent contemporary American cuisine, including the city's most formidable power breakfast.

3 **HOTEL DIVA**   *440 Geary Street (at Mason), 885-0200 or (800) 553-1900. From $99 to $275; major credit cards; 108 rooms. Mini-refrigerators and VCRs in all rooms; free limo service; use of IBM computers. Continental breakfast; valet parking.* It looks like a set for an avant-garde Italian movie. The Diva is a sleek creation in stainless steel, chrome, and glass; its colors are glossy black lacquer, burgundy, and gray. This art nouveau hotel recently won "Design of the Year" award from *Interior Magazine.*

It's commodious as well as stylish, with down comforters and surprisingly cushy furniture. Some describe the look as "Euro-modern"; others compare the rooms to upscale New York apartments. The Diva is in the city's main shopping area, a block from Union Square.

4 **DONATELLO**   *501 Post Street (at Mason), 441-7100; or (800) 792-9837 in California and (800) 227-3184 outside. From $155 to $200; major credit cards; 95 rooms. Mini-bars and tape decks. Ristorante Donatello and cocktail lounge; valet parking.* The Donatello is in a league with the Mandarin Oriental and Campton Place as one of the city's premier mid-sized hotels. It exudes quiet elegance with its Fortuny fabric wall covering, Carrara marble and glittering lobby chandelier of Venetian glass. Room furnishings are elegantly modern, accented by European antiques and fine artworks.

The adjoining Donatello Ristorante, which we selected as the city's best restaurant (Chapter 5) rivals the hotel in popularity; indeed the hotel's name was changed from Pacific Plaza to Donatello in 1986. The restaurant is coiffed in 19th-century fashion; the menu is contemporary Northern Italian.

Mr. Donatello — should you wonder — was an Italian Renaissance artist.

5 **THE HUNTINGTON HOTEL** *1075 California Street (at Taylor), 474-5400; or (800) 652-1539 in California and (800) 227-4683 outside. From $170 to $230; major credit cards; 143 rooms. Some suites with kitchens or wet bars; limo service downtown; fitness club adjacent. Full breakfast; two restaurants, L'Etoile and the Big Four; cocktail lounge; valet parking.* The Huntington is a world-class hotel in everything but size, offering all the amenities of its larger Nob Hill brothers. The rooms — all with city or bay views — are artful blends of contemporary and classic European, with comfortable furnishings and fine artworks. Each room has its own distinctive decor. Free limo service is provided, rather stylishly, in a 1978 Rolls Royce.

Guests have a choice of two of the city's better restaurants; L'Etoile is noted for its *cuisine de France* and the Big Four, named for California's railroad barons, features Continental fare.

6 **HOTEL JULIANA** *590 Bush Street (at Stockton), 392-2540; or (800) 372-8800 in California and (800) 382-8800 outside. From $94 to $125; major credit cards; 107 rooms. Honor bars; two TVs in mini-suites; no-smoking rooms available. Continental breakfast; Palm Restaurant adjacent; garage parking nearby.* Fashioned like a high-style French pension, the Juliana sits atop the Stockton Street tunnel, a quick walk from Chinatown, Nob Hill, or downtown. The decor is cool European, with light woods, soft burgundies and pastels; the term "restful elegance" comes to mind. The rooms feature color-coordinated drapes and spreads, with modern furniture; some offer city views.

The small lobby, with its pale marble fireplace, coffee and tea bar, and framed prints, is one of the most pleasing in the city. The next-door Palm restaurant serves Continental and American fare.

7 **MONTICELLO INN** *80 Cyril Magnin Street (lobby entrance on Ellis), 392-8800; or (800) 669-7777. From $99 to $169; major credit cards; 91 rooms. Writing desks and mini-bar refrigerators in each room; free limo service; no-smoking rooms available. Continental breakfast; Corona Bar and Grill adjacent; valet parking.* The Monticello, fashioned from a

1906 hotel, offers a light, cheerful early American look, from its quiet lobby parlor with its rich Colonial decor to the half-canopied beds and color-coordinated fabrics in the rooms. Visitors can end the day before a crackling fireplace in the library, sipping gratis wine and admiring historic prints and other Thomas Jefferson memorabilia. Although antiques grace the rooms, furnishings are modern and comfortable, with full baths and oversized beds.

It's one of the best located of our mid-sized hotels, on the edge of the Union Square shopping district, a block off Market Street and a quick walk to BART and the Powell Street cable car turntable. The adjoining Corona Bar and Grill is a popular upscale Mexican-Southwestern restaurant specializing in spicy seafood.

8 THE ORCHARD *562 Sutter Street (at Powell), 433-4434; or (800) 433-4434 in California and (800) 433-4343 outside. From $93 to $180; major credit cards; 96 rooms. Mini-bar refrigerators in rooms. Sutter Garden Restaurant; lobby bar; parking available.* Yet another old structure — this one dating from 1907 — was rescued with the recent opening of the Orchard hotel. There's a feel of old Europe in the lobby, with its crystal chandeliers and damask couches and chairs. The rooms are more contemporary, with pastel colors offset by rather striking dark mahogany furniture. Sutter Garden Restaurant offers assorted American and Continental dishes.

9 THE RAPHAEL *386 Geary Street (at Mason), 986-2000 or (800) 821-5343. From $89 to $109, penthouse $175; major credit cards; 152 rooms. Non-smoking rooms available; FAX machine. Mama's Restaurant adjacent; parking available.* The Raphael was the first of the city's new mid-sized hotels, dating back to 1971. The rooms have been redone recently, achieving a light Continental look: a mix of European and American contemporary. Paneled walls, a beadwork chandelier, and a print carpet give the lobby a pleasing turn-of-the-century European feel.

It's in an excellent location, in the heart of downtown. Mama's Restaurant serves Continental cuisine with an Italian tilt.

10 HOTEL VINTAGE COURT *650 Bush Street (at Powell), 392-4666; or (800) 654-7266 in California and (800) 654-1100 outside. All rooms $94; major credit cards; 106 rooms. Mini-bar refrigerators, non-smoking rooms available. Masa's Restaurant adjacent; parking available.* Vintage Court is one of the most charming little hotels in the city. The furnishings are modern, with European accents, and the rooms are color coordinated. We particularly like the hotel's wine theme. The rooms are named for California wineries, wine prints grace the walls, and gratis glasses of the grape are served before the fireplace in the attractive lobby each afternoon.

The adjacent restaurant needs little introduction; Masa's is one of the most expensive in the city, and some call it one of the finest French restaurants in the country. Plan on parting with upwards of $200 for dinner for two. Perhaps the hotel's modest prices will make dining more affordable. And here's a bargain: Vintage Court guests can order breakfast there for a mere $5.50 per person.

Architectural Delights and Disasters

LISTS OF THE CITY'S GREATEST AND GHASTLIEST BUILDINGS

Of all the efflorescent, floriated bulbousness and flamboyant craziness that ever decorated a city, I think San Francisco may carry off the prize.
— *New York Times* article, 1883

That writer was talking about the "new" gingerbread Victorians. Were he here today, he'd probably prefer those efflorescent structures to some of the drab slabs built recently. Frankly, we like those bulbous Victorians, and even some of the new high-rises that have stepped out of the Wheaties box mold to offer a little form and shape.

The city probably contains the greatest mix of building styles of any community in America. As we prowled about to research this book, wandering through the architectural museum called San Francisco, we began compiling lists of interesting buildings that caught our eye — both the awesome and the awful.

SAN FRANCISCO'S TEN MOST HANDSOME VICTORIANS

1 **HAAS-LILIENTHAL HOUSE**   *2007 Franklin Street (at Jackson), 441-3000. Tours noon to 4 a.m. Wednesday and 11 a.m. to 4:30 p.m. Sunday. Adults $3, kids and seniors $1.* Our premiere Victorian is a delightful clutter of all the elements of that architectural period: gingerbread trim, turrets, cupolas, dormer windows, and more filigree than you'll find in great-grandmother's hankie. It's colored a somber gray, probably more appropriate to the Victorian era than many present-day restorations with their Technicolor paint jobs. It's also a museum of period furnishings. Built in 1886, this Queen Anne classic now houses the Foundation for San Francisco's Heritage.

2 **HENRY OHLOFF HOUSE** *601 Steiner Street (at Fell).* Another elaborate architectural mix of towers, cupolas and bay windows, this house sports a distinctive multifaceted roof. The colors are rust and light gray. It's a Queen Anne–Romanesque mansion, now housing an alcohol rehabilitation center operated by the Episcopal Diocese of California.

3 **ITALIANATE-STYLE HOUSE** *817 Grove Street (at Webster).* This structure wins our vote as one of the most attractive small Victorians in the city. The restrained and tasteful use of colors on the little false-front home — gray, blue, and white — is particularly eye-pleasing. Italianate homes typically have straighter, less elaborate lines than the more complex Queen Annes of the later Victorian era; they were often built with false fronts to conceal the pitch of the roof. Our candidate here is one of three matching row houses.

4 **QUEEN ANNE–STYLE HOUSE** *1701 Franklin Street (at California).* Built in 1895 and now housing law offices, it's a particularly noteworthy example of the Queen Anne style, with twin towers and a decorative frieze that circles the structure just under the roof line. "Queen Anne" refers to the closing era of the Victorian period, identified by rounded turrets and towers and curved bay windows. Queen Anne ruled before Victoria, but the more elaborate styles of earlier periods were returned to popularity in England during the later years of Victoria's reign; they were then copied in California.

5 **"RUSSIAN CONSULATE"** *1198 Fulton Street (at Scott).* A large four-story Italianate mansion built in 1875 to house the consular corps of Imperial Russia, this structure characterizes the San Francisco Stick style. It is slender with many vertical lines, including a particularly striking square lookout tower. The building is privately owned.

6 **SPRECKELS MANSION BED AND BREAKFAST** *737 Buena Vista West (off Haight), 861-3008.* Built in 1887 for sugar baron Adolph Spreckels, this great square-shouldered Victorian has several cupolas cut into the roof and Colonial columns at the entrance, supporting an unusual half-moon portico above. It's one of our Ten Best bed and breakfast inns (see Chapter 19).

7 **"TOWER HOUSE"** *573 South Van Ness Avenue (at 16th Street).* Surrounded by a rather scruffy commercial neighborhood, this elaborate Victorian is a fine example of a "tower house," with one or more towers as a predominate architectural feature. The ornate red and white frieze adds a touch of brightness to this carefully restored 1878 Queen Anne.

8 **"GINGERBREAD VICTORIAN"** *1057 Steiner (at Golden Gate).* It is probably the most elaborate, gingerbready Victorian in the city, a fun conglomeration of cupolas, witches'-hat towers, balconies, and gabled roofs, decorated with wrought iron, crests, friezes, leaded glass, and curlicues. The color scheme of this four-story mansion is busy as well: assorted shades of brown, burgundy, green, and turquoise. It's as close to a fairy-castle Victorian as you will find.

9 **VICTORIAN DUPLEX** *2527–2531 Washington Street (at Fillmore).* Many Victorians survive in the Fillmore District on the edge of Pacific Heights, and this is one of the more curious examples. It's a perfectly symmetrical duplex, a fusing of two skinny garage-over San Francisco Stick Victorians, with scalloped columns supporting twin entries. The purple paint job is rather gaudy, but the distinctive "vertical duplex" design makes it worthy of our list.

10 **HAIGHT-ASHBURY VICTORIAN** *500–502 Cole Street (at Page).* The former haven of the Flower Children offers another extensive collection of Victorians, and current gentrification of that neighborhood is leading to many restorations. Our favorite in this area is a gabled and turreted four-story mansion with curved glass bay windows and a cut-stone chimney; the colors are turquoise, gray, and beige.

THE CITY'S TEN MOST ATTRACTIVE COMMERCIAL OR PUBLIC BUILDINGS

1 **THE AUDIFFRED BUILDING** *100 Embarcadero (at Mission Street).* This French Renaissance office building with its green inset columns, red brick, and filigreed mansard roof is indeed the most attractive commercial structure in the city. It was built in 1889 by Hippolite d'Audiffred, who started his fortune selling charcoal to Chinatown merchants. The building was saved from the 1906 earthquake and fire when the operator of a ground-floor saloon bribed the fire laddies with booze to keep them from blowing it up as a firebreak.

International Longshoremen's Union president Harry Bridges occupied upstairs offices during the 1934 waterfront strike, and it thus became the focal point of that violent period. Professional offices occupy the building today; you can step into the foyer during business hours and view a small historical exhibit.

145

2 **ALCAZAR THEATER** *650 Geary Street (at Jones).* Sometimes whimsy can be handsome, but we fear for the future of this wonderful Moroccan filigree of a theater. It houses a rental car office, and the building is looking alarmingly scruffy. Built in 1917 as an Arabian-style Shriner's Temple, the Alcazar offers just what architectural critics need: an outlet for their sense of humor (if any). Picture if you will a Mideastern lace facade with filigreed arches and balconies above, topped off by a big blueberry ice cream scoop of a dome. The color scheme is blue, tan, and violet. Try it on visually; you'll love it!

3 **CONSERVATORY OF FLOWERS** *John F. Kennedy Drive, Golden Gate Park.* A grand greenhouse in the old English manner, the oldest structure in Golden Gate Park was supposedly fashioned after London's Kew Gardens Conservatory. Ordered as a gift to the city of San Jose by early real estate magnate and philanthropist James Lick, it was built in Europe, taken apart, and shipped around Cape Horn. Lick had a falling out with San Jose officials and, in a huff, left the thing in its crates, where it remained until his death.

In 1877, a group of San Francisco businessmen bought it from Lick's estate and had it assembled in Golden Gate Park. The big wedding cake of a conservatory contains 33 tons of glass, held together by three tons of putty. (I'll never complain about caulking the shower stall again.)

4 **LEVI PLAZA** *Just off the Embarcadero, near Pier 23.* It isn't a building but a comely collection of structures, done up in smoked glass and brick with gently rounded corners. The circular brick columns in this upscale commercial center are a particularly striking feature. Terraces, patios, and a waterfall-fountain add an open-space feel to the attractive facility. Why can't all new business complexes look like this?

5 **101 CALIFORNIA PLAZA** *101 California Street (at Davis Street).* The 101 California building offers a fine example of the proper use of space in a downtown high-rise. The most impressive feature here is the plaza, a huge wedge of open space with granite slab terraces, an overflow fountain, and plenty of potted plants. Although the high-rise portion is a lofty glass tower, its surface is broken by varying terraced levels. The ground floor features a sloping glass roof sheltering a virtual greenhouse of potted trees and plants.

6 **THE PALACE OF FINE ARTS** *Baker Street near Marina Boulevard.* This great Romanesque colonnaded rotunda stands before a reflecting pool in the Marina District. It was built as a temporary showplace for the 1915 Panama-Pacific International Exposition, then restored in 1962 for $4 million, ten times the original cost. If you live in the Bay Area, you likely know that it isn't an art gallery, despite the name; the rear portion houses the Exploratorium science museum (see Chapter 2).

7 **RAMADA RENAISSANCE** *55 Cyril Magnin Street.* One of the city's most striking hotels, the Renaissance features ranks of bay windows that pay homage to San Francisco's architectural trademark. Like 101 California, the structure's sides are terraced to avoid the ugly blockhouse look. The base is set with columns and arches, with three scalloped burgundy awnings over the entrances.

8 **RINCON CENTER** *Mission Street between Spear and Steuart.* Not only did the builders of the new Rincon Center preserve a landmark, they improved it. The result is an effective fusion of the classic art deco Rincon Annex post office built in 1939 and a modern atrium shopping and business complex, completed in 1988. Both the facade and the lobby of the old post office have been preserved, along with the California history murals created by Russian artist Antone Refregier, perhaps the finest example of New Deal WPA artwork in America. The old post office lobby remains intact, although boutiques now lurk behind the closed postal windows. Graphics describe the Refregier murals and several display cases contain relics of early San Francisco.

The new Rincon Center continues the art deco look, with squared columns, angular planters, and a galleria roof. In complement to the Refregier murals, a decorative frieze of modern San Francisco scenes enhances the new center's atrium lobby.

9 **ST. MARY'S CATHEDRAL** *1111 Gough Street (at Geary Boulevard). Open to the public 9 a.m. to 5 p.m. daily; call 567-2020 for details.* St. Mary's is perhaps the most striking example of modern church architecture in the west, with winglike rooflines that sweep up into a cross. The massive yet graceful structure occupies two city blocks and soars skyward 200 feet, presumably toward heaven. Inside, the lofty conception continues as your eyes trace four brilliant strips of leaded glass up the walls to the top of the distinctive square-fluted dome.

10 **TRANSAMERICA BUILDING** *Corner of Columbus, Washington and Montgomery streets.* No, not the notorious Pyramid. We've nominated an intricately designed stone office building opposite the pointed highrise, which once housed Transamerica Corporation offices. Its fluted inset columns, black and gold circular stairway, and elaborate stone walls are an eye treat. A slender wedge of a building, it was built to conform to one of the pie-shaped corners created by the diagonal swath of Columbus Avenue.

SAN FRANCISCO'S TEN BEST ARCHITECTURAL UGLIES
Since architectural beauty and the lack of it are in the eye of the beholder, we list these diplomatically in alphabetical order.

1 **CALA FOODS** *California and Hyde streets.* Who's responsible for this ungainly critter, anyhow? With its painted window panels and indented, upswept roofline, it looks like a psychedelic owl that crash-landed on a vacant lot. The recent additions of green, yellow, and brown half-circles on the glass panels do not help.

2 **FINANCIAL DISTRICT–CHINATOWN HOLIDAY INN** *750 Kearny Street (at Washington).* Most Holiday Inns are merely functional; this one is ugly. Its boxlike tower juts skyward in gross disruption of the fine old Chinatown neighborhood that it invaded several years ago. Its base splays out in a curious spraddle-legged fashion; it looks like a man with one foot on the pier and the other in a boat. Or something worse.

3 **GALAXY THEATER** *Van Ness Avenue and Sutter Street.* This is a quick lesson in how to construct a new-wave theater building. Find a giant child with poor eye-to-hand coordination, give him a set of huge glass building blocks and turn him loose. See? He can't even get any symmetry in his stack. The silly thing's lopsided.

4 **HILTON HOTEL TOWER** *333 O'Farrell Street (at Taylor).* The new rose-colored addition to the Hilton Hotel complex, with its glow-in-the-dark dome, is sort of an improvement. Sort of. But the original tower — an aluminum-colored square stump — still dominates the skyline. The windows are boring little squares with no trim. It's the quintessential architectural cube.

5 **SAN FRANCISCO MARRIOTT** Fourth and Mission. Herb Caen calls it the "Jukebox Marriott," an apt description for this new high-rise hotel with curious glass accents, which opened for business in 1989. The mix of glass and granite might have been pleasing, but it's topped by irregular spires and glass facades that fan out, offering the impression of a jeweled Egyptian death mask or the wizard's castle in Oz. Or perhaps a galleria stood on end.

6 **IMPERIAL SAVINGS, NORTH BEACH BRANCH** *Corner of Green, Columbus, and Stockton.* Here we have an example of a structure that's ugly primarily because it's in the wrong place. It's a curious creature with arched glass window-walls and a three-domed roof; it looks like a surrealistic beehive. And it's plopped right in the middle of North Beach, near some fine old bay-windowed Victorians. It would look better elsewhere. In Utah, for instance.

7 **KING OF CHINA RESTAURANT** *Clement Street at 11th Avenue.* We praised the King's dim sum in Chapter 8, but, good grief, the look of the place! This shiny curiosity, with its silos of stainless steel and gaudy expanses of glass, is a head-on collision between art deco and Oriental excess. An oversized bulge of a bay window is the focal point of the futuristic two-story design, with an incongruous dragon crest above. Flanking the bay window are two glass and stainless steel columns that look like outside elevators with nowhere to go.

8 **460 MONTGOMERY BUILDING** *Montgomery at Sacramento.* This has to be the most abrupt and jarring fusion of architectural styles in the city. In an effort to preserve an old cut-stone Colonial-style building, architects stuck a square, drab Wheaties-box high-rise right on top of it. The effect is like an elaborate wood carving sprouting a two-by-four.

9 **NEIMAN-MARCUS STORE** *Geary at Stockton.* We have here another example of architectural fusion that leads to visual confusion. Attempting to preserve the look of the old City of Paris rotunda (the store it replaced), Neiman-Marcus sports a curious glass silo that emerges from a flat-sided building. The effect is inelegant, like a well-dressed woman wearing gaudy glass beads. The alternating dark and light brown granite diamonds decorating the exterior walls would look better on a pack of playing cards.

10 **ROSALIE'S RESTAURANT** *1451 Van Ness Avenue (at Bush).* The pre-cast doughy-looking concrete portal to this upscale restaurant resembles the entrance to an amusement ride in a 1930s fun zone. All that's missing is a papier-mâché fat laughing lady above that cavelike entrance. It gets curiouser inside. Wait until you see the cement tent maître d' station and the Reynolds Wrap palm trees.

Take a Hike or Pedal a Bike

THE TEN BEST PATHWAYS

I love this hilly city of yours. When you get tired of walking around, you can lean against it! — tourist quoted in *Herb Caen's San Francisco*, 1957

The hills haven't gotten any flatter since the city's pundit laureate wrote his affectionate guide to San Francisco more than 30 years ago. With its lumpy but compact terrain, it is a wonderful walking city and a cyclist's haven. So enough of this passive sightseeing, bar-hopping, and stuffing ourselves; it's exercise time!

To find the Ten Best routes, we hiked and biked San Francisco from bay to ocean, and crossed the Golden Gate Bridge into Marin County. Where pathways get complicated, we've sketched maps to help you find your way. We recommend transferring our street directions or sketches to a more detailed city map, using one of those highlighter pens. (AAA's San Francisco map is best, but you have to be a member to get one.)

THE TEN BEST HIKE ROUTES

Herewith, the Ten Best places to take a hike in San Francisco. We're serious walkers, so most of these outings are designed to give you a good aerobic workout. But we've included some moderate ones for those who just want to stroll around and enjoy some city scenery.

1 **THE FIRST SAN FRANCISCO HILL STRIDE ROUTE** *Moderate to strenuous; 6.8 miles. (See "Festivals of the Feet" in Chapter 16 for details on the annual walking race.)* In the summer of 1985, *CitySports*, a magazine not intended for couch potatoes, sponsored the first San Francisco Hill Stride, with the focus on power walking instead of running. It has since grown to the City Stride, one of the world's largest walking events, held yearly in several cities. *CitySports* is still a major sponsor.

Striding isn't strolling, incidentally; it's stepping out at a brisk four-mile-

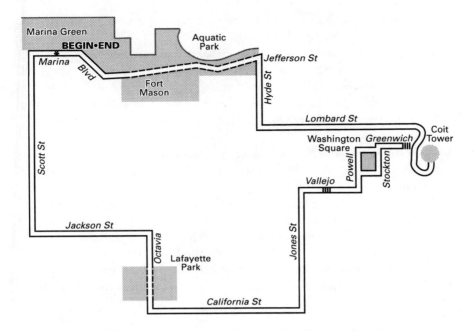

an-hour clip. Doctors and fitness gurus call it the ideal aerobic workout, without the spinal stress of running or the physical limitations of swimming.

The City Stride, held each August, has been expanded to more than seven miles, but we'll walk the original course, which is a bit less challenging for the novice power walker. It's an ambitious and complicated route beginning and ending at the Marina Green; it takes you over seven hills, with awesome vistas along the way. Some steep climbs are involved, but much of it is level or downhill, and you'll pass through some nice parks.

You'll note as you transfer this outline to a regular map that one stretch along Vallejo seems to go where there is no street; that's because it goes up a set of steps. That's right; *up*. We said it was a good workout. On the final leg, you descend Scott Street, with visions of the bay dancing before you. When you crawl back to your Marina Green starting point, you'll know you've done a day's work.

2 THE SQUIGGLY LOMBARD, COIT TOWER, EMBARCADERO WALK

Easy stroll to moderate climb; about a mile; a tough 2 miles if you do it round trip. This little hike contains a section of the original Hill Stride. Begin at Hyde and Lombard by walking down the "Crookedest Street," and just keep tooling along Lombard until you hit a set of concrete steps, then follow a shady pathway leading up to Coit Tower. After enjoying the vistas, follow the Filbert Steps down toward the waterfront. They begin at the point where the road enters the Coit Tower parking lot; look for a "Greenwich and Telegraph Hill" sign.

You'll clump down several flights of steep steps past hillside homes and landscaped terraces. You have several choices because the steps wander all over the side of Telegraph Hill, but eventually you'll emerge on level land at the Embarcadero. If you want to retrace your route, bear in mind that the trek back up to Coit Tower involves 494 steps. See you at the top.

3 **WHARF RAMBLE**   *Completely level; 2.5 miles.* This stroll along the Embarcadero is so obvious that we hesitate to include it, but it *is* a pleasant walk.

Begin at the concrete promenade built by the San Francisco Port Commission, just south of the Ferry Building. Then start strolling—leisurely or briskly, as you wish—toward Fisherman's Wharf. Places to pause along the way include Ferry Plaza, the historic Ferry Building, Justin Herman Plaza with its funny boxy fountain, handsome brick Levi Plaza opposite Pier 23, tacky Pier 39 if you must, Fisherman's Wharf, and the historic ships of Hyde Street Pier.

4 **GOLDEN GATE PROMENADE**   *An extension of the Wharf Ramble; a breeze to walk and pretty as a picture; 3.5 miles.* When the Golden Gate National Recreation Area was created, officials designated a walking and running trail from Hyde Street Pier to Fort Point beneath the Golden Gate Bridge. You're never out of sight of the bay on the Golden Gate Promenade, and the views are wonderful. Although it can accommodate bikes, we prefer to follow it on foot because it's too crowded and contains some sandy and gravelly stretches.

The route is easy: from Hyde Street Pier, walk toward the Golden Gate Bridge, past Aquatic Park, over a green Fort Mason hill, through the Marina Green, and along the Presidio shoreline. The path is marked here and there with gold, blue, and white signs. If you lose track of the route, just keep edging toward the bay. But stop short of getting your feet wet.

5 **MEXICAN MURAL WALK**   *Mostly level; about 3 miles. The Precita Eyes Mural Center at 348 Precita Avenue (285-2287), a nonprofit group dedicated to mural creation and preservation, conducts walks past the Mission District murals on the first and third Saturday of each month at 1:30 p.m.; $3 for adults, less for kids and seniors. Also, a $2 pamphlet from the Mexican Museum in Building D at Fort Mason Center (see Chapter 17) shows the location of many of these outdoor paintings.*

More than 200 murals are scattered throughout the city's Mission District. To see about 50 of the more interesting ones, follow the route we've

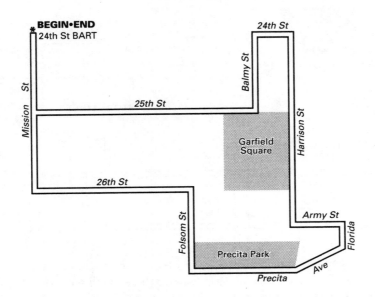

outlined below. You'll be trekking through a simple working folks' neighborhood and some of it's a bit scruffy, so don't expect a lot of fancy vistas. Murals range from strong political statements and slices of Latin life to simple whimsy; they're wonderful examples of Mexican-American folk art.

Begin by hopping a Daly City–bound BART train, and get off at 24th Street. You'll see your first mural, just above the station, showing humanoid T-columns holding up BART tracks. (BART on the backs of the people?)

As you walk and gawk about our mural route, note three areas in particular: Garfield Square park at Harrison and 26th, with several murals on park buildings and a nearby housing project; the beautifully decorated Leonard R. Flynn Elementary School near Precita Park at Precita Avenue and Harrison; and Balmy Alley, with an astonishing 30 murals in a one-block stretch. Sadly, some murals have been defaced with senseless graffiti, but most are intact.

6 VICTORIANA TO THE HAIGHT HIKE *Level to moderately steep; 3.4 miles.* On this walk, you'll get a look at some of San Francisco's finest Victorians and the Haight-Ashbury district where the Flower Children once reigned.

Begin beside Alamo Square, a Victorian historic district where Pierce Street T-bones into Hayes. This is the best vantage point for viewing the famous Painted Ladies, those six matching Victorians on Steiner Street that you often see on postcards. After following our route around the Alamo Square neighborhood, which brims with Victorians, take a long hike on

153

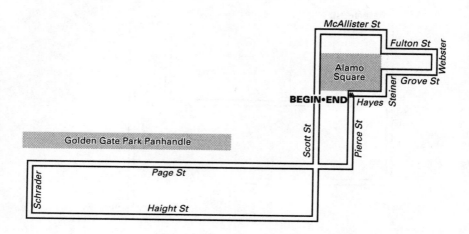

Haight Street into Haight-Ashbury, with its funky shops, galleries, and bookstores. Then return along Page Street, where you'll see more Victorian beauties in their bright makeup.

7 **WILDERNESS COAST IN THE CITY HIKE** *Some up and down, but mostly level; 9.2 miles. The Golden Gate National Recreation Area brochure, available at most GGNRA facilities, shows the two Coastal Trail sections of this hike.* The same folks who brought you the Golden Gate Promenade also carved out the Coastal Trail that follows sea cliffs above the Pacific on the northern and western edges of the city.

The trail begins at the Golden Gate Bridge viewpoint near the toll plaza and ends at Fort Funston near Lake Merced. It isn't all signed, but when in doubt just scuff along the beach or follow a city street until you can find another chunk of this seacoast trail.

From the bridge viewpoint, follow the trail under the bridge anchorage, past a maintenance yard, then travel along the edge of Lincoln Boulevard in the Presidio until the trail drops down to Baker Beach. There, you'll catch some great views of the bridge over your right shoulder. The vistas become even more dramatic if you back-track up the beach a few hundred yards. You'll also encounter some summer views of sunbathing in the buff, so just keep staring at the bridge if that sort of thing bothers you. Or pick a cold day to do your hike.

Continuing south on the trail from Baker Beach, you'll emerge at the swank Sea Cliff residential community. Follow El Camino del Mar, then pick up the trail again near the edge of Lincoln Park Golf Course. From here, it's up-and-down hiking through a beautifully craggy area of steep headlands with rocky, surf-pounded beaches below. The bridge-and-sea views are tremendous. Eventually, you'll reach the Cliff House; now follow Ocean Beach below the Great Highway to Fort Funston.

GGNRA rangers asked us to warn you *not* to climb over rocky outcroppings above the surf or wander off the trail where it's notched into sea cliffs; they're steep, slippery and dangerous. Rangers have to make several rescues a year, and some hikers have been killed.

8 | **URBAN WILDERNESS HIKE** *Very steep in parts; various lengths.* Mount Sutro Forest, on the slopes below Twin Peaks near the University of California Medical Center, offers a virtual wilderness in the heart of the city. Sutro Forest has many trails and partial trails that take you into thick stands of evergreens and eucalyptus. It's intriguing to lunge through a primeval thicket, then top a ridge to be greeted by a panoramic cityscape.

We won't attempt to outline a formal route here; we instead suggest a rather random exploration of the slopes and ridges around the Med Center. A good starting point is Belgrave Avenue. To get there, drive up Market Street, take a half right onto 17th (at Castro), and turn left onto Stanyan. Go up a steep grade to Belgrave, turn right, and you'll run out of street. Before you is an inviting trail into an urban wilderness.

You'll probably get misplaced wandering around here, emerging unexpectedly onto the Medical Center grounds or into one of the hillside residential areas. Take along a detailed city map to help maintain your bearings.

At the other end of Belgrave Avenue, incidentally, is a trail that takes you up to Tank Hill, whose vantage point we raved about in Chapter 3.

9 | **CHINATOWN STROLL** *Easy walk; some hills; probably less than a mile.* It's both simple and complicated to outline a route through Chinatown. The simple part: start at the "Gate of Chinatown," Grant Avenue at Bush Street. Follow Grant to Broadway, go up a block, and double back on Stockton. The complex part: after doing that, prowl every cross street and alley of Chinatown to capture the *real* flavor of this place.

Some things to look for:

■ The wonderfully cluttered gallery of Asian artifacts in the cellar of Canton Bazaar at 616 Grant.

■ The naughty netsukes (tiny ivory Japanese figurines in compromised positions) in display cases at Empress Fine Arts at Grant and Clay.

■ The "produce corner" sidewalk markets at Stockton and Broadway.

■ The Great China Art Company herbal shop at 857 Washington, where clerks still use hand-held balance scales.

■ A noodle factory at 12 Beckett Street.

■ A fortune cookie factory at 1328 Stockton, where you'll finally discover how they get those little messages inside.

155

10 **ORIGINAL SHORELINE HIKE**   *Flat and easy; about 2 miles.* As our map indicates, much of San Francisco's present downtown area was under water at the time of the Gold Rush. The shaded area indicates the original shoreline. Filling the bay began rather inelegantly; debris and sand were dumped onto the hulks of ships that had been abandoned by their crews, who had stampeded to the Sierra gold fields.

The heart of the Financial District extends about eight blocks into what was once shallow bay water and mudflats. If the original shoreline were intact, the Transamerica Pyramid would get its big buttresses wet, for that area was an inlet called Yerba Buena Cove.

It's interesting to zigzag along the original shoreline; the streets we've marked follow it rather closely. At the corner of Bush and Market, you'll find a bronze plaque detailing the pre–Gold Rush shore. As you wander through the area, watch for other plaques heralding anything from the inventor of the slot machine (Market at Battery) to the original office of the Pony Express (marked by several plaques on the California National Bank building at Clay, just up from Montgomery Street).

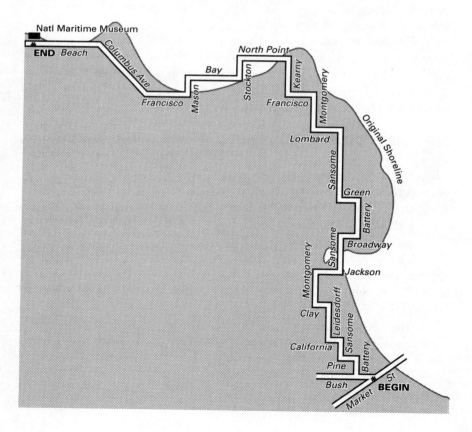

THE TEN BEST BIKE ROUTES

We're assuming that you'll buckle your bike rack to your car and drive to starting points, so we've tried to select places where ample and unmetered parking is available. All our routes are round trip, so you can return to your Belchfire V-6. These routes can be negotiated quite easily with a standard three-speed or ten-speed street bike; some are even suitable for single-speed cycles. If we had our way, we'd do all of our city biking early on a Sunday morning, the most traffic-free time of the week.

One of our routes takes us across the Golden Gate Bridge, then two others explore next-door Marin County.

For bike rentals, contact Park Avenue Cyclery at 1269 Ninth Avenue (Lincoln Way), 665-1394; Avenue Cyclery at 756 Stanyan (Waller), 387-3155; or Presidio Bicycle Shop, 5335 Geary Boulevard (17th Avenue), 751-3200.

1 **POTRERO TO THE WATERFRONT** *Level, with moderate upgrade on return; 10-mile round trip.* We love to pedal along the waterfront early on a sunny Sunday morning, passing tired old freighters dozing at dockside, pausing at the handsome Embarcadero Promenade, getting to Fisherman's Wharf ahead of the tour buses.

Our route is a simple one, filled with rewarding views. Begin at the corner of Mariposa and Missouri, in the city's Potrero District. It's an area of Victorians and hilly streets, but the route down to the waterfront is a gradual decline. Pedal down to Mariposa, noting views of the city skyline off to your left. Avoid the two-lane left turn at Third Street, keeping to your right until you hit China Basin. Now turn left and follow along the waterfront.

Your wharfside route blends into the Embarcadero, taking you past magnificent views of the bay, ships at anchor, the venerable Ferry Building, and the sleek Embarcadero Center. Ultimately, you arrive at Fisherman's Wharf, where aromas of crab cookers fill the air.

Two good suggestions for breakfast along the route: Mission Rock Resort (Chapter 9) just after you turn onto China Basin, for outside bayview dining; or the Buena Vista Cafe (Chapter 13), just up from Fisherman's Wharf at Hyde and Beach. Now, retrace your route back to your starting point.

Warning: Many railroad tracks crisscross the waterfront; they often cross streets at odd angles, and a track groove can cause a bad spill.

2 **CLIFF HOUSE TO LAKE MERCED** *Level except for one slight upgrade; 3.5-mile round trip.* This is another simple route, with views of the restless Pacific instead of the bay. It's nearly always windy out there, so take a wrap.

Begin just below the Cliff House on the Great Highway, where you'll find plenty of unmetered parking for your bike-toter. Ride south along the highway, catching glimpses of the sea between grassy dunes. You might like to pull over occasionally, tie your bike to something and take a beach walk. At Sloat Boulevard, you can swing up and make friends with denizens of the San Francisco Zoo.

Continue along the Great Highway to its junction with Skyline Boulevard near Lake Merced, then return to your starting point, or merge onto our Bike Route No. 3 below.

3   **LAKE MERCED CIRCLE**   *Completely level; 4.4-mile loop trip.* Begin in Harding Park on Lake Merced's shore just off Skyline Boulevard. An asphalt biking-walking trail circles the lake; follow it clockwise, making right turns to stay near the lake shore.

You'll start riding alongside Skyline, shift to Lake Merced Boulevard, then join John Muir Drive, and finally return to Skyline. It's a pleasant, traffic-free route, sometimes shaded by over-hanging cypress and eucalyptus. You'll pedal past Harding Park Municipal Golf Course, the back door of San Francisco State University, and the residential towers of Parkmerced. If you combine this with the Cliff House to Lake Merced route, the total distance is about eight miles.

4   **LAKE TO LUXURY ROUTE**   *Mostly level, with some moderately steep but short hills; 3-mile loop trip.* Lake Street, which parallels California in the Presidio Heights area, is one of the few city streets with a separate bike lane. The bonus is that it's in a beautiful neighborhood.

Start at Park Presidio Boulevard, near Mountain Lake Park, a little jewel of a greenbelt surrounding a pond. Pedal toward downtown on Lake Street, go left on Arguello, then left again into Presidio Terrace. This circular lane takes you past some of the city's most opulent homes, including the over-sized Hansel and Gretel cottage of Mr. and Mrs. Richard (Dianne Feinstein) Blum at 30 Presidio Terrace.

After wishing you could afford one of these mansions, pedal out of the Terrace and down Washington Street, passing more upscale real estate. Turn right on Laurel for one block, right onto Clay, and return to your starting point. (Clay blends into Lake Street.)

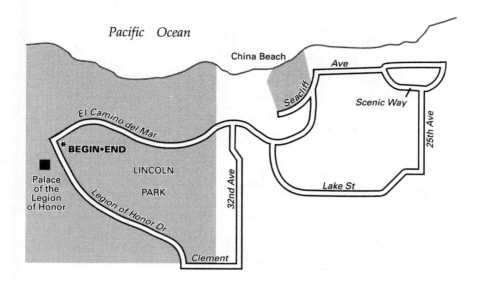

Pacific Ocean

LINCOLN PARK TO LUXURY ROUTE   *Somewhat hilly, but nothing terribly steep; 3-mile loop trip.* Sea Cliff rivals Presidio Terrace in opulence and offers ocean and bridge views as a bonus. To explore this haven of the rich, unload your bikes at the Palace of the Legion of Honor parking lot on Lincoln Boulevard, then follow the course we've outlined here. It's one of our prettier routes, with views of Pacific blue, golf course green, and all those stylish homes.

Our map doesn't attempt to show specific routes through the complex streets of Sea Cliff. Just pedal randomly until you've had your fill of envy, then pick up El Camino del Mar and return to the Legion of Honor. Pause to study the emotionally moving Jewish Holocaust Memorial just below the parking area.

PEDALING THE PRESIDIO   *Some gentle hills and a couple of moderate ones; 5-mile loop trip.* Begin at a dirt parking area on Merchant Road near an old gun battery. Pedal down Merchant and merge onto Lincoln Boulevard, then turn into the Presidio on Kobbe Avenue near a World War II monument.

By following our map through the Presidio (most of it on Washington Boulevard), you'll pedal beneath pretty forests-in-the-city and catch some surprise vistas of cityscape, sea, and bay. The route takes you through the main part of the old military post. We suggest a pause at the Presidio Army Museum (see Chapter 17).

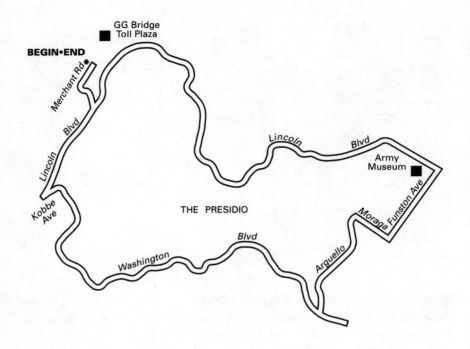

GG Bridge
Toll Plaza

BEGIN•END

Merchant Rd*

Lincoln Blvd

Lincoln

Lincoln Blvd

Army Museum

Kobbe Ave

THE PRESIDIO

Moraga

Funston Ave

Blvd

Arguello

Washington

7 **PEDALING THE PARK**   *Golden Gate Park; level but busy with other bikers on weekends; 7.5 miles or more.* This is old stuff to Bay Area cyclists, but if you've just arrived from Madera, you'll enjoy pedaling in Golden Gate Park.

The main route, John F. Kennedy Drive, is closed to motor vehicle traffic on Sundays, but that doesn't mean it's deserted. You'll encounter legions of other cyclists, ghetto-blaster-toting roller skaters, skateboarders, striders, and runners. So it's hardly a wilderness, but the park is beautiful. Start at McLaren Lodge near Stanyan and follow J.F.K. Drive to the Great Highway, then return along South Drive. That route will cover a bit more than seven miles.

Don't limit yourself to these two main routes. You'll find a dozen or so smaller roads and bike paths that zig and zag through the scenery and greenery. Of course you'll lose your way, but it's a pleasant place in which to go astray. The park is long but narrow, and even if you become totally misplaced, you'll shortly emerge onto a familiar street.

8 **ACROSS THE BRIDGE AND INTO THE WILLOWS**   *Mostly level, with one steep downgrade and upgrade; 8-mile round trip. Sausalito*

160

means "little willows" in Spanish, and the ride across the Golden Gate Bridge into this pretty bayside town is one of the area's classic bike routes.

We start at the Golden Gate Bridge toll plaza and follow the bike route across the bridge. Pause at Vista Point on the far side, then take the marked bike route down Alexander Avenue, which blends into Bridgeway in Sausalito. Pedal along the handsome Riviera-style bay front and past the town's cutesy boutiques, many in century-old buildings. Zack's Restaurant off Bridgeway is a good sunny-day lunch stop, offering excellent hamburgers and an open deck over the bay.

Our turn-around point is the Army Corps of Engineers' Bay Model at 2100 Bridgeway (open Tuesday–Friday from 9 a.m. to 4 p.m., weekends and holidays from 10 a.m. to 6 p.m.; shorter hours in the off-season; call 332-3870). The corps built a two-acre scale model of San Francisco Bay with its in-flowing streams to study the effect of tidal action, silting, and such. An excellent graphic exhibit traces the development of life from the sea; a film on the model's function is shown on request.

9 **STRAWBERRY TO TIBURON**   *Level; 5-mile round trip.* Start at the Strawberry Shopping Center off U.S. 101 (take the Blithedale-Tiburon Boulevard exit), and follow Tiburon Boulevard into the hidden hamlet of the same name. As you pedal along the boulevard, you'll pick up a bike path near Greenwood Beach park, and this takes you traffic-free into Tiburon. The village is just as cute as Sausalito, and it's generally less crowded.

A couple of good lunch stops are Sam's Anchor Cafe and Guaymas, both on Main Street and both offering decks with views of the distant San Francisco skyline. You can sip wine samples and buy the bottles you like at Tiburon Vintners tasting room in a stately Victorian a couple of blocks away.

10 **ANGEL ISLAND AMBLE**   *Level with some hills; 5-mile loop trip. The Red and White Fleet departs for Angel Island from Pier 41 in San Francisco; call 546-2815. The Tiburon Ferry offers service to the island from Tiburon; call 435-2131. Both operate daily in summer and weekends only in the off-season, and both can accommodate bikes. For general information, call Angel Island State Park at 456-1286.*

Angel Island is that large, green 758-acre lump in the northern corner of San Francisco Bay, off the Tiburon peninsula. It's a state park with hiking trails, picnic areas, abandoned forts, and an exciting 360-degree view of the bay.

The main route around the island is very bike-able; this is one of the most popular rides in the Bay Area, so it's best to avoid it on summer weekends, if possible.

The Good, the Goofy, and the Strange

LISTS OF THINGS THAT FAIL TO FIT INTO OTHER LISTS

Toto, I don't think we're in Kansas anymore.
— Dorothy, in *The Wizard of Oz*

THE TEN BEST PLACES TO SNUGGLE WITH YOUR SWEETIE
Feel a romantic urge? Want to slip away with someone special for a few moments, a few hours? Here are our favorite hidden corners:

1 **The Best Place to Study the Stars Together: THE STAR-GAZER SUITE** *Spreckels Mansion Guest House, 737 Buena Vista West (off Haight Street); 861-3008.* The Spreckels Mansion and its next-door guest house are side-by-side bed and breakfast inns near Buena Vista Park. Most rooms are snuggly Victorians with fluffy down and frilly lace, but the Star-gazer Suite is a modern hideaway with warm woods, a private fireplace, and a skylight above the bed and above a Japanese-style bath. A romantic night spent staring at the stars — and at one another — will cost $185. Call well in advance to reserve your own special spot beneath the Milky Way.

2 **The Best Place for an Intimate Dinner: FLEUR DE LYS** *777 Sutter (at Jones), 673-7779. Dressy, jackets for gentlemen; see detailed listing in Chapter 5.* Settle into a plush booth at a candlelit table, and beneath the sensual fabric canopy of this posh French restaurant, and let romance happen. Fleur de Lys is not only a romantic spot, it was voted as the best restaurant in the city in a poll of cafe executives and celebrity chefs in our other book, *San Francisco's Ultimate Dining Guide*. The menu is pure French, but in a lighter nouvelle style, so you won't doze off as you flutter your eyelashes at your partner.

3 | The Best Place to Sit and Sip with Someone Special: MASON'S COCKTAIL LOUNGE AT THE FAIRMONT HOTEL

950 Mason Street (at California), 392-0113. Mason's on the arcade level of the Fairmont offers all the ingredients for an intimate cocktail lounge: soft lighting, table candles, overstuffed sofas piled with throw pillows, and Peter Minton at the keyboard of the grand piano. Peter, who holds court Wednesday through Saturday, will play romantic ballads while you exchange dreamy glances. Mason's is also an upscale restaurant, but the cocktail lounge is completely sheltered from the tinkle of silverware. It's an elegant little bar and gentlemen are requested to wear jackets.

4 | The Best Place to Share the Sunset: MARIN HEADLANDS

The turnouts along the Marin Headlands road can get awfully cluttered with camera-clutchers during the daytime, but they're surprisingly uncrowded at night. The view of the sun slipping into the Pacific, the bridge standing below you, and the lights of the city beginning to twinkle will stir the romantic soul in anyone.

5 | The Best Place to Greet the Sunrise Together: ATOP TANK HILL

This is a little-known promontory below Twin Peaks, which we nominated as the city's best vista point in Chapter 3. It's a wonderfully private place to greet the new day. The air may be chilly at that hour, but all the more reason to snuggle.

To get there, drive up Market to Castro, and veer slightly to the right onto 17th; follow this to Stanyan, turn left, and go up a steep grade to Belgrave. Go left again and, still climbing, drive a few blocks to the end of the street. Before you, on the left side of the street, is a trail sloping upward to Tank Hill. Take your partner's hand and walk toward the new day.

6 | The Best Place to Be Alone Together in the City in a Dark Thicket: SUTRO FOREST

This thick stand of eucalyptus on the steep flanks of Mount Sutro is surprisingly remote. It's a nice place to walk hand-in-hand; you can climb to high vantage points and gaze down at the city. To find it, follow the directions to Tank Hill above, but turn *right* onto Belgrave and follow it to the end of the road. There before you is your trail into privacy.

7 | The Best Place to Sit and Simmer with Your Sweetie: IN A RENTAL HOT TUB

Grand Central Sauna and Hot Tub, 15 Fell Street (at Market), 431-1370; The Hot Tubs, 2200 Van Ness Avenue (at Broadway), 441-8827. Or look under "Spas & Hot Tubs, Rentals" in the Yellow Pages. Can't afford to have a hot tub installed in your crabgrass patch? These two companies rent hot tubs and sauna space by the hour, in cozy private rooms.

8 **The Best Theater in Which to Snuggle and Ignore the Movie: THE BALBOA** *3634 Balboa Street (at 38th Avenue).* This handsome old art deco theater has rocking chair loges for two, high up in the back rows. They're great places to cuddle, so pick a dull movie.

9 **The Best Place for a Romantic Beach Stroll: CHINA BEACH** Situated below the cliff-hanging homes of Sea Cliff, China Beach is a pretty little rock-bound cove offering striking views of the Golden Gate Bridge and San Francisco's craggy coastline. Although it's busy with sunbathers on warm summer days, it's practically deserted on windy, cool days—the perfect time to bundle up and stroll arm-in-arm. Sea caves and rocky overhangs offer places to snuggle against the wind.

Although this is a small cove hemmed by rocky cliffs, you can amble for about a third of a mile when the tide's not too high, perhaps pausing to study a starfish or gaze at the mist-shrouded bridge beyond. Since it's outside the Golden Gate, China Beach is washed by a modest surf. It earned its name during the California Gold Rush, when Chinese fishermen camped here to provide seafood for the growing young city.

To reach China Beach, drive out Geary Boulevard to the Richmond District, turn right onto 26th Avenue and follow it until it T-bones into Sea Cliff Drive. Go left to the end of Sea Cliff (veering right at a Y intersection). You'll find a small parking area and a set of railroad-tie steps leading down to the beach.

10 **The Best Place for an Overnight Escape: CLAREMONT RESORT AND SPA** *Ashby and Domingo avenues, Oakland, 843-3000.* With its brand new $6 million spa, night-lighted tennis courts, bay view restaurant, and modern rooms furnished with antiques, the Claremont has become *the* hideaway resort in northern California. Romantic souls can percolate in a hot tub, get an "aromatic massage," dance to a fantastic Bay Area vista, or just stroll the 22-acre grounds. And it's just half an hour from San Francisco.

All this happens amid the historic ambiance of a resort hotel dating back to 1915. It has undergone a complete restoration, from its monumental lobby to its spacious rooms tucked behind those wonderfully silly little cupolas. (See Chapter 24.)

DRIVING YOURSELF TO DISTRACTION: A MOTORING AND PARKING GUIDE

We prefer riding Muni or BART, or walking in the city. If you *must* drive here, these Ten Best driver's pointers may save you a lot of grief. They're listed in no particular order.

1 THE BEST PLACES TO FIND PARKING PLACES On weekends, daytime parking around the Civic Center is pretty open, and it's a short stroll or brief Muni or BART ride downtown. Catch BART at the Civic Center station or Metro Muni at the Van Ness station. Parking also is available during weekends along Mission Street, south of Market. And you can find slots during evenings and weekends in the Financial District.

For weekday evening parking in the downtown area, use a trick employed by locals: edge into one of the 4 to 6 p.m. tow-away zones about 5:45 and spend a furtive 15 minutes watching for the parking patrol.

2 THE BEST PLACES TO FIND TOURIST AREA PARKING Fort Point always has more parking available than the more popular Golden Gate Bridge view area just above it, and there are no meters. If you're visiting the Marina Green and can't find a spot, drive into Fort Mason Center; it's just a couple of blocks away. If the Palace of the Legion of Honor parking lot is full, drive down along El Camino del Mar; there's plenty of legal parking along the shoulder.

3 THE BEST TIMES TO FIND NOT-QUITE-LEGAL FREE PARKING The odds of getting an overtime parking ticket drop considerably on weekends because the parking patrol ranks thin out then. Most meters go to sleep after 6 p.m. Monday through Saturday and all day Sunday, but *not* in popular tourist spots. We've gotten occasional tickets for expired meters on Saturdays, but we've never been ticketed in an unmetered time-limit zone on weekends or evenings. (But be warned: This can change; please do not forward parking citations to the authors.)

4 THE CHEAPEST PARKING GARAGE Portsmouth Plaza Garage at Kearny and Washington on the edge of Chinatown charges a mere 75 cents an hour.

5 THE BEST STREETS ON WHICH TO GET FROM HERE TO THERE During non-rush hours, drop over to Howard (southbound) or Folsom (northbound) instead of struggling up Market or Mission. If you're headed into Chinatown or North Beach, the Stockton and

Broadway tunnels cut out a lot of stoplights. The problem is, you can't find a parking place once you get there.

6 **THE WORST STREETS ON WHICH TO GET ANYWHERE** The city Traffic Engineering Department says the most heavily traveled street is Van Ness Avenue between McAllister and Lombard. Franklin Street and 19th Avenue aren't exactly speedways, either.

7 **THE BEST PLACES TO EXPERIENCE GRIDLOCK** The most congested intersections, says Traffic Engineering, are Lombard at Van Ness, the Broadway-Columbus-Grant confrontation, and 19th Avenue at Lincoln.

8 **THE BEST DRIVING MAPS** The California State Automobile Association (150 Van Ness Avenue at Hayes) produces the best maps of San Francisco and other Bay Area cities and counties, but you have to be an AAA member to get one.

9 **THE BEST WAY TO MAKE FREEWAYS WORK FOR YOU** The Central Freeway—an octopus-like tangle of I-80, I-280, and U.S. 101—can come in handy for hopping quickly about town during non-rush hours. Study your map and you'll see that the spaghetti sprawl does a rather good job of feeding into various areas.

10 **THE BEST WAY TO GET OUT OF TOWN HEADED SOUTH** Let's face it: going north and east, you've got two bridges between you and the rest of the world; if they're jammed, you're stuck. If you're headed south, however, take I-280; it's less crowded and prettier than U.S. 101. You can pick up 101 again just south of San Jose, and also miss that growing city's traffic.

TOURIST BUSING: THE TEN BEST MUNI RIDES

If you grow weary of the quest for a place to park your Belchfire V-6, you can do considerable touring on the assorted buses, streetcars and—of course—the cable cars of Muni, the San Francisco Municipal Railway system.

The first trick is to buy a monthly Fast Pass, available at a variety of banks and stores, or from a booth at City Hall. It allows you unlimited rides on the entire system. The price was $28 as we wrote this.

At 85 cents a ride, it takes 33 Muni trips to use up the price of a Fast Pass. But even if you use it fewer times, it's a great convenience since you don't have to fumble for change (which drivers do not make). Also, the pass gets you onto cable cars, which normally cost $2, and it's good on BART service within San Francisco. Muni route maps cost $1.25. To find out where they're available, and to learn anything else about the system, call 673-MUNI.

Okay, Fast Pass in hand? Let's use Muni to play tourist. Here are our Ten Best routes:

1 **76-MARIN HEADLANDS** This special bus, which runs Sundays and holidays only, takes you across the Golden Gate Bridge to the outer reaches of the Marin Headlands. The terminal is at Fourth and Townsend, south of Market Street.

2 **J-CHURCH** The Muni Metro system travels under Market Street, and this particular line emerges to rumble through the Mission District on Church Street. You can jump off at Church and 16th and walk a block down to Mission Dolores. The terminal is at the Embarcadero Muni/BART station at the foot of Market. You can catch it at any Muni/BART station along Market, or at the Market and Van Ness Avenue Muni station near the Civic Center.

3 **L-TARAVAL** If you're into tunnels, the L-Taraval Muni Metro takes you through the Twin Peaks tunnel and out to Ocean Beach, where you're within a short walk of Lake Merced. The terminal and other Market Street stops are the same as J-Church above.

4 **18-46th AVENUE** You can travel to Sutro Heights, the Cliff House, along the edge of Golden Gate Park, down the Great Highway, and around Lake Merced on this one. A good place to catch it is at the Palace of the Legion of Honor parking lot in Lincoln Park.

5 **29-SUNSET** Take this bus through the Presidio, along Lincoln Boulevard with ocean and Golden Gate Bridge views, across Golden Gate Park and down Sunset Boulevard to Lake Merced. Catch it in the Presidio on Lombard, near DeWitt Road.

6 **30-STOCKTON** The famous "Orient Express" travels through Chinatown into North Beach, terminating at Broderick and Beach. If you're in the downtown area, a good place to catch it is at Stockton and Sutter, just before it enters the Stockton Street Tunnel.

7 **37-CORBETT**   Panoramic views are the lure on this bus, which travels through the hilly Buena Vista Park/Haight-Ashbury neighborhoods, then climbs up into the Twin Peaks area. It passes quite near the Twin Peaks lookout, and you can hop out for a view. A good place to catch it is at Market and Church.

8 **38-GEARY**   This bus serves the heart of downtown, then roams out Geary Boulevard past Japan Center to Ocean Beach, within a short walk of the Cliff House and Golden Gate Park. It launches from the Transbay Terminal at Mission and First, or you can catch it anywhere downtown along Geary.

9 **42-DOWNTOWN LOOP**   We think of this as the San Francisco "sampler" because it wanders around a good part of downtown, skirts briefly along the Embarcadero, passes through Fisherman's Wharf, follows Van Ness Avenue through the Civic Center, then prowls south of Market. Catch it downtown on Sansome at California, or anywhere along Van Ness Avenue between Bay Street and Market. It runs in a continuous loop.

10 **44-O'SHAUGHNESSY (via Glen Park BART station)**   This is an interesting cross-town route that winds through a pretty ravine in Glen Canyon Park, passes landscaped homes of the Twin Peaks area, then crosses through Golden Gate Park near the major museums, Japanese Tea Garden and Academy of Science. To catch it, take a Daly City–bound BART train to Glen Park station, then board the 44 on Bosworth Street, headed uphill.

The Bottom Ten

LISTS OF THE LEAST OF THE BEST

Even paradise can have potholes. — Don W. Martin

For 22 chapters we've verbalized the virtues of San Francisco. We aren't suggesting that it's flawless, only that it's wonderful. There *are* a few things up with which we'd rather not put. Much of it is centered on Fisherman's Wharf, which has become a tacky shadow of its former self. A few other areas could use a bit of brushing up as well.

THE TACKY, THE TAWDRY, AND THE TOLERATED

1 **The Tackiest Street: JEFFERSON AT FISHERMAN'S WHARF** What once was a charming tourist attraction of friendly Italian seafood restaurants and a working fishing fleet has become a tacky collection of wax museums, cheap souvenir shops, and trinket peddlers passing themselves off as street artists. The cafes and some of the fishing boats are still there, and the smell of the crab pots is still wonderful in the morning air. But Jefferson Street junk shops and so-called museums have turned the place into a cheap carnival.

2 **The Biggest Clutter of Useless Souvenirs: THE BAY COMPANY** *211 Jefferson Street, Fisherman's Wharf.* This is the ultimate trinket parlor, awash with silly souvenirs that range from pointless to inappropriate to crude. Most of the other Wharf "gift" shops go through the motions of offering something useful. But the Bay, the biggest of them all, is a mere supermarket of schlock: the personification of what our once-charming Wharf has become.

3 **The Tackiest Shopping Center: PIER 39** *Off the Embarcadero.* When Pier 39 was opened in 1978, many observers — including Betty and I — judged it to be rather tacky and garish with its odd

169

pier-piling architecture, noisy video game parlor, and a carousel with plastic horses. Then the place began to grow on us — and we've always liked some of its specialty shops and restaurants.

Unfortunately, like its synthetic carousel ponies, the pier has come full circle and is looking shabby as well as tacky. The splintery decks, steps, and railings are in bad need of maintenance, and some of the shops are rather scruffy; caricature artists and arcade games attest to a rather cheap carnival atmosphere.

4 **The Most Boring Tourist Attraction: RIPLEY'S BELIEVE IT OR NOT MUSEUM** *Jefferson Street (at Jones), Fisherman's Wharf.* "Mrs. Birdie Cassells of Ireland sat on a nest of eggs for three weeks and became the mother of chicks. Believe it or not." About $6 buys you the privilege of walking by a miserable collection of freaks, distortions, and wax figures, and learning the wonderful news about Mrs. Cassells.

5 **The Saddest Street: MARKET BETWEEN POWELL AND VAN NESS** Market Street should be our Champs Elysées or Canal Street, with its brick sidewalks, polished granite benches, and designer trash cans. For many visitors, arriving by bus or cab from the airport or wandering from their downtown hotels, Market provides one of their first impressions of the city.

But middle Market from the Powell Street cable car turntable to Van Ness Avenue remains a sad gathering place of the unwashed and the unwanted, the despairing and disturbed castoffs of society. They shuffle about aimlessly, extending soiled hands for coins, sipping from bottles in brown paper bags, and upending the fancy trash cans in search of some grubby treasure.

The homeless sleep in littered doorways or stretch out on the dirty bricks, sometimes startling our clean-scrubbed visitors from Kansas.

6 **The Ugliest Beach: OCEAN BEACH** With scalloped breakers washing over miles of broad strand, Ocean Beach should be a pretty place and a haven for families. Instead, it attracts bands of scruffy types who look like rejects from outlaw motorcycle gangs. Their idea of a day at the beach is to perch on the graffiti-ridden seawalls, turn up their ghetto-blasters, and guzzle beer. The beach area has become a dirty wasteland, trashed and vandalized by these punks.

7 **The Worst Defacing of Public Property: MUNI BUSES** Is it really that difficult to keep the felt pen punks (probably the same ones who hang out at Ocean Beach) from defacing our buses? Must we surrender to this civic ugliness? And why are the BART trains and cable cars virtually unmarred?

8 **The Worst Places to Find Parking** Parking is nearly impossible in Chinatown, North Beach, Nob Hill, and Russian Hill almost any time; downtown and the Financial District are difficult during working hours. Next time, take the bus.

9 **The Most Crowded Parking Garage: PORTSMOUTH PLAZA GARAGE** On the edge of Chinatown, it's the least expensive garage in the city (Chapter 22) and bargain-seekers line up around the block on Friday and Saturday nights and most weekday afternoons. We've always wondered why management doesn't raise the rates. If you *do* want cheap parking, try the garage about mid-morning, after commuters have settled in.

10 **The Worst Time of the Year: SUMMERTIME** San Francisco's "summer" is really in the fall; our nicest weather is from September through early November. The normal July-August summer is marked with unpredictable weather and crowded streets. You try to guess how to dress but the elusive sun always fools you. You hope for a nice weekend; Saturday dawns brightly and you head for Baker Beach. But a cloud bank is just offshore, lurking and smirking. At noon, the wind blows the clouds ashore. Come on, September, hurry up!

THE TEN DUMBEST THINGS YOU CAN DO IN SAN FRANCISCO

1 **PARKING IN A TOW-AWAY ZONE DURING RUSH HOUR** Now, that's *dumb!* The fine is $40, but that could be just the beginning of your misery. If you're towed, you'll have to pay $50 or more to liberate your Belchfire V-6 from the towing company's garage, plus a daily storage fee if you don't pick it up right away. The only good news is that, periodically, a moratorium is called on towing because the city often has trouble negotiating contracts with towing companies. But don't count on it.

2 **FAILING TO CURB YOUR WHEELS** This law may not exist where you come from, but there's a $20 fine for failing to tuck your car's wheels against a curb on a steep street — to keep your car from going somewhere without you. The law says the wheels must touch the curb, and the city's Traffic Engineering Department defines an enforceable hill as one that's steep enough for a pencil to roll down; specifically, it's a 3 percent grade.

171

3 **WAITING IN LINE FOR A CABLE CAR**   Why queue up with the herd at the Powell Street cable car turntable? As we suggested in Chapter 2, catch a less-crowded California Street car at its California and Van Ness terminal. Then if you must ride the better-known Powell Street line, hop off at Powell and California to catch a wharf-bound or downtown car — and don't forget your transfer.

4 **PAYING $2.60 FOR A SO-CALLED BART "EXCURSION FARE"**   This is penny-ante stuff, I suppose, unless you're traveling with a family of six or a Marine regiment on liberty. A $2.60 BART "excursion" ticket allows you to travel throughout the system as long as you enter and exit from the same station. You can accomplish the same thing for 80 cents by entering one station, riding around until you're properly bored (as long as you don't exceed a three-hour time limit), then emerging one station down the line. The Market Street stations of Embarcadero, Montgomery and Powell are just a short walk apart.

5 **GETTING ONTO THE BAY BRIDGE DURING RUSH HOUR**   Rush hour, incidentally, starts around 4 p.m. If you'd like to experience *terminal* gridlock, try getting onto the bridge between 4 and 6 p.m. during the first rainstorm of the season.

6 **GETTING STRANDED IN AN INTERSECTION**   A recent law makes it an infraction to enter an intersection — even on a green light — if you cannot make it all the way across before the light turns red. This is an attempt — usually futile — to prevent rush-hour gridlock and traffic officers *will* issue citations.

7 **TRYING TO PARK AT FISHERMAN'S WHARF ON A SUNNY WEEKEND**   Wharf parking is virtually impossible on good-weather weekends, particularly in summer; don't even attempt it. The same holds true for the Coit Tower parking lot.

8 **DRIVING ALONG CHINATOWN'S GRANT AVENUE ON FRIDAY OR SATURDAY NIGHT**   Friday and Saturday are banquet nights for the Chinese, who come from all over California to attend catered affairs in Chinatown's restaurants. It's back to gridlock again. And don't even *try* to get into Portsmouth Plaza Garage.

9 **WEARING A DODGER CAP...**
at a San Francisco Giants' game.

10 **CALLING IT 'FRISCO** What's wrong with that? For one thing, the city is named for a saint — Francis of Assisi — so it's in poor taste to abbreviate it. For another, only sailors on shore leave and Southern Californians use that awful abbreviation. It is *never* used by a San Franciscan. However, it's semi-trendy to call it SFO, the official airport destination. If you're *really* a San Franciscan, you refer to it as "the city."

After all, is there any other?

An Ode to Oakland

SPENDING A DAY ACROSS THE BAY

Gertrude Stein was misquoted.
— Robert Maynard, publisher, Oakland *Tribune*

It's difficult enough living in the shadows cast by San Francisco's glitter, but living with the memory of Gertrude Stein's famous quote makes it even worse. She wrote in her biography: "Anyway what was the use of my having come from Oakland....There is no there there."

Oakland *Tribune* publisher Robert Maynard once commented that Stein's statement wasn't intended to knock the East Bay metropolis. She simply meant that when she returned to the Oakland neighborhood where she grew up, after 40 years' absence, she found that everything had changed. Her childhood home was gone, and there was nothing *there* to which she could relate.

We'll let historians argue over Gertrude's meaning. Oakland *does* offer some interesting lures. Also, local tourist promoters claim that hotel rooms are less expensive, suggesting that visitors can stay in Oakland and commute quickly by BART to San Francisco. I can say from personal experience that Oakland has a far superior and less crowded airport and generally — dammit — a better baseball team.

The visitor bureau in the Trans Pacific Center in downtown Oakland (1000 Broadway) can tell you more about the city's objects of intrigue. Call or write: Convention and Visitors Bureau, 1000 Broadway, Suite 200, Oakland, CA 94607-4020, (415) 839-9000. Tell them Gertrude sent you.

Here then, with considerable help from that bureau, are lists of the best lures in Oakland and neighboring Berkeley.

THE TEN BEST ATTRACTIONS IN OAKLAND AND BERKELEY

1 **THE OAKLAND MUSEUM**   *1000 Oak Street (at Tenth), Oakland, 834-2413. Open 10 a.m. to 5 p.m. Wednesday–Saturday and noon to 7 p.m. Sunday. Free; charges for some special exhibits.* The Oakland Museum is California in a capsule, reflecting the history, art, cultures, lifestyles, and natural sciences of the Golden State. It's the only major museum in the world devoted to a single subject, the state of California.

No musty collection of bric-a-brac and butter churns, the Oakland Museum features innovative, full-dimensional exhibits. A focal point is the Hall of History, which ingeniously carries out a "California Dream" theme with tableaux of lifestyles through the generations. Equally intriguing are the dioramas and realistic environmental displays depicting California's various biotic zones, in the Natural Sciences Gallery. They graphically depict the climate, geology, flora, and fauna of this incredibly complex state, from the Pacific to the Great Basin.

The museum covers the complete California picture, including an Indian acorn granary, a Mel's Drive-In sign, low-rider hotrods, and mementos from the Gold Rush, the gay community, and, yes, even the yuppies.

It's also an architectural landmark. The structure looks like it emerged from the earth instead of being built upon it. Covering four city blocks, it's a three-tiered complex with hanging gardens, terraces, and lily ponds. Your first impression is that you've come upon a park instead of a museum.

2 **CLAREMONT RESORT AND SPA**   *Ashby and Domingo avenues, Oakland (take Ashby north from I-80); 843-3000.* The Claremont is the Bay Area's only full-scale resort, with a new $6 million spa, tennis courts, Olympic-sized swimming pools and elegant rooms. It's also one of the East Bay's Ten Best attractions, worth a visit even if you aren't planning to stay. This great white castle snuggled against the Berkeley Hills has been a landmark since its completion in 1915. With a recent $27 million restoration, it's even more opulent than before. The chateau-like main building is massive, 800 feet long and more than 100 feet high. The look is both regal and whimsical, with a grand entry and curious little cupolas popping out of the steeply raked roof.

Stroll about the monumental lobby and the 22 acres of manicured grounds; have a cocktail or meal and enjoy awesome views of the Bay Area. For a fee, you can use the spa and other resort facilities without an overnight stay.

Of course, the best way to experience the Claremont is to spend one or more nights. Go there to unwind, go for a beauty treatment, or put yourself back together with a fitness program that includes aerobics, brisk hikes, and health-oriented meals.

3 **EAST BAY REGIONAL PARKS** *Headquartered at 11500 Skyline Boulevard, Oakland, 531-9300.* Alameda and neighboring Contra Costa counties got together several years ago and formed a joint parks district. Twenty-seven parks covering 50,000 acres are now scattered over the two counties; many are linked by hiking or biking trails. Some of the largest and woodsiest preserves are in the Oakland and Berkeley hills, offering commanding Bay Area views.

A trip to Tilden, Redwood, Joaquin Miller, or Chabot parks offers instant wilderness relief from the pulsating urban sprawl below. For a stunning panorama, drive along Skyline and Grizzly Peak boulevards, which follow the twisting ridge line of Oakland, passing through these parks.

To get there, head southeast through Oakland on I-580 until you hit the Golf Links Road turnoff. Go east (inland) on Golf Links for about two miles, then swerve left onto Grass Valley Road. This blends into Skyline Boulevard. Just keep following it north along the ridge line; it eventually becomes Grizzly Peak Boulevard.

4 **JACK LONDON SQUARE/JACK LONDON VILLAGE** *Along the Oakland estuary.* The story is that hell-raising author Jack London used to run with the oyster pirates off the Oakland estuary. He sailed from here on many of his worldwide adventures. As a teenager, he'd hang out at a rat-trap saloon called Heinhold's, sipping beer and thumbing through Johnny Heinhold's thick dictionary, shaping his future as a writer.

The square today is an attractive area of landscaped gardens, bayside walks, parks, curio shops, and seafood restaurants. More than the memory of London lingers here. **Heinhold's First and Last Chance Saloon** survives, and the barkeep regales visitors with tall tales of the wild young writer. **Jack London's cabin,** where the writer wintered during the Yukon Gold Rush, was discovered in Canada's wilds a few years ago, and its logs were shared with the people of Oakland and Dawson City. Oakland's share has been reassembled on the square, with additional logs added to make it whole again.

Jack London Village, a themed shopping center built in the manner of an old waterfront hamlet, is just south of the square.

5 **LAKE MERRITT AND LAKESIDE PARK** *In downtown Oakland.* Resplendent in its new "Necklace of Lights" that rims Lake Merritt, Lakeside Park is to Oakland what Golden Gate Park is to San Francisco. It's a city retreat for strollers, picnickers, joggers, cyclists, and folks who just like to sit on cool grass with their backs against real trees.

This park has a bonus: saltwater Lake Merritt with small-boat sailing, canoeing and shorelines where you can feed Wonder bread to the ducks. Old-fashioned Sunday afternoon concerts are held in Edoff Memorial Bandstand; you can ride around the lake on a silly old sternwheeler or hop aboard a kiddie train. There's a large playland with fairy tale–themed three-dimensional structures for curtain-climbers.

The Necklace of Lights was — and is again — a string of 5,000 small bulbs supported by Florentine lamp posts circling the lake. It was removed during World War II, then restored in 1987 to return a dazzling nighttime glitter to the park.

For those who love trivia — this is the "largest saltwater lake lying wholly within the boundaries of an American city," and it's the nation's oldest bird sanctuary. But the nicest thing about Lake Merritt is that it's smack in the middle of downtown Oakland.

6 **LAWRENCE HALL OF SCIENCE** *Centennial Drive near Grizzly Peak Boulevard, Berkeley, 642-5132 (taped information) or 642-5134. Open 10 a.m. to 4 p.m. Monday–Saturday and noon to 5 p.m. Sunday; $1.25 weekdays and $2.50 weekends.* Perched on the upper rim of the University of California campus in the Berkeley Hills, Lawrence Hall is a science museum with a focus on computers and state-of-the art research. Of particular interest to students, it stresses hands-on exhibits and discovery labs; there's a small observatory as well.

And once you've finished fiddling with scientific intrigue inside, you can step outside for a spectacular bay view.

7 **MORMON TEMPLE AND GENEALOGY CENTER** *4770 Lincoln Avenue (near the Warren Freeway), Oakland, 531-1475. Grounds open 9 a.m. to 9 p.m. daily. A free guided tour includes a slide show about the temple and its construction.* This modern granite temple is one of the city's most visible landmarks, with golden spires thrusting skyward from a shelf high in the Oakland Hills. It's particularly striking with its nighttime illumination. The grounds are carefully manicured and the Bay Area view from this high niche is impressive.

By prior arrangement, you can use the facilities of the genealogy center to trace your roots. After all, you might be kin to someone famous.

Or, more interesting, perhaps a horse thief.

8 **OAKLAND ZOO AND KNOWLAND PARK** *Golf Links Road (take the 98th Avenue-Golf Links exit from I-580 and go east), 632-9523. Open 10 a.m. to 4 p.m. daily; $2 for adults and $1 for kids and* seniors. *Park admission is $2 per car Tuesday–Sunday; free first Monday of the month; always free to pedestrians.* About 300 critters are housed in this zoo in the Oakland Hills. An aerial tram provides views of animals in their habitats below and the greater Bay Area beyond. The zoo also features a children's petting area; special elephant shows are scheduled on summer weekends.

Surrounding Knowland Park has a playground, picnic areas, a miniature train, and other rides for youngsters.

9 **PARAMOUNT THEATRE OF THE ARTS** *2025 Broadway, Oakland, 893-2300; box office, 465-6400.* Once a lavish 1930s art deco movie palace, the Paramount was rescued from redevelopers a few years ago and meticulously restored. It now functions as a major performing arts center and home of the Oakland Symphony.

You can peer at the wonderful detail of its Egyptian and art deco motifs without catching a concert, since guided tours are conducted the first and third Saturdays of each month at 10 a.m.; reservations aren't necessary.

10 **UNIVERSITY OF CALIFORNIA AT BERKELEY** *Ninety-minute campus tours depart weekdays at 1 p.m., and two-hour Lawrence-Berkeley Lab tours are available by appointment; phone 642-5215.* The senior campus of the University of California system occupies a sloping 720-acre site above Berkeley. More than a major learning center, it's also a repository of museums, gardens, and other things worthy of visitor interest. Here's a partial list:

University Art Museum, 642-1438, Bancroft near College Avenue. The museum exhibits Oriental and contemporary art and is open Wednesday through Sunday from 11 a.m. to 5 p.m.; adults $2; kids and seniors $1.

Pacific Film Archive (in the University Art Museum), 642-1412. The archive shows classic films nightly from its extensive collections. Adults $4.25; less for kids and seniors.

Campanile, 642-3666. This slender observation tower in the center of the campus provides Bay Area vistas. An elevator ride to the top (daily between 10 a.m. and 4 p.m.; closed second Tuesday) costs an entire quarter.

Lowie Museum of Anthropology, 642-3681, Bancroft at College Avenue. The museum features excellent exhibits on the study of man, and particularly California Indians. It's one of the finest museums of its type in the state. Open weekdays except Wednesdays 10 a.m. to 4:30 p.m.; weekends noon to 4:30 p.m. Admission is $1.50.

THE NEXT TEN BEST ATTRACTIONS IN OAKLAND AND BERKELEY

1   **BERKELEY MUNICIPAL ROSE GARDENS**   *Euclid and Bayview, Berkeley; open during daylight; free.* Go sniff more than 4,000 kinds of roses. The blooms are best from late spring to September.

2   **BRET HARTE BOARDWALK**   *Fifth Street between Jefferson and Clay, Oakland.* Author Bret Harte grew up here, and the area's Victorian homes have been refurbished and fashioned into boutiques and restaurants.

3   **GREEK ORTHODOX CHURCH OF THE ASCENSION**   *4700 Lincoln Avenue, Oakland, 531-3400. Open 9 a.m. to 4 p.m. Monday–Friday; free.* The copper dome of this Byzantine-style church is a dramatic Oakland landmark; inside are Biblical mosaics and a 12-foot Baccarat crystal cross.

4   **DUNSMUIR HOUSE AND GARDENS**   *2960 Peralta Oaks Court, Oakland, 562-0328. Open Sundays only, from Easter to September, noon to 4 p.m. Guided tours scheduled at 1, 2 and 3 p.m.; small admission charge.* This 37-room Colonial Revival mansion in the East Oakland foothills resembles a relic of the ante-bellum South, with its thick white columns and second-floor balconies. The surrounding 40-acre garden contains more than 70 types of trees and shrubs hauled in from all over the world. Hiking trails curl around the borders of this large estate.

5   **KAISER CENTER**   *Lakeside Drive at the end of Lake Merritt, Oakland. Art gallery open weekdays 8 a.m. to 6 p.m. (271-2351); roof garden Monday–Saturday 7 a.m. to 7 p.m.; both free.* Once the largest office building west of Chicago, the dramatically curving Kaiser Center provides two reasons for tourists to enter: the second-floor art gallery and a pretty roof garden with pleasant views.

6   **MILLS COLLEGE**   *MacArthur Boulevard and Seminary Avenue, Oakland; art gallery open Tuesday–Sunday 10 a.m. to 4 p.m. during school term.* Mills College occupies a pretty wooded campus in the Oakland hills; the gallery offers a variety of changing exhibits.

7   **MORCOM AMPHITHEATER OF ROSES**   *700 Jean Street, Oakland, 658-0731. Open during daylight; free.* Landscaped pools and walks set off this garden; late spring to summer are the best blooming times for its 8,000 rose bushes.

8 **OAKLAND-ALAMEDA COUNTY COLISEUM COMPLEX**
Hegenberger Road off I-880, 639-7700. Home to the Oakland
Athletics and Golden State Warriors, this modern complex has hosted more
pro sports champions during the past decade than any other in the nation.
The A's, the Warriors, and the now-departed Raiders won 12 world titles
during the 1980s. It's also the birthplace—perhaps unfortunately—of the
"human wave," started here on October 15, 1981, by A's cheerleading
mascot "Crazy George" Henderson.

9 **OAKLAND CHINATOWN** *From Eighth to 11th streets between
Broadway and Harrison.* Although it lacks the glitter and silly dragon
lanterns of San Francisco's Chinatown, Oakland's version is every bit as
ethnic. It brims with excellent restaurants, and they're generally less
expensive than those across the bay.

10 **TAKARA SAKE** *708 Addison Street, Berkeley, 540-8250. Open
noon to 6 p.m. daily; free.* Sip a little sake and watch a slide show in
California's only Japanese rice wine distillery.

THE EAST BAY'S TEN BEST RESTAURANTS
What the world is now calling California cuisine began in Berkeley with the
inventive creations of Alice Waters of Chez Panisse. We consider it to be the
finest East Bay restaurant, but there are many other excellent dining places
across the water as well.

Our selections are a mix of our own choices and those from *San Francisco's Ultimate Dining Guide,* a book we compiled from surveys of people
in the food and hotel business.

1 **CHEZ PANISSE** *1517 Shattuck Avenue (at Vine), Berkeley, 548-
5525. California cuisine; expensive; wine and beer. Dinner 6 to 9:15
p.m. daily. Reservations essential; MC, VISA, AMEX.* For years, Alice Waters and her chefs have created new taste sensations every night, with her simple philosophy of obtaining the freshest ingredients and combining them
creatively. The $45 prix fixe dinner may feature warm puff pastry with
sweetbreads and artichokes; fennel, carrot, and spinach soup; blood orange
salad; a foil packet of sea bass with julienne carrots, scallions, thyme, and
lemon.

The Cafe at Chez Panisse, occupying the upper floor of Alice's simple
shingle-sided cottage, is less expensive but equally creative. It focuses on
California-Mediterranean items such as grilled fish, interesting salads, along
with calzone and pizza from a wood-burning oven.

2 **BROADWAY TERRACE CAFE** *5891 Broadway Terrace (at Clarewood), Oakland, 652-4442. California grill; moderate; wine and beer. Dinner 5:30 to 10 p.m. Wednesday–Saturday and 5 to 9 p.m. Sunday. Reservations essential; no credit cards.* This is California cuisine done on a grill in a woodsy setting. It specializes in mesquite grilled fish, chops, and birds, accompanied with fresh salads, pastas, and desserts. Restaurateur Albert Katz creates such tasty curiosities as Gorgonzola with romaine, fruit, and nuts; a corn and bell pepper custard timbale, and for dessert, chocolate soufflé cake with blood oranges.

The restaurant seats only 34, so reservations are a must.

3 **GERTIE'S CHESAPEAKE BAY CAFE** *1919 Addison Street (at Martin Luther King Jr. Way), Berkeley, 841-2722. Seafood; moderate; wine and beer. Lunch 11:30 a.m. to 2:30 p.m. weekdays, dinner 5:30 to 9:30 p.m. weeknights and 5:30 to 10 p.m. weekends. Reservations advised; major credit cards.* If you're thinking that Oakland and Berkeley restaurants serve only California or Southwestern cuisine, this pleasant little place takes us to the East Coast for crab cakes, Maryland crab soup, steamed mussels, and other regional favorites of the Chesapeake Bay.

It also features Down South specialties such as pan-fried oysters, gumbo, and Southern fried chicken. The look of the place is art deco modern, and diners adjourn to a patio when the weather's right.

4 **HUNAN** *366 Eighth Street (at Webster), Oakland, 444-9255. Northern Chinese; inexpensive to moderate; wine and beer. Open 11:30 a.m. to 10 p.m. Wednesday–Monday. Reservations accepted; MC, VISA.* We mentioned above that Oakland's Chinatown has some tasty and inexpensive places to eat, and this is our favorite. It specializes in spicy north China fare such as Mongolian beef, hot and sour soup, and pot stickers; a few milder Cantonese dishes also are on the menu.

Hunan is typical of small, inexpensive Chinese cafes: a blend of bentwood chairs, vinyl tables, and the ubiquitous red-tasseled lanterns; not a decorator's delight, but the food is great.

5 **JUAN'S PLACE** *941 Carlton Street (at Ninth), Berkeley, 845-6904. Mexican; inexpensive; wine and beer. Open 11:30 a.m. to 10 p.m. weekdays and 2:30 to 10 p.m. weekends. MC, VISA.* Locals like this casual little cafe for its basic California-Mexican fare, all created on the premises. The servings of chiles rellenos, flautas, burritos, and such are monstrous, and dinners average around $6.

The decor is a bright blend of wonderful Mexican clutter.

6 **PLEARN THAI CUISINE**   *2050 University Avenue (at Shattuck),
Berkeley, 841-2148. Thai; inexpensive; wine and beer. Lunch 11:30
a.m. to 3 p.m. Monday–Saturday; dinner 5 to 10 p.m. daily. MC, VISA. San
Francisco Chronicle* restaurant critics call Plearn the best Thai restaurant in
the Bay Area, and we're inclined to agree. And its tasty fare is served in a
modern, attractive environment, instead of a scruffy Formica cafe.

Entrees include a variety of barbecued satays in peanut sauce, fresh seafood seasoned with lemon grass, and assorted spicy curries.

7 **SANTA FE BAR & GRILL**   *1301 University Avenue (at San Pablo),
Berkeley, 841-4740. American regional, specializing in smoked meats;
moderate to moderately expensive; full bar. Lunch 11:30 a.m. to 3 p.m.
weekdays; dinner 5 to 10 p.m. Sunday–Thursday, until midnight Friday and
Saturday; Sunday brunch 10 a.m. to 3 p.m. Reservations essential; all major
credit cards.* Fazio Poursohi, whose smoked meats and brick-oven fish
created raves at Faz in San Francisco, has taken his talents to Berkeley's
Santa Fe. Some of the original Southwestern menu remains as well, and the
place offers homemade pastas and pizzas.

Its appearance is rather striking: sort of Southwestern Byzantine with
Spanish arches, a domed roof, and an outdoor patio.

8 **SEDONA GRILL AND BAR**   *2086 Allston Way (at Shattuck Avenue), Berkeley, 841-3848. Southwestern; moderate; full bar. Lunch
11:30 a.m. to 2:30 p.m. Sunday–Friday, dinner 5:30 to 9 p.m. Tuesday–Sunday. Reservations advised; MC, VISA, AMEX.* Southwest cooking is a close
cousin to California cuisine, and this is the specialty of Sedona Grill (formerly the Dakota). Situated beneath the lofty Ionic columns of the venerable
Shattuck Hotel, the restaurant features creations such as salmon with
mango and chili sauce; buttermilk-cornmeal crepes with diced asparagus;
and zucchini in a goat cheese and red bell pepper sauce.

Designers have created a striking indoor desert garden and added warm
Southwest colors to the lofty reaches of the old hotel.

9 **SKATES**   *100 Seawall Drive (at University Avenue), Berkeley, 549-
1900. American regional; moderate; full bar. Open 11 a.m. to 11 p.m.
daily. Reservations essential; MC, VISA, AMEX.* Folks go to Skates for the
scene as much as for the food. It's an upscale, trendy palace of noise perched
on piers at the Berkeley Marina, with glass-walled views of the bay. In fact,
the ambiance is probably better than the food. The menu tries to cover all
the trendy styles: California cuisine, Southwest, Cajun, sushi, kiawe-wood
grilled, yuppie nouveau.

At times, the fare at this corporate creation is rather good, and the scene is always fun.

10 **SORABOL**   *372 Grand Avenue (at Perkins), Oakland, 839-2288. Korean; moderate; full bar. Open 11:30 a.m. to 9:30 p.m. daily. Reservations accepted; major credit cards.* We've had several pleasing meals at this handsome place near Lake Merritt. Much of Korea's fare, like the notorious kim chee, is hot and spicy, apparently to get citizens through those cold Korean winters. But once can balance a Sorabol meal with milder dishes. Try the gentle *bul-gokee* (thin-sliced rib eye steak), fluffy *beandu duk* (egg pancakes), and spicy *sengsun guyee* (whole rock cod). Incidentally, beer is the best accompaniment to Korean food.

Sorabol is styled to resemble a royal Korean courtyard, with carved wooden panels, Korean prints, and a ceramic tile false roof.

CHAPTER TWENTY-FIVE

Beyond Paradise

THE TEN BEST REASONS TO GET OUT OF TOWN

San Francisco has only one drawback — 'tis hard to leave. — Rudyard Kipling

We've done San Francisco and even Oakland. Perhaps it's time to slip away for a few days. If you're new to Northern California, just about any area of the Golden State will be a discovery. But if you're a Bay Arean, you've probably grown tired of Tahoe, and you've been to Yosemite so many times you're beginning to recognize some of the bears. The art colony of Mendocino is old hat, and *nobody* goes to Carmel anymore because it's too crowded.

What follows is a list of *new* escapes: places you may have overlooked. They're all within long weekend or mini-vacation range, from two to eight hours' drive from the Bay Area.

1 **REDISCOVER THE GOLD RUSH IN HISTORIC COLUMBIA**   *A 2½-hour drive from San Francisco. Contact Columbia State Historic Park, P.O. Box 151, Columbia, CA 95310, (209) 532-4301. For Fallon Hotel or City Hotel reservations, contact City Hotel, P.O. Box 1870, Columbia, CA 95310, (209) 532-1479.* Tucked into the woodsy foothills of California's Sierra Nevada range, Columbia is a historic jewel, a living museum of the great California Gold Rush.

A Wells-Fargo stagecoach rumbles and squeaks along Main Street while gingham-gowned ladies sell scented soaps and homemade candies in iron-shuttered stores. Visitors can sleep amidst 18th-century finery in the City or Fallon Hotels. You can dine in 1860s splendor at the City Hotel Restaurant, or enjoy fine Mexican food in a converted 19th-century home at El Sombrero Restaurant.

Dramatists perform in the Fallon Theater, a blacksmith hammers visitors' names into hand-forged horseshoes, and miners demonstrate gold-panning. Western bands twang happily away in the St. Charles Saloon, as elbow-bending good old boys raise a little harmless hell. It's a place where yesterday still happens.

Gold was discovered here in early 1850; by the time the mines ran dry, $2 billion in bullion (at today's prices) had been taken from the ruddy soil. During its rowdy heyday, Columbia was one of the largest cities in California, ranking behind San Francisco, Sacramento, and Stockton. It dwindled to a sleepy, scruffy hamlet; then the state bought many of its sagging buildings in 1945, and restoration began. Through the years it has become a fascinating one-of-a-kind place: part living-history museum, and part lively community, where residents buy groceries at the corner Mercantile and pick up their mail at a century-old post office.

The people of Columbia dwell in a gentle time warp, living for today but cherishing yesterday. They welcome visitors the year around, and particularly during their old-fashioned festivals. Come celebrate the Fourth of July with greased-pole climbing and watermelon-eating contests. Experience a country Christmas with the scent of pine boughs, a grand Gold Rush feast, and a living Nativity scene.

Columbia folks like to think they've found paradise, and, as a matter of fact, they have. The town was used as the historic model for the "Paradise" television series.

2 **WANDER NORTHERN SONOMA'S WINELANDS** *A 2-hour drive from San Francisco, north on U.S. Highway 101. The best guide to the area is a brochure called* Russian River Wine Roads, *listing wineries, lodgings and annual events. Send a stamped self-addressed business-sized envelope to Healdsburg Area Chamber of Commerce, 217 Healdsburg Avenue, Healdsburg, CA 95448; phone (707) 433-6935.*

The vineyards of the Napa and Sonoma valleys are beautiful and the wineries are fun to visit; but, good grief, the weekend crowds! Next time, explore the winelands of northern Sonoma County. The area isn't much farther, the countryside is equally attractive, the wines are excellent, and the wineries aren't as busy.

Northern Sonoma's winelands begin in the Russian River Valley north of Santa Rosa; most are centered around Healdsburg and Geyserville. This region has more wineries than the better-known Sonoma Valley and — except for some summer and fall weekends — they're rarely crowded. If you plan a couple of days for this vineyard country ramble, you'll find that bed and breakfast inns and good restaurants are cropping up like crocuses.

Here are some of our favorite northland wineries:

J. Pedroncelli Winery, a mile north of Geyserville at 1220 Canyon Road; tasting daily from 10 a.m. to 5 p.m.; tours by appointment; (707) 857-3531. John and Jim Pedroncelli continue a tradition of fine wines started by their father, who must have been the original Italian optimist. He started their winery during Prohibition. Generous sips of their award-winning varietals are poured in a sparkling new tasting room.

Hop Kiln Winery, 6050 Westside Road, Healdsburg; tasting 10 a.m. to 5 p.m. daily; informal tours; (707) 433-6491. Hop Kiln's tasting room is located in the loft of an impressive triple-towered 1905 hop-drying barn that's been selected as a National Trust structure. Art exhibits brighten the walls of the tasting room and picnic tables outside invite visitors to linger.

Chateau Souverain, just south of Geyserville on Independence Lane; tasting 10 a.m. to 4:30 p.m. daily; (707) 433-8281, and 433-3141 for restaurant reservations. This modern winery was built to *look* like a hop kiln (leading you to assume — correctly — that this area used to be hop country). You can dine beside a vine in Souverain's attractive indoor-outdoor restaurant, open for lunch and dinner daily except Monday.

Korbel Champagne Cellars, 13250 River Road, along the Russian River west of Santa Rosa; tours 10 a.m. to 3 p.m. daily, tasting 9 a.m. to 4:30 p.m.; (707) 887-2294. This handsome vine-covered stone winery complex looks like a transplant from the Rhine. Korbel specializes in champagne and brandy, and the tour provides a good study of the champagne-making process.

Some places to stay:

Lytton Springs Inn, 17698 Healdsburg Avenue, Healdsburg, (707) 431-1109. This Mediterranean-style ranch house offers warm hospitality and an impressive view from a bluff above the Alexander Valley. A hot tub, a champagne breakfast, and cocktail-hour tapas served on the patio are among its lures.

Hope-Merrill House, 21253 Geyserville Avenue, Geyserville, (707) 857-3356. It's a beautifully restored and elegantly furnished Victorian, with whirlpool baths, a swimming pool, and a gazebo suitable for sitting and wine sipping.

Ridenhour Ranch House Inn, 12850 River Road, Guerneville, (707) 887-1033. A ranch-style bed and breakfast furnished with antiques, it's located near Korbel Champagne Cellars. Offerings include a hot tub, old-fashioned lawn croquet, and a full breakfast.

3 **SAMPLE SHAKESPEARE IN A HAMLET**   *A 7-hour drive from San Francisco. Write Oregon Shakespearean Festival, P.O. Box 158, Ashland, OR 97520-0158; or call (503) 482-4331 for a thick brochure listing the current season's events, plus hotels, motels, and restaurants. For general information on the area, contact the Southern Oregon Reservation Center, P.O. Box 477, Ashland, OR 97520, (800) 547-8052. For information on music festivals in neighboring Jacksonville, contact Peter Britt Festivals, P.O. Box 1124, Medford, OR 97501, (800) 882-7488.*

Quick quiz: Where is America's largest annual drama festival held? The answer surprises us, too. It occurs in the small lumber town of Ashland, Oregon, just across the northern California border. This town of 15,000 souls lures *300,000* visitors a year to its Oregon Shakespearean Festival.

The drama fete runs from late February through October, with about a dozen plays in repertory, ranging from Shakespeare and his contemporaries to modern classics to avant-garde to brand-new works. Its highly polished company, which has won a Tony Award and other accolades, performs in two indoor theaters and a large outdoor Elizabethan stage (which operates in summer only).

The entire town has taken up Shakespeare's tune, with fluttering banners, cross-timbered buildings, madrigal singers, and Elizabethan dancers. The festival began in 1935, the brainchild of local drama teacher Angus L. Bowmer.

About 15 miles down the road, visitors can prowl along the funky 19th-century main street of Jacksonville, a Gold Rush town that's been designated as a national historic landmark. Like neighboring Ashland, Jacksonville has a cultural tilt: it presents summer music festivals in its Peter Britt Gardens, with programs of classics, jazz, and bluegrass.

4 **DROP ANCHOR IN AVILA BEACH** *A 6-hour drive. For information, contact the neighboring San Luis Obispo Chamber of Commerce, 1039 Chorro Street, San Luis Obispo, CA 93401, (805) 543-1323. For San Luis Bay Inn accommodations, contact San Luis Bay Inn, P.O. Box 189, Avila Beach, CA 93424, (805) 595-2333.* Flanked by more popular Pismo Beach and Morro Bay, Avila Beach is a scattering of old homes and a few stores on a sloping hill next to a pretty crescent bay. The weathered main-street shops and old concrete beach promenade are right out of the thirties, and the wide, clean strand is rarely crowded, although it gets busy on sunny summer weekends.

Most travelers on nearby U.S. 101 bypass this small enclave on San Luis Obispo Bay. Its ominous neighbor, the Diablo Canyon nuclear generating plant, is much better known. But the town is charming and definitely suitable for a weekend retreat, with its oak-thatched rumpled hills sloping down to peaceful beaches.

There's little to do here, and therein lies the area's charm. It's a place to stretch out on the strand, stroll along the beach and scuff at seaweed, and perhaps wander over to the old pier at Port San Luis, about a mile away. San Luis isn't a town; it's a harbor and pier with a couple of seafood restaurants. Nearby San Luis Obispo is also worth a look, with its old mission, pretty creekside park, and a couple of rustic-themed shopping centers.

You can lounge in luxury at the San Luis Bay Inn, a handsomely appointed resort with its own golf course and sea-view rooms on a bluff above Avila Beach.

5 **COOL IT IN CAPITOLA**   *A 3-hour drive. Contact Capitola Chamber of Commerce, 410 Capitola Avenue, Capitola, CA 95010, (408) 475-6522. For Shadow-Brook Restaurant reservations, call (408) 475-1511.* If Avila Beach is too much of a stretch for your weekend, hop down to Capitola, one of our favorite Northern California seaside cities. This gem of a town is built along a wooded ravine and a small harbor at the mouth of Soquel Creek in Santa Cruz County. Like Avila Beach, it's only a few miles from a much more famous resort — Santa Cruz in this case — and it's considerably less crowded.

Beach seekers have a choice between freshwater dipping in Soquel Creek lagoon or the salty sea just beyond a sandbar. We like the town for its wonderful examples of Victorian homes, its art and crafts galleries, and a pretty sheltered walkway along Soquel Creek. This is begonia country, and the town celebrates with its Begonia Festival every September.

Our favorite restaurant here is the Shadow-Brook, snuggled against a shaggy hillside above Soquel Creek. Patrons reach it by parking above and taking a tiny red funicular down to the dining room.

6 **CLIMB THROUGH A LAVA CAVERN**   *A 7-hour drive. For information, call Lava Beds National Monument, (916) 667-2282.* On its busiest days, Lava Beds National Monument is practically deserted. Yet this intriguing area has two major lures. It's a place where Mother Nature tortured the earth's crust with a volcanic fury that left a barren world of broken lava, cinder cones, and hundreds of lava caves. And it is the site of one of the country's last Indian wars. But since it's tucked into a remote corner of northeastern California, most of the world passes it by.

Visitors to this dark, tumbled land can prowl through a score of lava tubes, created when rivers of liquid basalt hardened on the surface but continued flowing beneath to leave natural tunnels. These aren't "developed" caves with guided tours and fancy indirect lighting. To explore the tubes, you should first stop by the monument's visitor center to borrow a strong lantern. And you can buy, for about $2, a hard plastic "bump hat" that will prevent the low, jagged ceilings from giving you an Excedrin headache.

Just over a century ago, a Modoc Indian named Captain Jack liberated his people from a hated reservation and led them into the Lava Beds wilderness, where he defied the U.S. government to root them out. Using the natural fortifications of caves and lava trenches, he held off the Army for five months in a miserable war that one park ranger described as "an American Indian Vietnam." Fewer than 60 Modocs defied an army of 600 soldiers, inflicting 237 casualties while losing only 16 of their own. But, chilled and starved by a merciless winter, the band was rounded up; Captain Jack was hanged.

In a natural lava fortress called Captain Jack's Stronghold, numbered markers help visitors reconstruct those fascinating days of 1872 when — for a brief and angry moment — a band of frustrated Indians kept the government at bay.

Lava Beds isn't a resort. The camping crowd can feel at home here, but the area has no lodging, no stores, and nothing to drink but water. Tiny Tulelake, California, has a couple of motels and restaurants, about 15 miles north. The nearest town with a reasonable assortment of motels and restaurants is Klamath Falls, Oregon, another 28 miles north.

7 SEEK SHANGRI-LA IN THE SIERRA   *A 5-hour drive. Contact the Sierra County Chamber of Commerce, P.O. Box 555, Downieville, CA 95936, (916) 289-3560. For Sierra Shangri-La reservations, contact Sierra Shangri-La, P.O. Box 285, Downieville, CA 95936, (916) 289-3455.* You've noticed that our theme here is to find fascinating but uncrowded places. One of the least-visited and prettiest parts of the great Sierra Nevada is in the northern end of this rugged mountain range, in an area appropriately called Sierra County. If you like swift-running streams, untrammeled hiking trails, funky old Gold Rush towns, and pine-clad mountains that reach for the stars, this is your place.

To find this undiscovered land, head east on Interstate 80, then turn north onto State Highway 49 at Auburn. Stay on 49, the historic "Golden Chain" highway, and you'll find yourself in a beautiful river canyon in the uppermost reaches of the Gold Country. Here, you can fish, wade in chilly waters, camp, picnic, and even pan for gold. Downieville, with 400 residents, is the Sierra County seat, sitting in a narrow, wooded valley at the confluence of the Downie and Yuba rivers. It's one of the prettiest settings for a town in the entire west. In 1988, it took a major step toward yesterday when utility lines were sent underground and boardwalks replaced sidewalks. With its iron-shuttered rough-cut stone stores and steepled churches, it looks little changed from the 1850s, when it was a thriving mining camp.

A bit farther upstream is Sierra City, a slightly smaller version of Downieville, and just beyond that, an excellent historic park called the Kentucky Mine Museum. Above Sierra City, you can hike, backpack, fish, and generally explore the wilds and alpine lakes of Tahoe and Plumas national forests; particularly appealing are the Gold Lakes area and a rugged outcropping called the Sierra Buttes.

One of our favorite hideaways in all of California is Sierra Shangri-La, a resort perched above a rocky gorge in the Yuba River between Downieville and Sierra City. It offers kitchen cabins with pot-bellied stoves and smaller motel-style units. Most have their own decks, some right over the roaring river.

8 **SAUNTER THROUGH SACRAMENTO**   *A 2-hour drive. For details, contact Convention and Visitors Bureau, 1311 I Street, Sacramento, CA 95814, (916) 442-5542.*

We aren't suggesting that Sacramento is a little-known place. But you may not know that it has several major tourist lures. So all right, it isn't Carmel or Mendocino. But our capital city, spraddled over the flatlands of the Sacramento Valley, can keep the visitor occupied for a weekend or even a week.

Begin with Old Sacramento, a gathering of boutiques, shops and galleries in carefully restored, century-old brick and clapboard buildings along the Sacramento River. Clump along boardwalks, clatter across cobblestone streets, and pretend you just got off a riverboat. Spend some time at the California State Railroad Museum, with one of the largest collections of trains and railroading memorabilia in the world. Through the ingenuity of modern museum-makers, you'll hear the lonely call of a distant whistle and the rumble of voices in a 1930s train station; you'll even feel the rhythmic sway of a 1929 sleeping car as you stroll past its curtained compartments.

Reserve most of an afternoon for a tour of the impeccably restored State Capitol, about a mile from Old Sacramento. At a cost of $68 million, the domed French Revival structure was carefully returned to its 1874 elegance. More than 2,000 craftsmen labored five years to complete the most expensive and meticulous restoration of a public structure in the country's history.

Pause a while at Sutter's Fort at 27th and L streets, a re-creation of the civilian fortress built in the 1840s by Swiss fortune-hunter John Sutter, one of the major early colonizers of California. It was his plan to construct a sawmill in the Sierra Nevada foothills that led to the discovery of gold by his mill foreman, James Marshall.

9 **STAND IN A SEQUOIA'S SHADOW**   *A 5-hour drive. For general park information, contact Sequoia/Kings Canyon National Park, Three Rivers, CA 93271, (209) 565-3341. For lodging, contact Guest Services, Inc., Sequoia National Park, CA 93262, (209) 561-3314.* If you're a Californian, you know that you practically have to take a number to get into Yosemite National Park these days. Sequoia National Park, only two hours farther from the Bay Area than Yosemite, is equally intriguing and not nearly as crowded.

A wonderful nature's brew of giant Sequoia trees, cascading streams, aspen-rimmed meadows, and the high granite wilderness of the Sierra Nevada, this is a park for all seasons. You can hike in the summer, photograph golden aspen in the fall, shoeshoe or cross-country ski beneath cinnamon-barked sequoias in the winter, and watch wildflowers march across spring meadows.

10 **SHOP UNTIL YOU DROP IN SOLVANG**   *A 6-hour drive. Contact Solvang Chamber of Commerce, P.O. Box 465, Solvang, CA 93463, (805) 688-3317.* Solvang is another of the state's unexpected delights: a recreation of a Danish village in the green farmlands of south central California, in Santa Barbara County. It was established in 1911 as the site for a Danish school and farming community. It has since become a tourist-oriented Danish village, complete with cross-timbered houses, Scandinavian folk dancing, and enough smorgasbord to feed the Danish Navy.

It's a major shopping area, with more than 300 stores focusing on European imports and tasty Danish pastries. The town is particularly popular with credit-card clutchers during the Christmas spending period. Solvang also fosters a Danish Days celebration the third weekend of September and an outdoor theater festival in the summer.

Also interesting, but from quite another ethnic world, is Mission Santa Ines, established in 1804 as one of a chain of California's Spanish outposts. The surrounding Santa Ynez Valley features a growing assortment of wineries, many with tasting rooms open to visitors.

INDEX

194